"An excellent perspective on the role of alliances in strategy execution and ecosystem development. Gomes-Casseres's three fundamental rules are the basis for a pragmatic set of management tools, structures, and guidelines that equip leaders for a future in which collaboration between businesses is essential for survival."

—**CEES BIJL,** Head of Emerging Business Areas and
Head of Group Alliances, Philips International BV

"A terrific book with lots of insights and management tools, valuable to business leaders everywhere. Because I've been involved in several joint ventures, so much in *Remix Strategy* resonates with me, particularly the lessons on where joint benefits come from, on governing alliance strategy, and on dealing with uncertainty and change."

—**ASHOK KRISHNA,** Vice President, Downstream & Chemicals
Technology, Chevron Corporation

"*Remix Strategy* provides a clear framework focused on value creation that will support managers working with business combinations at all stages—from inception through deal negotiation and implementation to termination. The tools in the book address the day-to-day challenges of identifying, delivering, and sharing value in combinations. An entertaining read that will benefit everyone working with business partnerships."

—**NIGEL SHEAIL,** Head of Business Development & Licensing,
Bayer Healthcare AG

"The ideas in *Remix Strategy* are creative, unique, and perhaps transformative. Today's dynamic, shape-shifting business environment requires companies to acquire, divest, merge, ally, and partner, whether to innovate or just survive. This useful book reveals the fundamental laws of collaboration that lead to success."

—**ROSABETH MOSS KANTER,** Professor, Harvard Business School;
author, *MOVE, Supercorp,* and *Confidence*

"A fascinating roadmap to creating and capturing value through business combinations. Gomes-Casseres provides the tools you need to identify, govern, and share joint value and illustrates through numerous case studies how to make critical choices in designing and executing business combinations."

—**MARTIN FLEMING**, Chief Economist and Vice President, Business Performance Services, IBM Corporation

"A powerful paradigm for prospering in a rapidly changing environment, rooted in three critical tools to evaluate and develop strategic business options. Gomes-Casseres shows how these tools can be applied in different scenarios with practical, real-world examples."

—**STEVE STEINHILBER**, Vice President, Industry Solutions Partner Ecosystems, Cisco Systems, Inc.; author, *Strategic Alliances*

"The first book to explain the critical concepts behind successful business combinations—and provide immediately actionable insights. *Remix Strategy* is a must-read for managers in business strategy, corporate development, and corporate alliances."

—**RUSS BUCHANAN**, Vice President, Worldwide Alliances, Xerox Corporation; Chairman Emeritus, Association of Strategic Alliance Professionals

"Whether you are an investor assessing the value of a business combination, a director reviewing the firm's alliance strategy, or an executive considering a partnership, *Remix Strategy* gives you the tools to understand and unlock value. Gomes-Casseres (re)mixes case studies with practical tools that you can use right out of the box. It's modern business thinking for modern business times."

—**MIKE BELLISSIMO**, Enterprise Vice President, Humana Inc.

REMIX
STRATEGY

REMIX STRATEGY

The Three Laws *of*
Business Combinations

BENJAMIN GOMES-CASSERES

HARVARD BUSINESS REVIEW PRESS

Boston, Massachusetts

Library of Congress Cataloging-in-Publication Data

Gomes-Casseres, Benjamin.
    Remix strategy: the three laws of business combinations / Benjamin Gomes-Casseres.
        pages cm
    ISBN 978-1-4221-6308-5 (hardback)
    1. Strategic alliances (Business).   2. Business networks.   3. Strategic planning.   I. Title.
    HD69.S8G663 2015
    658'.046—dc23

                                                            2015004987

The paper used in this publication meets the requirements of the American National Standard for Permanence of Paper for Publications and Documents in Libraries and Archives Z39.48-1992.

ISBN: 9781422163085
eISBN: 9781625270573

For Susan and Rachel

Contents

Part Three

How Remix Strategy Changes
the Way You Compete

Complete Collection of
Remix Strategy Tools

Part One

Creating Value by Combining Resources

I N CONTEMPORARY MUSIC AND ART, A *REMIX* IS A PIECE OF media that is created by combining bits and pieces from other media. A collage is a remix of pictures. New songs can come from remixing the sound tracks from other songs. Even text created by cutting and pasting is a remix.

In this book, I use the word to describe *the mixing of resources, assets, and capabilities of one organization with those of another to create value.* It happens through business combinations of various sorts. An alliance between Apple and IBM. A joint venture of Novartis and GlaxoSmithKline. A merger of Walgreens and Boots. A partnership of Oxfam and Marks & Spencer. A consortium of General Electric and internet-of-things players Verizon, Intel, and Cisco. Joint development by NASA and SpaceX. In today's fast-paced, interconnected business environment, this remixing of assets is fundamental to competitive advantage. It brings in new ideas, provides access to new capabilities and markets, and lets companies leverage what they do best.

Most likely, you have considered acquisitions, alliances, joint ventures, and other kinds of business combinations. The key strategic questions you face are not whether combinations such as these are necessary but, rather, how will these business combinations create value, and how are you going to capture that value?

As executives look to external partners for acquiring resources and capabilities, what they need most is a practical roadmap to key questions: What combinations do we need? How do we manage them over time? What profits will we earn? Will they justify our investment? Part one introduces a simple but powerful framework to help you make these critical decisions. This roadmap—and the practical tools that follow in subsequent chapters—will show you how to profit from your own business remix.

Chapter 1

The Three Laws of Business Combinations

BUSINESS IS BEING TURNED OUTSIDE-IN. ACQUISITIONS, mergers, joint ventures, alliances, partnerships, and other business combinations are bringing in resources from outside the firm. And they are no longer exceptions in most businesses—they have become central to gaining competitive advantage.

This is not surprising. At the most basic level, new value often comes from combining ideas and effort from disparate sources. Labor and capital. Technology and brand. Hardware and software. Global and local. In today's world of fleeting advantage, combining assets, capabilities, markets, and talent pools is even more important than ever. This combining of resources to create new value is what I call the business remix.

Every technology company knows what I mean—the firm is often inundated by deal opportunities, and its success usually depends on a network of allies. (Think of Google and its Android partners.) Large companies surrounded by start-up innovation have learned to tap into new ideas. (Think of big pharma's many investments in biotech start-ups.) Combining assets in older, industrial companies is no different; these manufacturing firms of ten have global supplier networks and partners in emerging markets. (Think of General Motors and Shanghai Automotive Industry Corporation.) Service industries, too, have their own way of combining forces through networks and joint projects. (Think of Star, oneworld, and SkyTeam, the three global airline alliances.) The business remix applies to everyone.

Although the remixing of businesses is not a new phenomenon, we have not previously recognized fully how to use it to advance strategy. The real issue is not whether you should be looking outside your walls for resources. The question is how are these ventures going to enhance your competitive position? How will they create value? And how are you going to capture that value? Whether you are at the top of the company driving the remix, in the middle managing an acquisition or a partnership, or among the operating ranks keeping the pieces humming, you need to know the answers to such questions.

I wrote this book because, in my work with executives, I've noticed a distinct gap in their toolkits. Managers already have a great deal of information and best practices for implementing alliances and acquisitions. The strength of these playbooks is their concrete detail about the legal, managerial, and financial ins and outs of every deal type and the tips on how to manage people and cultures in these combinations on a day-to-day basis. But managers lack a set of guiding principles for actually making the deal create value for the company. That's what this book is designed to do. It gives you a simple but powerful framework to see clearly what the key decisions are and then to navigate those decisions successfully. I have dubbed these guiding principles *the three laws of business combinations.*

Successful business combinations—those that turn out to be a profitable use of resources—all follow the three laws. These laws are not formulated as commandments or orders, but are necessary conditions for success. All business combinations must have the potential to create joint value, must be governed to realize this value, and must share value in a way that provides a reward to each party's investment. Each law points to a set of practical implications:

> **First law: The value created by the combination should exceed the total value that would be generated by the players acting alone.** The first law asks these practical questions: How much more value can we create in the market together? What specific resources must we combine to create this value?

> **Second law: The combination must be designed and managed to realize this joint value.** Which partners and structures fit this goal best? How do we manage the risk and uncertainty inherent in such combinations?

> **Third law: Each participant must earn a return sufficient to justify the investment.** How do we divide the joint value created? How will value be shared over time?

I've arrived at the three laws of business combinations through my thirty years of consulting, teaching, and academic research on partnership strategy. Taken together, the laws provide a powerful, systematic approach for creating and capturing value from your partnerships. The management tools in this book help you apply the laws to specific decisions—from when to form a combination, to how to manage collaboration, to how to ensure that you get a return on your efforts.

Regardless of your actual role in combining businesses, you can benefit from the practical remixing approach that I advocate in this book. If you are a deal-maker at a company, then of course you must be able to make strategic decisions, such as selecting the right partner and the right structure for a deal. If you are managing an alliance or implementing an acquisition, then too, many decisions you will face need to be consistent with strategy and sometimes will need to reshape that strategy. Functional managers in sales, R&D management, finance, legal, and human resources will also make better decisions if they understand the strategic thinking behind a combination.

Your decisions—as a general manager, functional manager, or project manager—will shape how well your organization follows these laws. For example, think of the due-diligence task in an intended combination. This technical and complex task has been covered in other books and practical manuals. But you need to know the strategic elements in your research on a potential partner. What are potential sources of value? How well will the key resources of the partner fit with your own internal resources? This book will help you step back from the details of the deal and see how the deal affects your profitability overall.

The same is true of other tasks, such as financial analysis, legal agreements, and the implementation and governance of a combination. Each of these tasks has an impact on how value is created and earned by your company. Your decisions will depend, of course, on the competitive, regulatory, organizational, personnel, and cultural conditions you face—and getting these specifics right is essential to implementing any deal. But this book takes you up a few levels to give you a set of core principles to help you navigate the details. The approach can be applied consistently from one deal to the next and from one partnership to the next, so that you are not managing your combinations in an ad hoc way.

While this book is based on my own experience, observation, theorizing, and testing, I have also incorporated the thinking of fellow scholars, thought leaders from other fields, and the many practitioners with whom I have worked over the decades. I try to forge a bridge from the best thinking of researchers to the best practices that managers seek. My previous two books anchored the two ends of this bridge—*The Alliance Revolution* was an academic treatise, and *Mastering Alliance Strategy* offered how-to tips. This book brings the two perspectives together—a remix, if you will. It relies on research in economics, law, organization design, negotiation, and other fields, but does not present this material in an academic fashion. The theory is merely the foundation—the three laws, and their practical implications for you, are my focus. The book also presents telling and instructive examples from a wide range of cases and industries; these cases are meant to elucidate and illustrate ideas rather than to test their validity. Further evidence and key ideas from scholarly research are referenced in the back of the book.

Why Business Combinations Are Now Vital

Business combinations have long been recognized as a key factor in competition and innovation. The first to see this relationship was Joseph Schumpeter, the great political economist of the early twentieth century. He is well known today for the idea of creative destruction, a forerunner of what we now call disruptive innovation. In his lesser-known work on entrepreneurship, he described how the normal routine of a business could be upended by new combinations of the elements of the business. Entrepreneurs, he argued, are the ones who made these new combinations—combinations of existing and new manufacturing processes, of markets and new sources of supply, of new products and technologies, and even of new corporate structures and strategies. These new combinations were at the heart of his theory of innovation.

Schumpeter's observations still describe what is now happening all around us—but today it is not only start-up entrepreneurs who are coming up with the new combinations. Executives in established companies are now driving this innovation process too. The last decade has seen a proliferation of strategies of this sort—strategies that combine assets and resources from inside and outside a company. The details of these combinations vary: they may be temporary or permanent, be governed by a loose or an iron-clad contract, be exclusive or not, and so on. But, fundamentally, *they all seek to create value by combining or repurposing resources*. Here are just a few ways that companies do this:

- **Acquisitions:** Buying assets from another company, or buying the whole company

- **Outsourcing:** Contracting for another firm to perform a role in operations

- **Joint ventures:** Sharing the investment (and returns) in an operation or plant

- **Codevelopment:** Sharing R&D for a product, usually to be licensed

- **Comarketing:** Sharing the marketing or channel for a product

- **Licensing:** Buying or selling rights to use a technology (respectively, in-licensing and out-licensing)

- **Alliances:** Any external collaboration (also called partnerships or teaming)

- **Ecosystems:** Collections of external firms or technologies that support a firm

- **Consortia:** Multipartner organizations formed to develop technology or other common interests

- **Supplier networks:** Sequence and tiers of supplier relationships providing inputs to a firm

- **Open innovation:** Gathering ideas and technologies from sources outside a firm

To be clear, this book is not about the details of these alternative deal forms or how to choose among them. Rather, I hope to give you a way of thinking and a set of tools for managing *all* these choices strategically—how to create value with them, how to manage the remixing of assets, and how to gain benefits from the deal in the long term.

Why should you care about these deals? Because dramatic changes in the competitive environment may be putting the survival of your business at stake. Competition today has become a battle not of isolated firms against other firms, but of groups of firms against other groups. These groups represent bundles of resources that compete against other bundles. Deals like acquisitions and partnerships are some of the tactics you'll need in this battle, but you can't just be tactical in times of fundamental change. That's why remix strategy is so important. This book will show you how to dissect the logic behind each business combination you consider.

Understanding this logic is critical to success because the new style of competition is not business as usual. Most managers prefer strategies that rely on resources they own or that they obtain through contracts that give them substantial control over critical decisions. Dependence on a partner that has its own interests and goals seems risky. Sharing decision making seems like a recipe for delays and possible deadlock. Cultural differences between the parties add complexity and uncertainty to these deals. No wonder managers worry about the odds of success in alliances and acquisitions. This book will help you beat those odds. But I also believe that this worry is often overstated. The sidebar "Recalibrate Your Odds of Success" explains why.

I learned about remix strategy from the ground up. Early in my career, while I was working for the World Bank, I saw powerful examples of how combinations between foreign investors and local entrepreneurs in emerging markets created new industries, jobs, and profits. Later, I conducted statistical studies of thousands of companies and uncovered broader patterns of when, why, and how companies connected with others and what effects these alliances had on performance, particularly when entering foreign markets. I also investigated a number of cases in depth, including the joint ventures that Xerox and Honeywell each had with local partners in Japan. The explosion of the high-tech industry in the late 1980s and 1990s opened my eyes to how groups of allied firms competed in the computer industry, a phenomenon I wrote about in my first book, *The Alliance Revolution,* and in several articles.

In consulting and executive training with large companies, I got a chance to test the perspectives and tools from my academic work. In the process, I dug into the internal workings of about fifty large companies that were struggling in one way or another with business combinations. In particular, I learned much from the experiences in those years of Eli Lilly, Daimler, Motorola, Sun

Recalibrate Your Odds of Success

Every consultant gives the same pitch: "Your deals have an *x* percent chance of crashing—let us help you beat the odds." I made the same pitch. It gets your attention. But it's usually wrong. Not the numerical odds that are cited, although the evidence on these is mixed. What's wrong is the superficial interpretation of the numbers. Once you recalibrate your odds properly, combinations are not that scary.

Consider the available information: roughly speaking, between one-third and two-thirds of alliances break up within ten years. The precise divorce rate varies by many factors; there is no comprehensive data. Breakups can be costly, as you probably know from experience. In mergers and acquisitions, outright divorce is less common, though it is not unheard-of. More common are acquisitions that simply never cover their costs.

Does this mean that your company should avoid business combinations? Not in the least. To draw the right conclusions, consider these three questions:

What does the breakup of a business partnership really signal? Not much—it is a signal with a lot of noise. The breakup of an alliance can mean that the partners did not get along, and so left a potentially valuable joint project in tatters. But it can also mean that they got along well and developed new capabilities that made it unnecessary to continue the partnership. Or a breakup could mean that circumstances external to the deal changed, nullifying the purpose of the partnership.

Microsystems, and Hewlett-Packard. A second book, *Mastering Alliance Strategy,* and other articles came out along the way. Further teaching and research on key firms added another fifty firms to my informal sample, which by then covered major players in every industry, from information technology, media, and services to consumer goods, pharmaceuticals, cars, airlines, and energy.

What can be done to reduce the risk of a bad breakup? A lot. Better communication, reciprocity, forbearance, flexibility, and clarity on common goals all lower the relationship risk in a combination. A good deal of this book is devoted to making the deal right, as well as to making the right deal. In the last few decades, we have learned much about how to manage alliances better and how to implement acquisitions. Many companies have built strong capabilities to execute these strategies, with measurable improvement in their results.

What risk remains, even after our best efforts to reduce the risk of breakup? Even if the relationship risk were reduced to zero, most business combinations remain risky. The risk derives not from uneven management of the relationship, but from the very purpose of the combination. Business combinations always intend to do together what a firm cannot do alone—launching a new business, introducing a new product, reconfiguring the shape of a business, and so on. Risky businesses, all!

In the end, the key to understanding your odds lies in selecting the proper benchmark (see chapter 7). Compared with start-ups, business combinations have a great record; many more start-ups peter out or fail outright. Routine product launches also have a shaky record—many new products, new market entries, and new brand extensions fail, though the data on this is fragmentary. Against the backdrop of these other kinds of entrepreneurial ventures or the option of going it alone when you don't have the requisite skills, a well-managed business combination would seem like a low-risk move.

Through this work, I came to see that business combinations helped firms recombine resources to create new capabilities and improve their competitive position in the market. I was struck by the analogy to biology, where genetic engineers recombine strands of DNA to transfer traits from one seed or cell to another, making new organisms that are better suited to certain functions. And in science, too, the recombination of ideas can lead to new ideas. Another term for remix strategy is thus *recombinant strategy*.

Today, the role of remix strategy is greater than ever, across many industries. The strategy is particularly useful when new technologies shake an existing order—incumbents will then seek to protect their franchises by adopting features of the new technology. And start-ups usually need partners to make an impact on the market. This need was evident in the early days of the PC and internet and now exists with the mobile web, smart and connected devices, biotechnology, electronic cars, and clean energy. The appearance of new market opportunities likewise has been shown to prompt a rise in alliances and acquisitions—think China, emerging markets, and health care.

A more philosophical reason drives the current interest in collaborative ventures too. Advocates of sustainable business practices and the public roles of corporations often form alliances to involve multiple stakeholders. In many parts of the world, public-private partnerships and alliances with nongovernmental organizations (NGOs) are popular ways for a for-profit firm to address social needs. Oxfam, for example, has an alliance with Marks & Spencer to recycle used clothing. One start-up that spun out of Oxfam is working on an even more ambitious plan: to organize peasant farmers in Latin America and Africa into joint ventures that could attract investment in agricultural processing facilities.

The framework of remix strategy applies to all such situations. I use examples from many industries to show just that. Many examples are not new business cases—you've heard about them in the news. But it is precisely because of this familiarity, and the fact that we can see how these cases turned out, that we can leverage the examples to explain the three-law framework, which I describe in detail next.

The Three Laws

The three laws—no more, no less—emerged out of my years of study and practice.

First, to be successful, a business combination must have the potential to create an amount of *joint value* in the market that exceeds the total value that would be generated by the same resources without the combination. This law has significant practical implications. You need a good sense of how much more value can be created—and which important elements need to be combined—before proceeding to hammer out a deal.

Second, the way the combination is designed and managed must enable you to actually create the joint value. You will have to decide how you are going to encourage the fusion of the key elements and how you will mitigate risks that are inherent in combinations.

Third, each party involved in the combination must earn a share of the joint value produced—a profit—that provides the incentive for the party to commit its resources to the joint effort. You are going to have to decide, with your partners, how value will be divided among you. And then you have to keep an eye out for changes over time in what you gain from the deal.

Furthermore, you need to be mindful of the relationships between all these laws. The triangle in figure 1-1 represents a quick guide to the main themes of this book. The laws shown are necessary and sufficient conditions for success in any business combination, regardless of its form or purpose. As with most of the other images in the book, this abstract depiction of concrete conditions will vary according to the situation. To use it in making decisions, you need to adapt it to the situation at hand. The chapters in the book examine these laws and show you how to adapt them.

These three laws determine the success of *any* business combination, and at first glance, they're easy to grasp. But each is deeper than it looks. And living by them is tricky in practice. Often, one or the other gets short shrift in the rush to strike a deal or gets lost in the glare of a promising future. Another practical problem is that because each law revolves around a different school of thought in strategy and management science, experts in one area can easily miss cues in another and, in doing so, inadvertently plant the seeds for a costly retreat later on. To avoid these pitfalls, we will need to dig deeper before setting you loose with the three laws. So let's start by fixing some basic ideas about them.

FIGURE 1-1

| Management Tool |

The three laws of business combinations

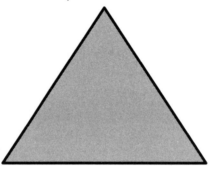

**Identify potential
joint value**

First Law
The combination
must have the potential to
create more value than
the parties can alone

**Govern the
collaboration**

Second Law
The combination
must be designed
and managed to realize
the joint value

**Share the
value created**

Third Law
The value earned by
the parties must motivate
them to contribute to the
collaboration

First Law: Identify Potential Joint Value

In casual conversation, the idea of creating value in combinations is often expressed as $1+1=3$, or some such mathematical metaphor. In fact, that isn't a crazy way to think about the three laws, at least for now. Let's look at how this idea manifests itself in the first law.

As explained, the first law for a business combination is that the remix must have the potential to create more value than the resources can generate when governed separately, that is, without being combined. In common business language, the combination has to produce *synergy*. I hesitate to use that term because of its reputation as a business buzzword. But as we will see, the bad rep comes from ignoring the complex processes involved in creating value in combinations. To actually produce synergy and achieve real results, you need to pay attention to all three laws.

The potential for joint value creation drives any business combination. Out of this value, each party might earn a return on its efforts. The simple way of summarizing this relationship is indeed $1 + 1 = 3$. But this statement is too abstract and simplistic. It begs many practical questions.

For example, how much more value is created by the combination? In our metaphorical formula, the extra value is 50 percent (3 is 50 percent greater than 2). But in a real situation, what is the actual amount of extra value created? That variable is clearly worth pinning down before you launch any new combination. If the increased value is great, then the risk of failure is probably lower and there will be more extra value to share in the third law. If the increased value is small, then everything must go right for the combination to pay off. Governance must be optimal and setbacks must be minimal. Furthermore, with such a narrow margin of error in the combination, a lopsided division of gains could well leave one party earning less from the combination than it would if the party kept its assets separate. Consequently, this party would be less likely to want to commit to the combination.

And there is an even more fundamental question: How do we even measure value in this context? The numerical metaphor makes it looks easy to add and compare values. But in fact, the benefits of a combination may come in various forms—from added cash profits or lowered costs to added learning or sustainability of an advantage. And not-for-profit partners will usually value outcomes differently still. Similarly, the inputs, or contributions, are also valued differently—these could be cash, technology, know-how, and so forth. In the abstract, you might think that all the benefits sought and the contributions made affect shareholder value or the market capitalization of a firm. But the steps from strategic benefits to market valuation are, in themselves, usually rough estimates at best. Furthermore, each partner may perceive the benefits from any given combination differently. One partner may estimate an outcome of 3 when the other sees only 2.5. Such differences may get resolved in the negotiation over the distribution of gains, but they make the initial evaluation of joint value murky.

To address these kinds of ambiguities, we need to focus concretely on the economic and competitive mechanisms that will drive the creation of joint value. This calls for fundamental strategic analysis. Why would combining resources yield an added benefit? What new competitive advantages are generated by the combination? Does it matter how the resources are combined? Which key levers affect the amount of value created by the combination? We'll examine these issues closely in chapter 3.

Second Law: Govern the Collaboration

The second law of business combinations is that they must be implemented in a way that creates joint value in reality, not just on paper. In other words, the combination *has to act as an integrated operation in those areas that count for value creation.* We might summarize this law as $1 + 1 = 1$, referring now to unity in the management of the combination, not to its economic rationale.

Effective governance means more than ensuring that the parties get along at the personal level or that their cultures mesh. Business combinations, of course, involve people, and "soft" factors related to culture need to be addressed with care. Important as these factors are, however, they do not predict success. Excellent combinations have been struck across wide cultural differences, and harmonious personal relationships have often failed to support poorly designed business combinations. I have observed that when "cultural differences" are cited to explain the failure of a deal, the phrase more often than not hides conflicting interests and incompatible strategies.

Alternatively, the effective-governance law might seem to depend mostly on the legal structure of a combination. After all, that structure will reflect some high-level decisions, such as whether to acquire part or all of a firm, how to share investments, and so on. But this too is only a partial condition of success. Joint value does not appear automatically when assets are combined; value creation and distribution also depend on how the combination is shaped and managed after the initial deal is concluded.

When the deal is an acquisition, for example, the acquired resources can be merged into existing units or not, and the management personnel and processes may be left in place or replaced by that of the acquiring firm. Alliances, by definition, leave the partners to be managed as separate firms, but there may be varying degrees of cross-holdings or shared ownership. Simpler transactions usually include little joint management, just an agreement to exchange value on prearranged terms. We'll take a closer look at these combination forms in chapter 2.

Across all these various forms, the elements that are critical to creating joint value must be managed effectively in a coordinated fashion. If the main source of joint value is economies of scale in production, for example, then the combination—whatever its form—must successfully integrate investment and management of the production facilities. If the joint value comes from sales, then that aspect of the deal, similarly, needs coordinated management. Often, the elements critical to a combination do not reside in every part of the value chain. Thus, many combinations can have successful outcomes even if they fall short of full integration and focus only on collaboration in selective areas. But in such combinations, too, excessive rivalry, conflict, or differences in management approach can doom the effort. We will look closely at these challenges in chapter 4.

Third Law: Share the Value Created

Even when joint value is created by a well-governed combination, your company might not receive a good part of the value. That's why the last law is certainly not the least: ultimately, the joint gains need to be divided in a way that leaves each party better off than it would have been without the combination. The share of profits is the reward, or incentive, that encourages each party to contribute its resources to the combination.

To continue the metaphor, the 3 in the $1 + 1 = 3$ of the first law needs to be divvied up. The shares are not always predetermined and don't need to be equal. So, perhaps the summary formula will look like $1 + 1 = 1.4 + 1.6$. The split can also be 50-50 or 80-20 or anything else. What matters is that each party earns a fraction high enough to convince it to redirect its assets and efforts from another use into the combination.

Determining this split of profits is often just as hard as estimating the joint value itself. Just as the joint value depends on future trends in the competitive environment, so too does the division of profits. The balance of power between the parties in the combination usually evolves, and with it, so do the profit shares. For example, a partner may go into an alliance with weakness at the bargaining table, but may gain strength over time—perhaps because its own business options are growing and its contributions to the alliance have become more valuable. As a result, whatever division of gains was agreed upon at the start may come under strain over time, with one party pushing for a renegotiation or angling for new ways to capture additional value. The survival of the alliance may then be at risk if the new conditions are not accommodated.

Changes in the division of gains over time are also common in acquisitions, though in these deals the changes express themselves differently. In a cash acquisition (or divestment), one party is paid its share and the other gets the remaining returns, including both upside and downside potentials. If the former owners of the acquired resources retain some ownership in the new combination, perhaps because the acquisition is financed by stock, then they share somewhat in the subsequent risk of the combination. In that case, over time, each party may realize more (or less) value than what was initially anticipated.

This third law of business combinations, therefore, is intimately tied to the other two laws. Because of these links, companies often look at the other two laws through the lens of what they will gain or lose in this final equation. In other words, they evaluate the potential for joint value with a keen eye toward what share of value each party will capture, and they consider governance in the same way. Chapter 5 will explore the details of this law.

* * *

The three laws are easy to grasp, but can be challenging to apply. The triangular depiction of the three laws in figure 1-1 does not give you a lockstep formula to follow. And you have to continually weigh trade-offs among the laws. But as you go around the triangle and back again, you can be sure that you are addressing all the critical questions for success. The sidebar "How to Use the Three-Law Model" gives tips on how to apply the framework in practice.

The Three Laws in Concert

The three laws apply to every combination and shape your whole approach to competition. One implication of the increased use of combinations is that competition is becoming a battle of groups of firms against other groups. These groups, composed of firms and their allies, have boundaries and structures that shift continually. For example, Samsung is clearly part of the Google's Android smartphone grouping, but that does not keep it from supplying Apple with components and from flirting with other smartphone standards. An even more fluid set of groupings is now forming around the internet-of-things industry. Remix strategy helps you succeed in this kind of competition by focusing your attention on the bundles of resources you need, regardless of where these are, inside or outside your company. The three laws are guides to how you create value, govern collaboration, and share profits in these multipartner groups too, as chapter 6 will show.

This book will also help you rethink core questions in your business strategy. I will argue that the idea of recombining resources—and the laws of how to do this right—should be an integral part of

How to Use the Three-Law Model

The three laws will remind you of the fundamentals of any business combination. In using them, consider the forces influencing each one (these are discussed in subsequent chapters) and the linkages between the laws:

- **It is fine to prioritize one corner of the triad, but be sure to follow the linkages.** For example, the first law on joint value will lead to deal-structure questions (the second law), which lead to how gains are divided (the third law). Or the division-of-profit law (third) will send you back to structure (second), which then depends on how joint value is created (first). Similarly, deal negotiations (second) lead to consideration of the division of gains (third); those depend on what joint value is created (first). Don't worry about where you start the analysis, but be sure to complete the cycle. In practice, I have found that managers remember one or two laws and forget at least one of the three—but which one they forget varies from person to person!

- **Examine each corner of the triad with its own logic and in light of its own external forces.** As suggested above (and explored in depth in the following chapters), each law revolves around a different set of external factors and follows the logic of a different discipline. Joint value potential depends on the economics of the business, effective governance depends on organizational dynamics, and the rewards

your strategic thinking. Because of this, remix strategy has implications for all of the big questions in strategy. Where does competitive advantage come from? How do you deal with change and innovation? How does governance affect competitiveness? How do you measure the return on investment in your strategic initiatives?

from sharing value depend on continual negotiations among the parties.

- **There is no requirement to maximize each law, certainly not in isolation of the other laws.** You don't need the highest potential joint value or the most effective governance, though shooting high generally helps. What matters more than maximization of each law is the overall fit among the choices you make.

- **One or another corner is not the pinnacle, or basis, of the combination, regardless of the upright layout of the graphic.** Every corner depends on the other two. Without effective governance and rewarding value sharing, joint value will not be created. Similarly, how value is shared depends directly on how the joint value activities are governed. The triad is a bird's-eye view; it is not a hierarchical structure rising up from the ground.

- **When you have multiple deals—as you probably will—the three laws also apply to the totality of your portfolio.** For your whole combination strategy to work, each deal in the portfolio must work. In addition, however, each deal is likely to be related to other deals: joint value in one deal will depend on activities in others, governance of one deal will affect the same in others, and so on.

You will gain a new perspective on these core issues in chapter 7, the concluding chapter.

Taken as a whole, the chapters in this book will help you navigate the landscape of related decisions shown in figure 1-2. Unfortunately, these decisions are sometimes treated as a linear

FIGURE 1-2

Management Tool

Key decisions in remix strategy

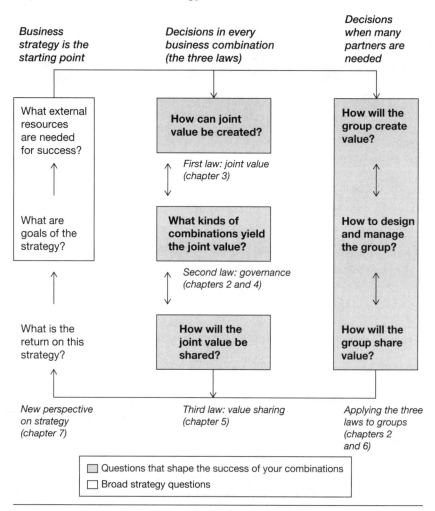

*Business
strategy is the
starting point*

*Decisions in every
business combination
(the three laws)*

*Decisions
when many
partners are
needed*

What external
resources
are needed
for success?

**How can joint
value be created?**

**How will the
group create
value?**

*First law: joint value
(chapter 3)*

What are
goals of the
strategy?

**What kinds of
combinations yield
the joint value?**

**How to design
and manage
the group?**

*Second law: governance
(chapters 2 and 4)*

What is the
return on this
strategy?

**How will the
joint value be
shared?**

**How will the
group share
value?**

*New perspective
on strategy
(chapter 7)*

*Third law: value sharing
(chapter 5)*

*Applying the three
laws to groups
(chapters 2
and 6)*

☐ Questions that shape the success of your combinations
☐ Broad strategy questions

sequence, whereas they clearly depend on each other. Worse, in many companies, the decisions are handed off from one division to another. But you are far better off sharing the reasoning and enabling iteration around the key decisions.

The map of decisions in figure 1-2 shows how your basic strategic goals and needs drive your firm's key decisions in making combinations—why make combinations, with which partners, how, and to what end? The principles that should guide your answers to these questions can be applied to single deals as well as to groups of deals. This book focuses on the questions that shape the success of your combinations (gray boxes), and it provides a new perspective on the broad strategy questions (white box).

What the Three Laws Look Like in Practice

To see how the laws work in practice—and what happens when combinations fail to fulfill them—let's look at some examples. These case studies can clarify the concepts and help you see how the three laws apply to the decisions you face.

Consider, for example, the combination strategies of Daimler and of Renault in the early 2000s. The companies' ultimate goals were roughly similar, but the decisions they made about business combinations were widely different.

Two Paths in the Global Automobile Industry

Leaders at Daimler and at Renault faced similar strategic issues. Both companies were strong in their home countries and in Europe generally, but were niche players elsewhere in the world. Each company's leadership team decided that it needed to expand its footprint globally and increase its volume of production. Organic growth seemed a slow and difficult way to achieve these goals. Both Daimler and Renault therefore sought combinations with existing companies that could help them expand production and sales globally. In other words, both companies saw a potential to create joint value through a business combination—the first law of every business combination. From there, however, they took different steps, which have led to widely different results.

Daimler proceeded by acquiring Chrysler in the United States and then buying a one-third stake in Mitsubishi in Japan. Later, it also took a minority stake in Hyundai Motors in Korea, formed a three-way auto-engine joint venture with Hyundai and Mitsubishi, and added joint ventures in China. Overall, Daimler created a complex network of alliances worldwide at the same time that it worked to integrate the whole of Chrysler's business.

Renault chose a different route for the governance of its combinations. It focused mostly on its relationship with Nissan, which was a substantially bigger player in Japan and worldwide than Mitsubishi. Renault acquired a one-third stake in Nissan for $5.4 billion. Later, the two companies created a fifty-fifty joint venture to run joint operations, and they invested directly in each other. The result was a more coordinated and balanced approach than Daimler's multiple, but relatively separate alliances.

The differing governance choices made by each leadership team were heavily influenced by the conditions of its combination partners. Daimler was a more powerful player than any of its partners. Renault was almost equally balanced with Nissan in terms of production volumes. Nissan was financially in distress, but it had a proud and successful history, good technology, and good brands.

With these governance choices, collaboration between Renault and its partner was much more successful than that between Daimler and its partners. Daimler's relationship with Mitsubishi unraveled after a few years; the German company later divested its ownership of Chrysler after pouring money into the American carmaker, at a deep loss on the investment. Renault, by contrast, successfully turned Nissan around and created an integrated global operation rooted in Europe and Japan. The second law of business combinations explains Daimler's failure and Renault's success.

The third law came into play too. Because the structures of the deals were different, value was shared differently in the two cases. To acquire Chrysler, Daimler paid off Chrysler shareholders with a one-third premium over market value; in other words, the returns to those former owners of the resource were fixed at this point. The residual returns to whatever joint value DaimlerChrysler might create would accrue to the shareholders of the combined company. Unfortunately, because the actual joint value created was negative, these shareholders were left with negative returns.

The Renault-Nissan partnership, by contrast, set out to create new value for all parties and to pay out benefits as the new value occurred. As a result, the structure of the alliance enabled both parties to gain (or lose, if that were the case) proportionally over time. Their mutual and partial shareholdings were the primary way in which they shared the returns of their cooperation.

The overall performance of the two companies reflected the results from these combinations, but corporate performance depends on much else. During the 2000s, Renault's stock performance exceeded DaimlerChrysler's. The latter's fortunes only turned after it divested Chrysler and in effect abandoned the whole combination strategy it had forged in the early 2000s. Renault held fast to its model. Nissan flourished, but Renault itself suffered renewed weakness in its European operations.

Still, Renault was clearly more successful with its combination strategy than Daimler. And the benefits of its alliance with Nissan still resonate today, as the partners continue to manage their global businesses together. Even Daimler has since invested in that combination, buying minority shares in Renault and Nissan. Could the outcomes of these parallel combination strategies have been foreseen? The answer is probably yes, even though business results are always subject to chance. Could the poor results have been avoided by application of a more coherent strategy? I think so, but to see how, we will need a more nuanced understanding of each of the three laws. Before digging deeper, it's worth examining how the laws work in a context very different from the mature auto industry.

The Progression of a Media Combination

A decade-long relationship between Pixar and Disney illustrates how the balance of power between partners can change over time, affecting all aspects of the combination.

Steve Jobs's start-up, Pixar, was still unproven when both Jobs and Disney executives saw the potential for joint value in a Disney-Pixar combination. Pixar's digital techniques could help strengthen Disney's traditional animation business, they reasoned. They signed a feature-film production agreement for up to three films. Disney held the bulk of the rights to the movies, their distribution, and control over decisions about their production. Predictably, the returns were to be lopsided too: Pixar would earn 10 to 15 percent of revenues, and the movie rights were owned by Disney.

All this began to change after the blockbuster success of the path-breaking film *Toy Story*. Because the movie was produced under the original agreement, Pixar received the minimal returns agreed upon. But on the strength of the box-office hit, Pixar went public, and the partners renewed their agreement under revised terms. The new coproduction agreement called for up to five films to be made under terms that gave each company nearly balanced ownership and say in a host of key aspects. Revenues and costs were to be divided fifty-fifty, there would be joint ownership of the new movies, and Disney would no longer enjoy exclusivity in distribution.

Under the new agreement, Pixar's successes continued unabated, with new box-office hits in *Toy Story 2, Monsters, Inc.,* and *Finding Nemo*. In the meantime, Disney produced a string of lackluster movies. Pixar's market value tripled in a few years, while Disney's stock remained flat.

Predictably, Jobs began to lobby for another revision of the deal with Disney. The tussle that subsequently unfolded between the partners was fodder for the gossip papers. At its root, however, this conflict was natural—the third law of business combinations was rearing its head. The way value was being shared was at stake.

A new deal was inked a few years later and represented a substantial change in value sharing as well as governance—Disney acquired all of Pixar for $7.4 billion in stock. The reasoning behind this deal is instructive. Prior experience had shown that Pixar and Disney could create substantial joint value. But as Pixar grew in capability, the friction in the earlier arrangements prevented deeper cooperation. In other words, the companies were not managed as if they were one entity—far from it. A full acquisition would achieve that unity. The acquisition was done with stock, which meant that (in concept at least) the shareholders of both companies would share in future returns.

Less than a decade later, the acquisition of Pixar was hailed as a great step in Disney's revitalization after a period during which it struggled to find its footing in new media. After the Pixar deal, Disney also acquired Lucasfilm, Marvel, and a series of smaller digital technology companies. These deals brought new assets and capabilities into the Disney fold and boosted the competitiveness of all its business lines, from movies and TV to theme parks in the United States and abroad. This trajectory shows how business remixes can spur change and innovation even in well-established, traditional companies.

How can you ensure that you end up like Disney, Pixar, Renault, or Nissan and not like DaimlerChrysler? Understanding the three laws of a combination in full detail is the key—you'll do that in subsequent chapters. Before we jump into those details, however, we need to understand the landscape of decisions that you face. How do combinations fit into your overall business strategy? What kinds of combinations should you consider? How might these combinations fit together? The next chapter defines the key decisions in remix strategy.

Chapter 2

Assessing Your Portfolio of Relationships

A S WITH ANY GOOD STRATEGY, REMIXING RESOURCES starts by identifying your options. Every decision you face will have trade-offs among the choices. The chapters that follow will show you in detail how to use the three laws to make these choices. Before you can apply these laws, however, you need to assess what kinds of combinations are available to you.

This assessment requires two steps. First, you need to examine the range of combinations that you currently have and might choose in future deals. Each deal type has distinct characteristics; selecting the right deal for the job is critical to creating value, as we saw in the automobile case discussed earlier. To help you select the right deal, this chapter introduces a useful way to array your choices on a spectrum. Later in the book, you will learn powerful tools for selecting your position on this spectrum.

The second step in your assessment is to examine the web of combinations that you have and that you might need. Here the focus is not on the characteristics of each individual deal, but on how multiple deals fit together as a network. Often, a business strategy will require you to gain access to the resources of multiple partners or to acquire a series of companies. Over time, these strategies build up your *relational footprint*—the partnerships that function as an extension of your firm. Later in the book, we will see in detail how the same three laws that apply in every business combination also apply to this network as a whole.

The Relationship Spectrum

One decision that often requires some back and forth before being settled is the form of the combination—broadly put, whether it will be a vendor relationship, an alliance, or a merger. All too often, corporate decision sequences settle the choice too soon by assigning the deal to the mergers-and acquisitions team, to the alliance team, or to the procurement team. And CEOs often bias this choice by the way they talk about one type of deal or another.

Five years after stepping down as CEO of Sun Microsystems, Scott McNealy tweeted: "Most overused phrase in business is 'strategic partner.' Favorite partnership for me is a purchase order. Defined charter, beginning, end." Those who knew him during his long tenure at Sun were not surprised—they had heard this perspective before. McNealy's words probably resonate with many senior managers. The term *strategic partner* is overused, and all too often, as he implies, it describes a relationship that lacks clear direction and, ultimately, leads to no great outcomes.

The fact is that McNealy is both right and wrong. To avoid flimsy strategic alliances you should know your phrases and use them wisely. But McNealy's view is also limited and constraining in its own way. It pays to step back and examine your options in a neutral fashion, as we will do in this book (especially in chapter 4).

Not every kind of relationship between two firms is a combination, as the term is used in this book. And often, you don't need a combination to produce synergy. A simpler transaction may also do the job—a trade or an exchange of products, money, and services. The difference between a transaction and a combination rests on how the resources of the firms are governed. If they are governed separately and only output is traded, we have a transaction. If they are governed jointly, then we have a combination.

Simple transactions, short of what we're calling business combinations, can indeed unlock joint value in many situations. The English economist David Ricardo described in the early nineteenth century how the simple trade of goods can bring benefits to two parties, each comparatively better at doing something the other needs. In his famous example, Portugal would make wine and England would make cloth and the nations gain joint benefits by trading—not by merging their territories. Today, we refer to this idea as the principle of comparative advantage. Because of differences in the natural resources of trading partners, or the scale or specialization of the partners, trade using simple transactions can generate synergy.

And so it is in relationships between firms too. Take autos and gasoline—a classic example of synergy, because each is much more valuable when used with the other, to state the obvious. Realizing this joint value does not require mergers between oil companies and automakers. All that is needed is for the consumer to buy the right type of gasoline at the pump.

But therein lies the secret. These products are now so standardized that gasoline specifications are readily available to run in all common internal-combustion engines. In many industries, the linkages between supply-chain stages are not so standardized. Synergy then requires that relationships between firms be deeper than a simple transaction. That is where business combinations come in.

Different Kinds of Combinations

A new combination thus occurs when assets previously governed separately are managed together in one way or another, as one bundle, so to speak. Let's consider what this means.

Software and hardware may be sold in a package or a bundle, such as when we buy a laptop or tablet with software installed. Or telecom companies might offer bundles that include internet, TV, and telephone services. These products and services are sold in this way because consumers are thought to benefit from the bundling, through a better integration of the systems, the cost savings from one-stop shopping, and so on. (In some situations, usually barred by antitrust authorities, the bundling is intended to exploit the monopoly power of producers.)

This notion of bundling is relevant to what we mean here by asset combinations, and I will also use the term *asset bundling* in this book. But in bundling assets, the benefits come not from how consumers use a product or service, but from how producers use the assets. When there are advantages to managing different assets in tandem, you might benefit from owning them all under one roof. But not always. You can also enjoy the benefits of asset bundling by coordinating the work of different asset owners.

In the example of autos and gasoline, there are no benefits to actually managing the assets of the producers in tandem; it is sufficient for consumers to simply combine the end products. But think of how each of those industries works. To make an automobile, producers need to coordinate production across a wide range of suppliers—that is a form of asset bundling, though the assets are not owned by one company. The same is true for the oil industry—the large oil companies usually do own many of the assets involved, but the firms also coordinate production with other resource owners.

These brief examples show that the *form* of an asset bundle—or a business combination—will vary. When a firm acquires external units, it combines the ownership of the new assets with its existing assets and, with that combination, unifies its management under one roof. When a firm invests in an equity joint venture or takes a minority position in another firm, ownership is not combined, but shared. The management of the asset bundle is then not unified, but is likely to be coordinated through some form of joint governance.

Other forms of combination are looser in terms of the ownership of assets, and the ownership may not change at all. A nonequity alliance, such as a joint R&D program or comarketing program, might comanage the assets, but might not share ownership. Still, nonequity alliances are combinations as the term is used here. Similarly, in a still looser relationship, your vendor or supplier might allocate assets to produce output for your firm, even though there may be little coordinated management of these assets and, again, no shared ownership. And open-innovation models, technology markets, and ecosystem communities often need nothing more than a common standard or legal framework to remix assets.

You can categorize most common business combinations according to two important parameters. The first parameter is the *duration* of the combination. The duration can range from a onetime transaction to a long-lived relationship. The second parameter is the *extent of joint decision making,* or the intensity of management coordination that is needed between the firms in the combination. Figure 2-1 shows where different business combinations fall in relation to these two parameters.

```
Management Tool
```

FIGURE 2-1

The relationship spectrum

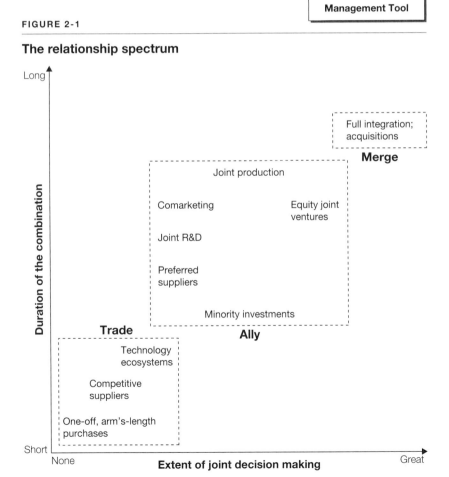

The terms used to describe similar types of combinations vary by industry. Automotive firms have preferred suppliers, for example, but in the airline industry, such a combination might be a type of code-share agreement. The defense industry uses teaming agreements, which telecom or software executives might call consortia. Even differences between legal departments of different firms will shape the conversation.

Because of these differences in jargon, it is more useful to think of the spectrum as representing three zones, labeled in figure 2-1 with the broader terms *trade, ally,* and *merge.* Firms *trade* when they simply buy and sell goods or services, as in simple outsourcing. They *ally* when they work together more closely, but remain separately owned units. And they *merge* when they combine all resources under one roof.

The spectrum shown in figure 2-1 does not say which form is best; moving higher in the chart does not imply greater value creation. The context and intent of a specific combination dictates which form will be more effective. The fit between task and form is what matters.

Let's take a closer look at the two axes on the chart to understand how they might affect the workings of a combination. In later chapters, we will return to this in more depth.

Duration of the Combination

The time frame of a combination shapes how and when it is used. The expected duration of a combination matters because the initial investments in making the combination usually take time to yield returns. In some situations, the returns to a combination come soon enough that long time horizon is not so important. But when a party needs to allocate special investments to a combination, it is unlikely to do so if the relationship will be short-lived. For example, when miners locate a capital-intensive processing facility close to a mine owned by another party, they will usually want a long-term supply agreement for the raw material, or the parties will form a joint venture to co-own the processing facility.

The duration of a combination may depend on the contract between the parties, and it may be cemented by an equity agreement and perhaps enforced with exit penalties. At other times, an implicit assurance of repeated transactions (say, with a preferred supplier) constitutes a long horizon even if the contracts themselves contain short-fuse exit clauses. Caterpillar's contracts with dealers, for example, traditionally had a thirty-day exit clause, but most dealers have been with the company for generations. Research on negotiation shows that repeated games engender more cooperation than do one-off games, in which one party can grab the spoils and leave town, so to speak.

In the end, few business combinations are "for life" in the way that marriages usually plan to be. Business combinations are marriages of convenience, and when circumstances change, it is reasonable to change the form of the combination or to end it altogether. As a result, long-duration combinations tend to be more appropriate for relatively stable industries, while short-duration deals are more often used in fast-changing environments. It is not surprising, therefore, to find the dynamic internet space littered with alliances that lasted at most a few years, while the more mature petroleum industry has joint ventures that are decades old.

So, the expected lifetime of a combination shapes how it will work. Even more important, however, are the internal moving parts of the combination. That's reflected in the horizontal axis of figure 2-1.

Extent of Joint Decision Making in the Combination

How often will the managers on each side need to communicate and negotiate with each other during the life of the combination, that is, after the initial deal is struck? That's the question that you need to ask to determine the extent of joint decision making for any potential combination. Joint decisions require continual interaction. Separate decisions don't—they just follow a template that is agreed upon at the start.

At the far left side of figure 2-1, you'll find arm's-length agreements, in which there is little coordination beyond the making of the deal. After the signing, each party will do what it agreed to do and then trade, sell, or buy outputs on specified terms. Competitive supplier relationships work this way, and when coordination fails, they may end up in court for enforcement. These are the rules of the road of standard market transactions, which is why relationships at this end are often referred to as *transactional*. In our terminology, the deals in this corner are examples of pure *trade* relationships—not combinations.

The relationships in the middle of the chart are different in that they involve more joint decision making. They only work if managers in charge of the resources in the combination coordinate their actions. Managers may need to match timing and volumes of production, tailor product specifications, invest in new assets, and so forth. If a combination requires such ongoing management coordination, then it belongs in this middle zone, labeled *ally* in the chart. The degree and form of coordination vary widely within this zone, from loosely organized joint programs in R&D and marketing to joint ventures governed with high-level boards and extensive staffing. But all these forms depend on some joint decision making after the deal is signed—much more than vendor and supplier relationships in the *trade* zone.

The combinations at the far right, grouped under the term *merge,* are of a different sort altogether. Here the assets of the parties have been combined under common ownership, so one cannot speak of coordination with an external party. There is still the need for management coordination among the assets being combined, and the assets often remain under a vestige of their old organization. But this coordination is now internal to the firm, where the degree of joint decision making is even higher than in the middle zone. Still, such internal coordination is by no means a given. Daimler and Chrysler, for example, struggled mightily to integrate their operations during their merger. Other companies have an easier time because their acquisitions are smaller or are in more homogenous assets. Cemex, for example, easily integrates assets acquired from external parties, in part because a cement plant in one part of the world looks very much like one in another.

Our discussion so far gives hints about how to shape a combination, but it does not create a complete picture. We have described the features of deals along the relationship spectrum, but we have not prescribed when you should use one type of deal or another. When should a combination be for a short or long time? When will it demand more or less coordination? What form improves the return to each party? How do you best manage each form? These questions go to the heart of the second law of business combinations—how to govern the combination so that joint activities indeed produce the promised synergy. We'll tackle that law in chapter 4.

As we will see, the forces that favor one type of deal over another are fluid; they vary with business objectives. Many industries have shifted over time from the top right of this chart to the bottom left—from deal types with maximum control to others with shared control. One reason for this shift is that information technology, better contract design, and the sheer growth of market choices now allow firms to coordinate activities with looser tie-ups than before. Thus, alliances are replacing mergers. By the same token, companies are now achieving levels of coordination that formerly might have required an alliance by using arm's-length trade agreements. Nevertheless, other conditions, such as the need for integration among technologies in an emerging industry, may argue for tighter control.

With this chart, you can measure the depth of any single business relationship. That is the first step in assessing what you are dealing with. Let's look now at the options you face in designing a portfolio containing many deals.

Relational Footprints

When you have many alliances and acquisitions, does each of these deals stand on its own, or are they interdependent? Do the activities and success of one affect one or more of the other deals? If your company is typical, then interdependence is the rule. Your deals depend on one another, and so you need to make sure that they add value to each other and don't conflict with or detract from each other. Another form of synergy potential arises here: the value created by several deals can far surpass the sum of the values created by each deal. In today's lingo, this is called a *network effect*.

To create positive network effects, you will usually need to design and manage your portfolio consciously. When you do that, you will be shaping the strategy of a *constellation* of firms. Like a single firm, a constellation is simply another organizational model for governing a broad combination of resources. The bundle of resources that competes against other bundles in any given market may be organized as a legal entity we call a firm and thus will be governed by ownership and "internal" management. But another bundle may be organized as a collection of separate firms that are managed as external relationships.

The airline industry provides a perfect example. Today, Star Alliance, with its twenty-nine partner airlines, competes with one-world (thirteen partners) and SkyTeam (nineteen partners) in the same global business. These groupings face competition from individual firms—sometimes from their own members acting on their own, but more importantly from unaligned companies, such as Emirates Airlines. The airline groupings and single firms each govern a similar set of resources—planes, landing slots, loyalty programs, brands, personnel, and the like—and compete on roughly similar criteria, including route structure, service, and price. The difference between these models lies in how these resources are managed—one relies on a multipartner constellation to do so, and the other uses the internal organization of a single firm.

The three main constellations also compete with each other on how they organize the resources of their members. In fact, they are remarkably similar in how they are run. Each constellation knows that if it falls behind in one aspect or another, such as route structure or service, there may be a snowball effect whereby its business falls off, partners peel off, and new members will be hard to find.

As a result, each constellation competes mightily with the others to add resources and members and perhaps to deprive the others of new members. Consider the bidding war that ensued between American Airlines (AA) and Delta over Japan Airlines (JAL). JAL had been part of AA's oneworld constellation for years, but when JAL found itself facing bankruptcy, Delta—a major partner in the SkyTeam constellation—did its best lure to the airline away from oneworld, at one point offering substantial payments. The negotiations went on for months, but in the end, JAL stayed in the oneworld constellation.

Competitive battles over partners are common in industries permeated by multifirm constellations. This leads to pitched battles when the rivals believe that the size or structure of their constellation might yield competitive advantage for them. The basic idea that the combination of resources delivering a product can be managed to strategic advantage is also relevant to industries with more traditional patterns of competition. There too, it matters whether you organize your collection of partners and subcontractors better than your rival organizes theirs.

Picturing a Relational Footprint

To gain an edge in such battles, you need to understand and shape your relational footprint—the map of relationships between your firm and other firms. (As discussed later in the book, this concept is related to, but different from, the idea of a business ecosystem.)

Fortunately, mapping relationships has become a popular new form of graphic entertainment. With the rise of social networking and the accessibility of online data, there is no shortage of charts showing how people, organizations, or ideas are connected to each other. The two types of charts most commonly used in business are shown in figure 2-2. They are both good starting points for capturing a relational footprint, but each also has its drawbacks.

A figure such as the one on the left side of figure 2-2—technically referred to as an *ego chart*—can help you see your immediate

FIGURE 2-2

Two perspectives on relational footprints

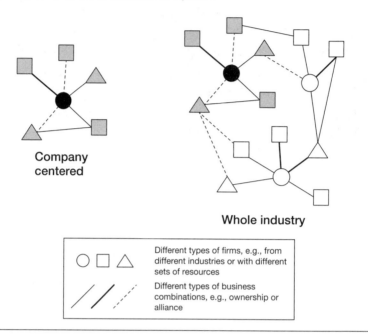

Company
centered

Whole industry

	Different types of firms, e.g., from different industries or with different sets of resources
	Different types of business combinations, e.g., ownership or alliance

connections clearly. But bear in mind, if one of your partners creates an ego chart, that chart will look different, because it will have that partner at the center. Lufthansa's ego chart will look different from that of its partner United Airlines, for example. Unless one company is clearly at the center of power and leadership in a constellation, ego charts aren't reliable for analytical purposes.

The *whole-industry* chart on the right side shows other linkages beyond your ego network, including networks that center on your rivals. Identifying such clusters can help you understand the main constellations competing in an industry and help you make more-informed decisions about your own partners. Unfortunately, a whole-industry chart can be dense and confusing. When everyone appears to be connected to everyone, and when every single connection is listed, regardless of the strategy it supports, you can easily lose track of the relative importance of any given connection.

The best way to use these two approaches—company-centered and whole-industry views—is in tandem. You can go back and forth between the narrow and broad view to get the most useful picture of your connections. Plus, it is important to consider the key success factors in your industry or competitive domain when visualizing your network of partners.

Competing with Constellations

You can add analytical power to these maps by pruning and reshaping them to show how each resource combination creates value in furtherance of a particular strategic goal. In terms of the three laws of business combinations, you can now assess the potential for joint value not just between two parties, but across the entire network.

For example, when an airline constellation considers whether to add a new member to its network, it will evaluate how that new member might add value to the business of each existing member. Doing so can get complicated, as sometimes a new member might add value to some but not all members or might even be costly for some members. When Singapore Airlines joined Star Alliance, for example, Thai Airlines, an existing Star member, was less than thrilled, as Singapore was a direct rival in its region. But the potential benefits that Singapore brought to the Star constellation exceeded the cost to one member. In other cases, a member might bolt from the constellation if it feels that it bears a big burden from a new combination among its partners. Continental switched from SkyTeam to Star Alliance when Delta merged with Northwest, making Continental feel like a fifth wheel in its original grouping.

To understand how additional members of a constellation add value to the whole, therefore, consider the competitive landscape of the group and its sources of advantage. For airlines, this means considering how a new combination affects a constellation's route structure across the globe. The constellations were created so that any allied airline could reach all corners of the globe seamlessly, so having major players in big markets is seen as one of the key to success.

The relational footprints of the airline constellations are shown in Figure 2-3. Because the alliances aim to combine firms from

FIGURE 2-3

Relational footprints of airlines in global air travel

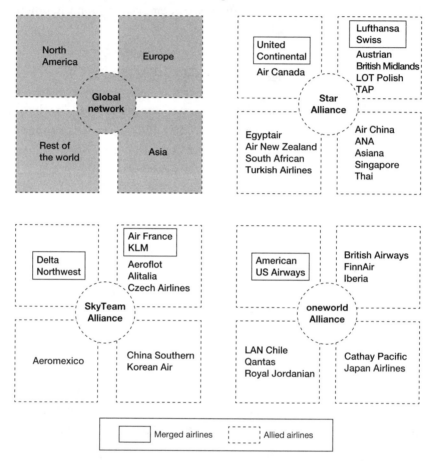

Source: Company websites and industry reports. Figure shows only the main members; each group may have additional associate members not shown.

each region into a global network, the depiction highlights the geographic dimension of their footprints. (In other situations, a footprint might highlight other dimensions, such as industry segments.) The competing airline constellations are patterned after the generic model at the top left of figure 2-3. Each airline has bilateral alliances with at least one member of its group and is a member of a joint organization. Some members have joint ventures with each other, and some members have merged.

Global travel is clearly the focus of figure 2-3, so the chart does not include each corporation's full set of connections. For airlines, this distinction may not matter much, as most of what they do is global travel, though their relationships in the cargo business might indeed differ from what is shown here. But for large, diversified companies, a generic relational footprint that includes all business connections is almost useless. General Electric, for example, has hundreds of relationships with external partners. But the main relationships that matter in its aircraft engine business are those with players in that business and in adjacent sectors. The same is true for GE's health-care software business and perhaps for its business in certain regions, such as Latin America.

Often, the key pattern to be highlighted is not geography, but segments of an industry or stages in a supply chain. In the emerging business of electric vehicles, for example, the auto companies each have significant relationships with the manufacturers of batteries, a key component that most automakers do not make in-house. Those relationships would be important to include on a relational footprint chart. A network of regional dealerships may be less critical to include for these products—in fact, Tesla is attempting to bypass regional dealers altogether and market its cars nationally on the web.

Building a New Business with a Constellation

To be useful, a chart showing your relational footprint needs to set boundaries around a specific relevant industry or competitive marketplace. That doesn't mean, however, that it shouldn't reflect ancillary industries that affect your business.

In many modern industries, key players exist well beyond your immediate value chain. Complementary technologies and products, for example, may come from other industries, adjacent to your value chain, but not directly connected. Nonetheless, they can be important considerations when you're shaping your relational footprint.

Google's smartphone business offers a good illustration. A different way to depict a relational footprint is shown in figure 2-4.

FIGURE 2-4

Relational footprint of Google in smartphones

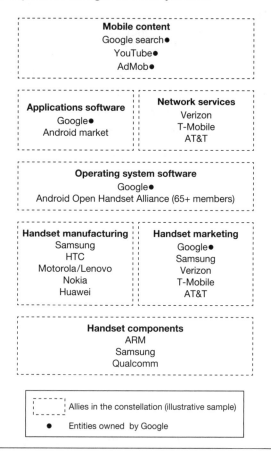

This figure organizes the main parts of the Google constellation across several complementary value chains. Without hardware and network services, Google's software will not work; without attractive applications, no one will be interested in it; and without a position in mobile advertising, Google may end up gaining little from launching its own smartphone.

For this reason, Google aimed to create a community of allies that together provides the full stack of components and services needed. (The concept of a stack is related to that of a value chain, as discussed in chapter 3.) To create this system of complementary businesses, Google used a remix strategy. Some of Google's combinations were acquisitions—the company integrated the capabilities of its acquisitions into its own operations. Other combinations were alliances, large and small, and constellations with multiple members. Each of these relationships represented a critical piece in the set of resources Google needed to assemble to build its smartphone business.

The layout in figure 2-4 highlights the partners in each layer and component of the stack. Loosely speaking, this is often called an *ecosystem,* a concept explored further in chapter 6. Relational footprints are useful for tracing the specific relationships inside such an ecosystem.

Google's relational footprint illustrates a more open model than many others. The Android Open Handset Alliance is an open marketplace for applications and for software development. Google also licenses technology widely to manufacturers and hopes to enable a large number of network providers to use its system. Such openness is neither good nor bad in itself—it is a feature of the competitive environment and Google's own position. The open model reflects the fact that Apple's iPhone was already strong in the field and that Google itself had little relevant technology. However, Google's footprint over time added tight linkages as well. The company acquired Motorola Mobility, but two years later sold most of its assets. The divestment was an implicit recognition that loose alliances with multiple partners may be a better remix strategy for Android than a tight combination with one player.

In your relational footprint map, it is useful to distinguish between such loose alliances and tighter linkages. It is also useful to highlight major and minor players, and the distinct role that each member plays in the network. Social network analysts have long debated whether the bare, graphical pattern of a network matters more or less than the identities of the players within it and the content of the linkages among them. For our purposes, the identities and nature of the linkages matter deeply.

Visualizing Your Relational Footprint

Armed with this basic understanding of what a relational footprint is, you can start exploring what your own dream team of partners would look like.

Your goal is to develop a chart for your own business by focusing on the most important operations—inside your company and outside of it—that could create joint value by being combined. Your chart and footprint will be unique, reflecting the capabilities, goals, and competitive position of the companies involved. As shown in other examples in this chapter, your footprint may include linkages to other firms in different value-chain layers, market segments, vertical markets, geographic areas, technical fields, and industries. A generic example to get your thinking started is in figure 2-5.

To develop and use the relational footprint of your business, start with a (large) blank page, and take the following steps:

1. **Define the goals and key success factors in your competitive domain.** These follow from your analysis of your own business strategy. Examine your competitive situation and potential competitive advantages; assess your internal capabilities, strengths, and weaknesses; and then identify gaps that may be filled by new combinations. What do you aim to achieve strategically, and what capabilities will you need to acquire from the outside to get there? This analysis will suggest the basic format for the mapping to follow, that is, whether to focus on value-chain segments, geographic areas, or other elements. Stick to a well-defined competitive domain, and organize your chart in any way that reflects the most important features of your business and competitive landscape. (If you don't, your chart will start to look like a bowl of spaghetti, and you'll quickly get lost!)

2. **Map your current combinations in this domain.** Now, assemble the data that shows how far your current network of partners gets you toward your strategic goals. Alliances

FIGURE 2-5

Management Tool

Mapping your relational footprint

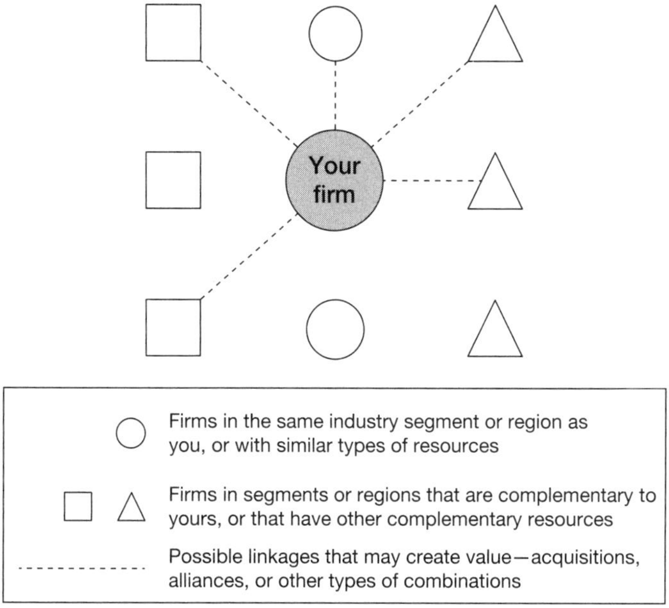

Firms in the same industry segment or region as you, or with similar types of resources

Firms in segments or regions that are complementary to yours, or that have other complementary resources

Possible linkages that may create value—acquisitions, alliances, or other types of combinations

of various sorts are obvious entries. But you should also include major suppliers and channels; you may decide to transform them into something different over time. Map recent acquisitions as well, to the extent that they are not already accounted for by your initial analysis of your internal capabilities. Note the relative strength of your existing combinations.

3. **Map potential alliances and acquisitions.** Often, preparing the map of your current combinations will suggest combinations that don't yet exist. This step should identify those potential combinations, including connections that might supplement or replace the weaker links you noted in the previous step. Where might new combinations create joint value?

4. **Evaluate critical links.** Step back and look at the maps. Some strategic needs are probably more urgent than others. Where are those key combinations? Which key combinations are weak? Sometimes one partnership leads to another. Which priorities among the new links ought to be developed?

5. **Map networks of your rivals.** Use your competitive intelligence to map the relationship footprint of your rivals and to identify the potential new combinations that would serve these competitors best. What might these rivals do in the near future? What might you be able to anticipate?

6. **Compare your footprint with those of your rivals.** This step is particularly important if competition in the industry takes the form of one group or camp against another, as in the global airline industry and in technology fields that are battling over standards. What competitive advantage does your constellation offer? And where are rivals threatening to overtake you?

This exercise will raise more questions than it answers, and for good reason: we are just looking ahead over the landscape here, not deciding what to do. To answer these new questions and make those decisions, we will need to understand the logic of the three laws better. It also helps to see some relevant examples and to have some basic tools in hand. All that lies ahead, in the next chapters.

Part Two

Using the
Three Laws
to Shape
Combinations

THE THREE LAWS ARE SIMPLE IN PRINCIPLE, PERHAPS even self-evident. Making concrete decisions that follow these laws, however, is challenging. Each law has its own logic, its own distinct set of important factors, and unique trade-offs. The three chapters in this part of the book address each law in depth. Along the way, they introduce new concepts and new tools that will help you make better remix decisions.

These chapters emphasize how the laws work in a wide variety of situations. The concrete details of each industry, company, and case vary tremendously. Each situation presents different conditions—different competitive forces, regulatory environments, financial and operational needs, and organizational and cultural factors. This book does not attempt to address all such details, even if they are important for success. Instead, part two focuses on the overarching logic that is common to a wide variety of situations. The guiding principles developed in this manner will help you navigate the complexities of your own case.

Because each chapter focuses on one of the laws, you may be tempted to ignore the relationships between the laws. But doing so would be a mistake. Often, the challenge of implementation lies in these relationships, because the best choice in one area might imply second-best choices in the others. For this reason, part two also highlights important relationships between the three laws.

Chapter 3

First Law: Identify Potential Joint Value

ALL BUSINESS STRATEGIES AIM TO CREATE VALUE. YOU can think of this in several ways. A popular meaning for value creation centers on improving the product or service that customers receive. But this kind of value creation is not an end in itself, at least not for profit-making entities. Ultimately, every strategy aims to create value for the firm. Often, you can indeed create value for the firm by first raising the value to customers. This strategy can increase demand and your customers' willingness to pay. In addition, however, you can also create value for your firm by lowering the costs of delivering the product or service and pocketing the savings. Either strategy, or both of them, will yield greater profits—and so a higher valuation for your firm. A firm's market value is another way to think about the idea of value creation.

How can a business combination create new value? Generally, it must deliver something more to customers or save something on the cost side. I call this *joint value* because you create it by joining forces. The creation of joint value is tricky, as it involves both the first and the second laws of business combinations—the potential for joint value must exist, and then the combination must be governed to make that potential real. Analytically, it is important to separate these two aspects of value creation. Here, we begin by focusing on how you can ensure that you follow the first law—you need to know where joint value will come from. (Chapter 4 will explore the second law—what you need to do to make that joint value actually appear.)

Value Creation in a Combination

Chester Barnard, the father of management studies, recognized the idea of joint value as the rationale for organizations in his 1938 classic *The Functions of the Executive*. He didn't use the term *synergy*; it hadn't yet been coined. But the idea that one person or group can't accomplish much without the cooperation (direct or indirect) of another was implied in all that he wrote.

Synergy is critical. In recent years, though, it has gotten a bad name. Big-ticket mergers promise synergy so that CEOs won't look like empire builders, but often, the new whole really isn't greater than the sum of its parts. Acquisition announcements tout expected synergies—and all too soon, analysts are smirking. Managers talk about synergy as if it's a panacea, but results often disappoint.

DaimlerChrysler, the failed merger discussed earlier, offers a classic example. Dissecting such a well-known story will help illustrate the concept of joint value. Let's look more closely at what happened.

When Daimler and Chrysler merged, the companies projected synergy to the tune of $3.8 billion per year. Of that total, $3 billion would come from cost savings in R&D, purchasing, financial services, and organizational efficiencies; the remainder was to come from added sales. These benefits were projected to come after Daimler spent $600 million in merger-related costs. By one calculation, the net after-tax flows of "yearly synergies" would have translated into a net present value of roughly $13 billion.

On the face of it, a $13 billion net benefit would be a substantial gain, given that the total market capitalization of Daimler and Chrysler before the merger was just under $77 billion. In other words, this projected synergy represented almost 17 percent of the combined market value of the companies before the merger. Remember our creative math? Here, it would have been: $1 + 1 = 2.34$.

If only it were that simple! It wasn't, because two realities intervened. First, those aspirational yearly synergies didn't materialize. Assets—even novel combinations of assets—don't create value by themselves, and they certainly don't automatically generate more value than they had in a previous situation or under previous ownership. The synergy has to be engineered. (In the private-equity world—where Chrysler ultimately ended up after being divested from DaimlerChrysler—creating this added value is generally called *sweating the assets*.) In this case, for DaimlerChrysler to generate the projected savings, the merger would have needed to consolidate R&D efforts across the two companies, centralize global purchasing, unify or closely coordinate selling and financing efforts, and so on. Doing so—across a proud American and a proud German company—proved too great a challenge.

Second, economic conditions turned against Chrysler, meaning that the assets Chrysler brought to the deal ultimately turned out to be less valuable to Daimler than first perceived. In the end, therefore, the $13 billion in predicted synergies simply did not materialize for the merged company.

But even that wasn't all. To have the right to the anticipated $13 billion in synergies, Daimler had to pay off Chrysler shareholders in the acquisition. This payoff is standard procedure in mergers and acquisitions. Shareholders of the target company are usually paid a premium on their shares to transfer ownership and control to the acquirer. In this case, the premium—28 percent of the value of Chrysler shares before the merger—translates into about $8 billion. Regardless of whether Daimler could realize the $13 billion in the years after the merger, therefore, the German company had already paid $8 billion of that projected amount to Chrysler shareholders from the start!

Daimler was not wrong to look for opportunities for creating joint value with Chrysler and other automakers with which Daimler tied up during its rush to expand globally. It had concluded, probably correctly so, that its own technology and brand could be extended beyond where it was being sold, and that another company may have had the scale and market access that could benefit from these Daimler inputs. That is the classic case for real synergy: you have a resource that could yield a greater return if it were combined with another company's resource. The problem was that Daimler and Chrysler executives didn't seem to know how to assess whether that vague, big-picture promise could really be fulfilled and what it would take to do so.

So synergy doesn't have a bad name because the concept is flawed. It has a bad name because too often, companies identify the potential value in a combination through an ad hoc process that relies on luck, not objective analysis. Many companies rely on various hunches to define the promise of a combination—feedback from customers, bright ideas from engineers, hallway conversations at conferences, epiphanies from visionary executives, smooth talk from an in-house champion who used to work for the other company. And once an executive has had that epiphany or conversation on the golf course and starts towards a deal, it may be hard to stop the momentum, especially if he or she is high up in the organization. Often, business leaders strike the deal without considering any alternatives; looking at other options is an afterthought, if anything. And often, the deal plays out poorly and ends up being bad for one or all parties.

That's why following the three laws is the key to creating real synergy. Doing so ensures that the potential value you're spotting is really there and that your pursuit of it—how you set your expectations and structure the deal—is intentional and purposeful. The rest of this chapter will focus on how you identify and scope out the joint-value potential in a combination. Subsequent chapters focus on the questions raised by the second and third laws.

Where to Look for Joint Value

The search for joint value has two stages: looking outside your company, and then looking inside. In the first stage, you scour the business landscape to find businesses that might complement your own. (In economic theory, two goods are complements when having one, or more of one, increases the value of having the other, or more of the other. Common examples: bread and butter, gasoline and cars, computer hardware and software.) In the second stage, you dive inside those businesses and inside your own to identify the components of the businesses that need to be connected to create joint value.

Firms that successfully make lots of acquisitions, as well as firms experienced in alliance strategy, employ both stages. They continually study their landscape, the industry's supply chain, their ecosystem, their vertical channels, and so on, to identify new uses of their products, new technologies to add value to their products, or new ways to improve delivery of products sold jointly with others. Importantly, however, they are also keenly aware that sometimes, managing the resulting interdependent relationships isn't all about coordinating complementary resources. It can also involve managing overlapping businesses—situations in which the success of one party detracts from or supplants the success of another. Classically, the idea of businesses combining to manage such overlaps suggests anticompetitive collusion and cartels. But as we will see, even within combinations of complements, firms need to suppress competition. Striking the right balance between cooperation and competition is not a simple matter; this question will stay with us throughout the book.

Look Outside for Complementary Businesses

Although every business is embedded in a unique landscape of buyers, sellers, technical linkages, and so forth, that landscape will probably look like one of the models in figure 3-1. The three models show the most common sources of complementarity among separate businesses. Through product flows or technical dependencies (linkages) in each model, one business is affected by the others. In the market model, businesses sell into the same market; in the

FIGURE 3-1

Every business is part of a system of complementary businesses

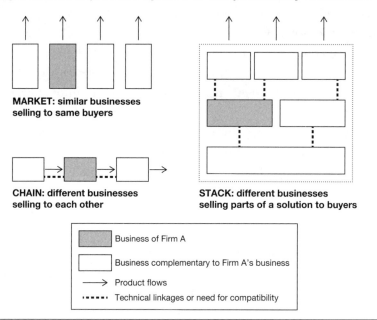

chain model, they sell to each other; and in the stack model, they sell in parallel to a final customer.

Figure 3-1 is, of course, simplified and abstract. In concrete situations, complementarity may arise from a combination of these sources, and from others not shown in the figure. Either way, to develop a relationship strategy toward outside firms, you need to identify the strongest sources of complementarity.

These three models correspond to three variants of interdependence described in the 1960s by the sociologist James Thompson. In one of the earliest theoretical analyses of business organizations, Thompson explained that organizations had to deal with pooled, sequential, or reciprocal interdependence among internal units. In pooled organizations, the work of several units depended on each other by drawing on a common pool of resources or contributing to a common output. In sequential organizations, the work of one unit provided input for another. In reciprocal organizations, the units each fed inputs to and from each other.

The most common way to think about a firm's environment is as a *market*. Except for rare monopolies, every business competes side by side with other firms in a market. These firms share what Thompson called pooled interdependence, though in a market, the businesses are mostly competitors. Still, there may be complementarities between these competitors if, for example, the businesses can benefit from scale economies by combining or if they shared common inputs. In that case, the combination of two competitors may create value by reducing costs—a classic example of the synergy typically cited in a *horizontal* combination: a merger or an acquisition between like businesses.

Of course, such a combination may also act to generate greater market power, extracting profits from buyers or sellers without creating new value. Horizontal business combinations often represent the trickiest balance between competition and cooperation, and thus often elicit careful scrutiny from antitrust authorities. Sometimes, the added market power of a combination is intended to counterbalance the market power of competitors, buyers, or suppliers. For example, Procter & Gamble acquired Gillette in part to increase P&G's power with large retailers such as Walmart. In airlines, antitrust authorities have allowed mergers and alliances that increased market power, partly to allow the applicants to compete better against other large players. At the same time, some proposed alliances have been blocked by antitrust authorities, such as the global shipping alliance proposed by Maersk—a proposal that threatened to concentrate the power of the shippers along key trading routes.

Another way to think of the environment of complementary businesses around your firm is as a *chain* where products or services flow from one business to the next. A supply or value chain of this kind generates opportunities for synergy when there are benefits from greater coordination or joint ownership of links in the chain, usually termed a *vertical* combination. One source of complementarity in such systems results when the amount, quality, and costs of products sold by one link affect the output and activities of the next link. Another source is technical complementarities between the links. Sometimes, the technical features of one link are highly dependent on technical features of a neighboring link. One link can then perhaps be tailored to better fit the needs of the other link, thus creating more value in combination. This system is a pure form of Thompson's sequential interdependence.

The market and chain models of business complementarity are well known because they represent age-old industries. Markets were around from the earliest trading days, and supply chains were popularized by the assembly technologies of the industrial revolution. In this sense, the *stack* model of complementarity among businesses is new, stemming mostly from the computer industry. But like the older models, the stack model, once popularized by this industry, clearly applies to other, older businesses too.

The stack model was so named in the computer industry because different parts of a computer system are put together (stacked) in order for the system as a whole to work. The PC stack, for example, at a minimum consists of a microprocessor, memory chips, input-output devices, the operating system, and application software. Today, larger and more complex stacks lie at the core of industries such as smart buildings and the so-called internet of things. Each of these stacks needs multiple components—from sensors and computer parts, to an infrastructure that connects the pieces, to devices that give users information and allow them to control the system. All these parts of the final system can conceivably be supplied from one firm to the other, as in a chain, with the last link serving the end user. But usually, the range of components is too broad and diverse for any one company to serve as the final assembler. As a result, the parts are often bundled together by a third party, a systems integrator, that doesn't manufacture anything. Or the parts are simply sold in parallel to the user. So, while the final system will eventually contain all elements of the stack, the parts are not always brought together by firms in a traditional supply chain. Stacks are increasingly common in modern competition in industries ranging from information technology to health-care systems.

In these stacks, there are strong technical complementarities between the components, or at least a strong need to coordinate decisions among producers of the components. The pieces need to be compatible with each other, and, in this context, that is akin to saying that they are complementary. Sometimes, this compatibility is black-and-white, that is, certain combinations work and others simply don't. At other times compatibility is a matter of degree, that is, stacks with a certain mix of components may work better than others. In Thompson's theory, the interdependence here is in part reciprocal and in part pooled.

Great opportunities for synergy can come from combining businesses in such stacks. But the range of these combinations, in reality, is neither horizontal nor vertical, as defined above. Maintaining the geometrical analogy, we would have to call these combinations sideways or parallel, but these terms are unwieldy except to those who loved eighth-grade geometry. So we will simply stick with the term *stack* combinations.

The Main Sources of Joint Value

The three models suggest *where* to search for business combinations that generate joint value—in industry segments that complement your business. You are likely to find potential allies, acquisition targets, or trading partners in these segments. But what might you seek to *do* with these partners? What strategies will actually create the joint value? Joint value typically comes from one of four sources: increased scale, expanded scope, improvements in management coordination, and expansion of future options. These sources are summarized in table 3-1.

Economies of scale. The most common—and varied—source of joint value is economies of scale, which allow for a reduction in the costs of either production or back-office operations. The tricky part is that the benefits of scale can arise at several points in the activities of a firm. To make a combination successful, you need to

	Management Tool

TABLE 3-1

Sources of joint value

Generic sources of joint value	Why value may be created when firms combine
Increased scale	• Savings in production cost from larger volume of operations • Increased market power from larger volume of sales or purchases • Specialization and focus that enables efficient scale of operations • Network effects from larger community of users
Increased scope	• Savings from sharing common resources in back office • Increased demand from cross- and joint-selling
Improved coordination	• Reduced uncertainty about supply and demand • Greater incentive for investment in specific assets • Reduced risk of dependence and holdup • Increased tailoring of output and activities
Expanded options	• Ability to hedge against uncertain outcomes in the future • Ability to respond to new information as it becomes available • Flexibility to change course as strategies and environment evolve

engineer the economies of scale carefully to target the potential source of joint value.

Economies of scale in production are often limited to the factory level; that is, they come from larger factories, not necessarily from larger firms. BASF, for example, has built the largest chemical plants in the world in Europe and China to exploit these kinds of economies. Pulp and paper producers such as Cellulosa Arauco in Chile are pushing the envelope on scale to lower costs of production.

Such scale economies in production may lead to business combinations when firms seek to share the high cost of investment. More often, business combinations seek to generate scale economies at the level of the firm and its capabilities that are spread across plants. Both Whole Foods and Starbucks grew through horizontal combinations—acquisitions of similar retail operations in different territories across the United States. The scale economies the two companies exploited lay in marketing and in management capability, as well as in supplier relations. Similarly, the sequence of mergers and alliances in the beer industry have been driven not by production economies (efficient beer plants are relatively small), but by the benefits of scale in marketing and distribution.

A different kind of economies of scale can appear on the demand side of the business, rather than the supply side. Business combinations that enlarge a customer base can sometimes lead to network externalities—an increase in the value of the product *because* there are more users. These sorts of effects are common in information and communication technologies, such as in popular software, social media, and user-generated entertainment. Combinations that generate more users in these industries raise the value received by each user and thus, in concept at least, the user's willingness to pay for the product. Stack combinations typically aim for such effects. For example, when eBay acquired PayPal, eBay's leaders hoped that jointly promoting transaction processing and auction services would increase the volume of business in both partners. More typically, firms will use alliances to increase the scale of a user base. Apple and Google formed alliances with application developers, telecom providers, and media companies to increase the user base for their smartphones.

Economies of scope. Economies of scope are an important derivative of economies of scale. You can think of the difference between economies of scale and economies of scope as the difference between "more of the same" and "more of something similar." With economies of scale, value may come from making more of the same product. With economies of scope, value comes from making a similar, or related, product. P&G's acquisition of Gillette, in this sense, also increased economies of scope—the acquisition enabled the combined entity to sell a wider variety of products that, though distinctly different, were related in certain ways, such as in branding, channels, and logistics. As a result, selling razors and men's deodorants (Gillette's line) could benefit from sharing overhead costs with selling lipstick and women's deodorants (P&G's line).

Aside from sharing costs, a combined entity pursuing scope economies could also engage in cross-selling, where customers of one line of products are drawn into buying the other line. Cross-selling is less likely among men's and women's deodorants, but it has been the reasoning behind mergers of financial service companies, such as when Citicorp and Travelers merged to become Citigroup. As the poor results from this case show, however, cross-selling benefits are often hard to achieve.

As Harvard historian Alfred Chandler has shown, the large firms of the early twentieth century depended heavily on scale and scope advantages. More recently, the role of scale and scope appears to be changing. The rise of new production technologies and of niche marketing and niche products has led to greater advantages to specialization, even at the expense of scale and scope. Smaller companies with excellent product design, marketing, and service can often outcompete larger firms that depend on their size for lower costs.

Paradoxically, therefore, scale and scope economies don't always lead to bigger and bigger firms. They can also anchor combinations that allow a company to specialize and focus more than it would be able to otherwise. ARM, the company that designs the microprocessors residing at the heart of many smartphones, is a case in point. ARM's network of allies allowed the company to develop distinct advantages in chips that consume little energy. Such an alliance would no doubt reduce production costs somewhat, but might be more important because it allows the chip company to deepen its expertise and R&D in distinct ways. Of course, increased scale also typically gives a company such as ARM increased market power in negotiations with buyers and thus yields yet another form of joint value.

Management coordination. Businesses enjoy the advantages of a simple form of coordination when horizontal combinations improve capacity planning in a market. A classic example is mergers among airlines that lead to the consolidation of their route networks, their airport gates, and their equipment. In addition, however, the businesses in supply chains and in stacks also depend on each other, and better coordination there can yield important benefits. A supplier has to produce its output in the right quantities, at the right time, and with the right specifications to be of use to a buyer in a chain; one layer in a stack has to be compatible with other layers; and so on. The quality of the linkages between the parts, therefore, can affect how well the system performs as a whole. As a result, combinations that improve the coordination between parts of such a system generate joint value. Both Toyota and Walmart are famous for their tight coordination with suppliers, which enables them and their suppliers to carry lower levels of inventory.

Vertical and stack combinations also enable improved coordination in investment. Improved coordination here allows each party to invest more in what economists call *specific assets*. This concept will be explained further in the next chapter, but in brief, specific assets are assets that are valuable (or the most valuable) in one part of the stack or chain because they serve a different part of the stack or chain in a specific way. For example, the asset may be tailored to produce an output that closely meets the needs of the next stage in a chain. Without that next stage, or if that stage required something different, the output would not be as valuable. As a result, the specific asset producing the output is itself less valuable outside the stack relationship.

In a situation like this, a firm in the first part of the chain is unlikely to invest in specific assets unless it has some assurance that the next part of the chain will be there to buy the asset's output. An example of this kind of interdependence in the values of assets in a stack is the relationship between electric cars and charging stations. A scarcity of charging stations will retard the adoption of electric cars; at the same time, investing in those stations depends on the cars being popular. Investments in each are valuable only if there are investments in both—in this way, both assets are specific to the relationship. This is one reason why Tesla is investing in a network of charging stations.

Better coordination here tailors product flows and lowers the risk each business would assume by depending on the other player—the risk of being "held up." Lowering that risk was another rationale behind eBay's acquisition of PayPal. Before this combination, PayPal was already handling almost two-thirds of eBay transactions, and there were few alternatives available to buyers should PayPal run into trouble or begin to raise its rates. eBay had tried but failed to develop its own payment system. As a result, eBay's auction markets, before the acquisition, were at risk of disruption from PayPal.

Future options. Future options are a less common source of joint value, but they are no less important. In fact, such options may become even more important in the coming years as firms seek better ways of dealing with risk and uncertainty.

Business combinations often open up new avenues for a company to pursue; their great benefit may lie in the options that the combinations create for future action. In financial markets, the value of options is well understood: for a small initial price, you purchase the right to buy or sell something later. The parallel in strategy is the concept of real options: for a small investment now, you buy the chance to expand a business later (or to let the option expire, just as with financial options). In this way, business combinations may generate value from the doors they open, so to speak, even if you were to wait until later to decide which door to enter and which others to close. eBay's acquisition of PayPal yielded this synergy too, though that may not have been eBay's intent from the start. As it turns out, PayPal has become a leading internet business in its own right, not dependent on eBay for transactions and opening up new avenues for international growth.

Gaining access to future options is especially important in emerging technologies. Firms like Cisco have long taken small bets on technologies that may become important—or that may fizzle out. If the idea pans out, Cisco has an early lead to use it; depending on the terms of the deal, the company may even have locked in an acquisition price. The current popularity of corporate venture-capital funds relies on precisely this argument. As the benefits of centralized, large-scale R&D have declined and those of distributed innovation by start-ups have risen, Google, IBM, Samsung, and countless others have developed portfolios of investments that, in essence, constitute options on future businesses.

As this trend suggests, the kinds of business combinations that help with future options will probably differ from those used for scale and scope. The form of the combinations is likely to be looser, and the amount of capital invested is less than for scale and scope. This difference can be confusing to corporate programs that lump together all combinations in one process. Alliances that are meant to develop future options are by necessity smaller, and most of them will "fail" in the sense that they will not be developed further. The objective in these alliances is the success of the portfolio, not of every individual deal. Combinations intended to exploit scale are larger and, thus, bear a higher burden of success.

Sources of joint value in not-for-profit enterprises. The way success is measured in a combination may also be complicated by the overarching goals of the organizations involved. The preceding discussion has defined value in terms most relevant to for-profit businesses. But the same sources of value can also apply to not-for-profit organizations such as philanthropic or nongovernmental organizations (NGOs) that target social or environmental improvements. There too, increased scale and scope, better management coordination, and expanded options can benefit the causes of the organization. But for not-for-profit organizations, value is just measured differently than in a classic for-profit firm.

To be sure, not-for-profit enterprises often need to cover their costs with revenues. In that sense, value for them is not measured much differently than it is in a for-profit firm—customer value, revenues, and costs can be important to NGOs too. But these organizations will have goals that are not measured by revenues and costs, such as environmental improvements, nature or energy conservation, educational and social advance, and poverty allevi-ation. Business combinations can help these organizations achieve these goals too, and often, sometimes a combination with a for-profit firm can yield different kinds of benefits to each side.

The Environmental Defense Fund (EDF) achieves this mix of benefits through an active program of partnerships with for-profit enterprises. The organization has a partnership with Walmart to reduce toxic chemicals in household products; with McDonald's, EDF has a long-standing partnership to reduce solid waste and the use of antibiotics in poultry; and EDF helped FedEx introduce hybrid diesel-electric delivery trucks. These alliances clearly have dual impact. They usually help the corporate partner save money or improve its reputation among socially concerned customers. At the same time, the partnerships contribute to the social or environmental goals of the NGO.

In these combinations of an NGO and a for-profit company—as well as in combinations between purely for-profit enterprises—success begins by being clear about what value is sought and where joint value may come from.

Look Inside for Value Elements

Even with clarity about objectives, however, you do not automatically create joint value just by combining one business with another in the same market, the same chain, or the same stack. The combination must actually reap benefits from deep inside—from the investments that are made together, from the way technologies are shared, from products that are tailored to each other, and so forth. In other words, putting together complementary businesses is only the first step in creating joint value. You need to construct synergy through the way resources and activities are integrated. To see how this second step works, you need to look inside your own business and that of your potential partner.

Synergy in new combinations comes from managing together the elements that yield competitive advantage to each business. In the examples above, one company's technology was linked with another company's marketing skills, or each company mastered one layer of a stack, or the assets of two companies came to be managed jointly. The key to constructing synergy, therefore, is to understand the building blocks of competitive advantage.

What are those building blocks? On this question, the study of strategy is, unfortunately, divided into two main camps. We will review the propositions from each side, but keep in mind that the best strategies for your company may draw from both sides.

One camp argues that competitive advantage comes from the unique *set of activities of a business*—how it organizes production, services customers, positions itself in the market, and so on. This camp is most closely identified with the work of Michael Porter at Harvard Business School. Porter and his colleagues have argued that the activities of a business distinguish it from its rivals, thus creating a greater willingness to pay among buyers or allowing the business to operate at lower costs. Oversimplifying, advantage comes from what you do, not from who you are.

The other camp argues that competitive advantage comes from the unique *set of resources of a business*—its tangible and intangible assets (e.g., large-scale plants and patented technology) and its organizational capabilities (e.g., management know-how and practices). Many scholars have contributed to this approach, starting with early work by Edith Penrose in the 1950s and continuing with more recent work by Jay Barney, among others. This *resource-based view* argues that the assets and capabilities of a firm set it apart from rivals and generate opportunities for profit. Oversimplifying again, advantage comes from who you are, not from what you do.

In between these two views is another camp, which argues that *capabilities* matter most. These are skills and organizational routines, which can be considered activities or resources. Newell-Rubbermaid traditionally relied on its capability to produce and sell staple products to mass-market retailers to create joint value through acquisitions. Similarly, Danaher touts its Danaher Business System as the reason that the firm has earned higher returns on its diversified portfolio of engineering and scientific businesses than other conglomerates. The well-known Toyota production system is another example of a capability.

This brief description of the academic camps in strategy research does not do justice to the nuances of each. But it is enough to make one thing clear: the arguments are not mutually exclusive and often even complement each other. For example, patents in pharmaceuticals are assets that yield value, but so is the marketing activity of a drug company. In fact, the two sources of value build on each other in this industry. In practice, therefore, strategists in pharmaceutical businesses had better pay attention to both—the businesses have to invest in unique technical assets at the same time that they develop a strong system of marketing activities.

To see more clearly how these camps fit together and how you can use the core ideas from both sides, we will consider a new way to map the building blocks of value inside a company.

The Value Stack

Some twenty-five years ago, Michael Porter introduced the value-chain model, borrowing the template of the traditional manufacturing supply chain to create an internal flow chart of the critical activities of a company. In the industry supply chain, of course, raw-material producers sell their output to manufacturers, which in turn sell their output to distributors. In Porter's model of the value chain of a business, a company procures inputs, transforms them, and then markets and sells the outputs. Value activities that span the full chain (human resource management, for example) support these steps.

In the same way, the new digital industries may now give us a new template, one that allows us to create a comprehensive picture that combines the two academic schools of thought on competitive advantage. As discussed, complementary businesses in digital industries often "stack up" to create value to the end user. The traditional notion of an industry supply chain is still relevant in parts of these industries, but it does not give us a full picture of how value is created. Furthermore, in an industry stack, one component or layer is often just as important as the next. Software needs hardware, and hardware needs software; neither is primary or sufficient on its own.

By analogy, therefore, we can envision a value stack at work inside every business, just like Porter envisioned a supply chain at work inside those businesses. In these *internal value stacks,* assets and capabilities work together to generate and support activities that yield outputs (figure 3-2). Materials do not need to flow from one of these building blocks to another, but each asset or capability needs the others to complete the system. And competitive advantage may lie in one or the other of the complementary blocks or, more likely, in their combination. In this model, the competing strategy camps are both right, but neither camp is 100 percent right by itself.

The value stack is a way to think about the sources of value inside a business. Figure 3-2 reminds us that competitive advantage may stem from specific resources, activities, and outputs. Inside a business, these elements are closely related, or are complementary: certain resources work best with other resources and with certain activities. The value stack does not require that one firm own all these elements, but just shows that all the parts of the stack contribute to the potential to create value.

FIGURE 3-2

Management Tool

Dissecting the value stack of a business

Concept: the value stack of a business		Example: exploration and production of oil and gas
Outputs	• Product • Service	• *Petroleum and natural gas*
Activities	• Operation that transforms inputs into outputs	• *Exploration* • *Drilling* • *Extraction*
Resources — **Capabilities**	• Skills • Know-how • Organization	• *Organization capable of operating exploration, drilling, and extraction*
Resources — **Assets** • Intangible • Tangible	• Brand • Rights • Technology • Capital equipment • Land	• *Sounding equipment* • *Drilling rig* • *Proprietary technology* • *Mineral rights*

The oil and gas exploration and production business serves as an example in figure 3-2. Working from the bottom of the stack upward, every exploration and production business starts with certain assets. These assets may be tangible or intangible—equipment and land are tangible; rights to exploit mineral deposits are intangible, as are proprietary technology and brands. These assets don't produce value by themselves—the firm needs an organization able to explore, drill, and extract minerals. These capabilities, together with assets, represent the *resources* in the resource-based view of the firm. The resources are put to work in the *activities* that are emphasized in the alternative view of competitive advantage.

The operations involved in the exploration, drilling, and extraction of minerals ultimately produce the *outputs,* which in this case are hydrocarbon products. Because these outputs are commodities, they themselves are hardly a source of advantage. But producing them at lower cost or in greater volume or improving their quality might be a source of advantage. The value-stack approach says that these sources might lie in resources or activities, or both.

Where is that deeper source of value in the stack? For a company that has privileged access to a particularly productive deposit, the advantage may lie at the bottom of the stack, in the very rights to exploit minerals. But advantage may also lie higher in the stack, in the way the activities are configured and positioned in the market. A company that specializes in difficult-to-exploit deposits, for example, will differentiate itself on those grounds. So the assets, capabilities, or activities by themselves are useful and can provide advantage; this has been the focus of most strategic thinking in the past decades. The idea of remix strategy asks us to focus on a different aspect of the stack—how the *interaction and combination* of the building blocks create value.

Combining Value Blocks

Because each of the building blocks of the value stack can be valuable, both the activities view and the resources view of the firm are right. So, putting that debate aside, let's examine how value can be created from a distinctive combination of these resources and activities.

As discussed earlier, joint value arises from different types of combinations. We saw how economies of scale and scope may result from better use of resources in multiple businesses, or how improved coordination may come from combined management of activities. Remix strategy thus creates value by mixing, matching, and marrying the building blocks in the value stack.

Economists and strategists have long accepted the notion that a certain combination of activities or resources may provide competitive advantage. Observers have traditionally seen this statement as a question of where to draw the boundaries of the firm and what to include in its scope. Firms have traditionally approached the issue by weighing the marginal costs and benefits of outsourcing an activity or doing it internally. We will return to this question later in the book.

In the remainder of this chapter, we will focus not on the question of a firm's boundaries, but on the idea that the bundles of activities and resources may create competitive advantage, over and above the advantage inherent in those activities and resources themselves. The whole edifice that is constructed from these components can be more valuable than the building blocks by themselves.

To see this, start by envisioning the work of an industry as being segmented into supply-chain stages, each of which is in turn composed of a stack of resources, activities, and outputs. Each cell in the resulting matrix might then be called a *value block*—a fundamental element that adds value to its stack that in turn adds value to adjacent stacks. In principle, the business of a firm could encompass this whole matrix or any particular part of it. Precisely where a business will operate is a strategic choice—the choice of what bundle to assemble from among the value blocks.

An illustration from the oil industry will help clarify this way of thinking. Figure 3-3 shows the full range of value blocks in the oil industry. The columns show the internal value stack in each segment of the industry supply chain that is depicted from left to

FIGURE 3-3

How oil companies allocate elements in the value stack

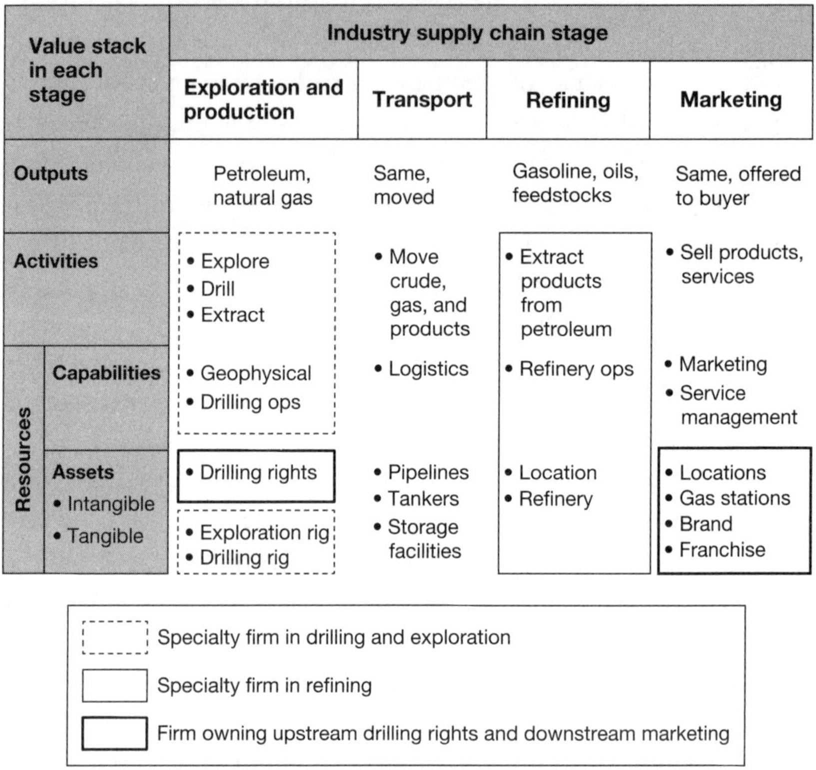

Value stack in each stage		Industry supply chain stage			
		Exploration and production	**Transport**	**Refining**	**Marketing**
Outputs		Petroleum, natural gas	Same, moved	Gasoline, oils, feedstocks	Same, offered to buyer
Activities		• Explore • Drill • Extract	• Move crude, gas, and products	• Extract products from petroleum	• Sell products, services
Resources	**Capabilities**	• Geophysical • Drilling ops	• Logistics	• Refinery ops	• Marketing • Service management
	Assets • Intangible • Tangible	• Drilling rights • Exploration rig • Drilling rig	• Pipelines • Tankers • Storage facilities	• Location • Refinery	• Locations • Gas stations • Brand • Franchise

⌐ ⌐ Specialty firm in drilling and exploration

☐ Specialty firm in refining

☐ Firm owning upstream drilling rights and downstream marketing

right—from upstream (oil exploration and production) to downstream (marketing of end products). The resulting matrix shows
the key elements of the industry that any given firm may choose to
own or not. If not owned jointly, the elements can still be combined
in looser ways.

At the risk of oversimplifying, the age-old strategy of big firms
in this industry has been massive vertical and horizontal integration. The Seven Sisters—the companies that dominated the
industry in the first half of the twentieth century—owned oil
fields, explored for oil themselves, transported and refined crude
in their own facilities, and distributed and marketed the final
products under their own brands. In other words, each of the
Seven Sisters owned a business that spanned the full area shown

this figure—sideways across the supply chain and up and down the value stacks in each stage.

But the value elements of this industry can also be combined in other ways, short of enveloping the whole matrix. One hypothetical firm, for example, might own the drilling rights, and the final marketing assets (represented by the box with thick solid lines in the figure), and trade with other firms for the services of the other value blocks. Another firm may only own exploration and drilling rigs, which it uses to service the owners of the drilling rights (the dashed-line boxes). Another type of firm may be a specialist in one stage of the supply chain—a specialist refiner is shown (thin solid-line box). The different firms still need to coordinate their activities to complete the supply chain and so will form other combinations with each other, short of ownership.

In fact, over time the oil industry's structure evolved and gave rise to all these different ways of bundling value blocks. As specialty companies sprang up along the value chain, the various elements of the value stack changed hands. The specialty companies focused on segments of the business or particular activities; and, they often managed their focused segment better than the soup-to-nuts majors did.

The de-integration of the oil industry was accelerated by the power of national governments over their natural resources—this power forced an early break between ownership of fields and industry operations. Furthermore, the national governments used their bargaining power to force the Seven Sisters to provide selective services in parts of the supply chain and to share selective capabilities. Finally, industry technologies and practices began to diffuse out of the Seven Sisters, as often happens when an industry enters a mature stage. In other words, the de-integration separated not only the supply-chain stages, but also the value-stack elements (outputs, activities, capabilities, and assets).

Today, it is common for different parts of the oil industry to be owned and controlled by different entities. BP's Gulf of Mexico oil spill brought this trend to light in excruciating detail. BP owned the drilling rights together with Anadarko and operated the concession for the joint venture. Halliburton was in charge of the activities on the Deepwater Horizon drilling rig, which in turn was owned by Transocean. Similarly, a different set of companies is often involved in transporting crude oil, and yet another set specializes in refining.

Divestments: The Mirror Image of Combinations

In remix strategy, deciding what *not* to include in the scope of the business can be just as important as deciding what to include. Many vertically integrated companies have divested pieces of the value stack to focus better on others. This strategy is often the other side of the coin of an acquisition strategy. To focus on one piece of the business, the firm will divest unrelated pieces; at the same time, the divestments may generate cash to invest in acquisitions.

A number of chemical companies have used this process to redirect their business from basic commodities to newer sectors. Dow Chemical, for example, planned to sell its plastics business to the Saudis and use the cash to acquire Rohm and Haas, a specialty chemicals company. (The sale fell through during the economic crisis, but the acquisition proceeded.) Bayer gradually divested its chemicals and materials businesses and ended up a pharmaceutical and crop-science giant. In other industries, divestments paired with acquisitions also led to corporate transformations. IBM sold off several hardware businesses, including PCs, at the same time that it refocused on software and services. As these examples suggest, when divestments go hand in hand with acquisitions, they can help reshape a company.

Divestments also complement acquisitions in another sense— they are often two sides of one transaction. When General Electric divested its ownership of NBC, for example, the broadcast network was acquired by Comcast. Sometimes transactions such as these are paired with a sale in the other direction, creating a swap. In a package deal valued at over $25 billion, Novartis sold much of its cancer business to GlaxoSmithKline, which in turn sold its vaccines business to Novartis. At the same time, the two firms put their consumer health-care businesses into a new joint

A similar kind of de-integration also happened in the computer industry, where vertical integration gave way to an industry structure "blown to bits" in the phrase of one observer—specialists took over in every component and layer. The model's applicability to these very different cases of oil and computers suggests that

venture. Novartis also sold a business to Eli Lilly as part of this package.

Because divestments and acquisitions are often mirror images of each other, we can use the same framework to understand both. This may seem paradoxical. The purpose of a business combination is to create joint value. How does a business breakup do that? Does the first law of combinations apply? The answer is yes. Divestments can create value too—if the businesses are worth more separately than they are together (using our earlier analogy, when the existing combination of 1 + 1 is worth less than 2). An asset sale will be profitable if a business is worth less in one asset combination (that of the divesting company) than in another (that of the acquiring company). The business may even be worth more by itself, as a stand-alone, in which case the divestment is a spin-off. A spin-off may need to acquire new pieces to build scale, as Covidien did after being spun off from Tyco International. The divestment was only the beginning of a combination strategy for Covidien.

Divestments therefore often also need to comply with our second and third laws, even if in reverse, so to speak. The divestment needs to have the potential to add value to the now-separated assets as noted (first law). But the split also needs to be governed effectively to achieve that (second law)—assets need to be disentangled, new companies need to be launched, and the newly separated units must follow new policies to take advantage of their independence. Furthermore, the way the divestment is done will leave some value in one company and the rest in the other (third law). Remix strategy thus involves unbundling as much a rebundling of assets and resources. For clarity, this book addresses only one side of the coin explicitly—the combination side.

it also applies to many other industries. In the airline industry, ownership of airplanes today is often divorced from the capability to operate them, as they can be leased. Flight operations can be divorced from marketing operations, as when code sharing lets one airline sell seats on a plane operated by another airline. In pharmaceuticals, some companies specialize in drug discovery, others in clinical trials, and others in marketing; the soup-to-nuts model is changing there too. Every story in the daily papers about foreign outsourcing highlights how some of the activities of a business can be divorced from its competitive assets. Nike designs, brands, and sells, but does not actually manufacture any shoes. On the other side of the coin, Flextronics manufactures electronic products, but for the most part does not design, brand, or sell them. And so on.

Even if our analysis is generally applicable, it oversimplifies dramatically. No industry can be described in one matrix. Each component can surely be dissected further, and the linkages between the pieces are always more complex than shown here. But the lesson is that remix strategy involves changing the configuration of value blocks that you own and manage. In our illustration, you apply a remix strategy by adding and subtracting blocks from the scope of your business and by changing the relationship between the blocks in your business. So, in addition to making acquisitions and forming alliances, you will also need to divest assets from time to time. In fact, divestments are conceptually the other side of the coin of business combinations (see the sidebar "Divestments: The Mirror Image of Combinations").

Finding Promising Combinations

To apply the ideas in this chapter to your business, you need to start by mapping the value stacks inside both your own business and the businesses complementary to yours. The tool presented in figure 3-4 can help you identify high-potential combinations.

To use this tool, you will first look outside your business to find combinations with the potential for synergy. The synergy—or

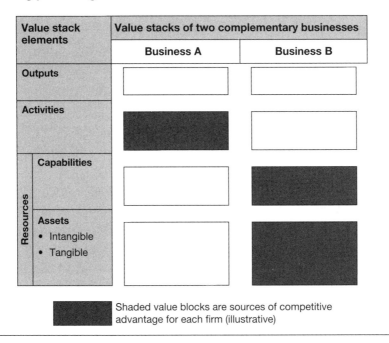

FIGURE 3-4

Management Tool

Finding promising combinations

Value stack elements	Value stacks of two complementary businesses	
	Business A	**Business B**
Outputs		
Activities		
Resources — **Capabilities**		
Resources — **Assets** • Intangible • Tangible		

Shaded value blocks are sources of competitive advantage for each firm (illustrative)

joint value—may come from economies of scale and scope, from improved coordination, or from an increase in the number of new options. A handy way to organize your search is to create a map of your industry that shows the value stacks of complementary businesses in your markets, chains, or stacks (as shown in figure 3-4). Move systematically across these structures, and ask if your firm can generate new value by joining parts of the industry or, alternatively, by splitting them up.

Then, look inside the businesses you've mapped (including your own) to identify the value blocks that need to be linked to construct synergy. To do this, first be clear about the elements of the stack that give your firm competitive advantage, and the elements that perhaps you might need to bring in from the outside. Second, examine the value stacks of external businesses that are complementary to your business. Finally, evaluate whether a combination of your internal blocks and those of the external business may create joint value.

The gray boxes in figure 3-4 illustrate sources of advantage for two businesses that are potential partners. Which value blocks need to be linked to create joint value? For example, if the key to joint value is to combine the brand of one firm with another firm's manufacturing know-how, the figure will help you see the relevant blocks that need to be combined. This mapping will be useful in designing the form of the combination, as discussed in chapter 4. Keep in mind that the chart is an abstraction that needs to be adapted to your business.

As this tool emphasizes, finding joint value is a two-step process; first, identify complementary businesses, and then link the value blocks. Skipping either of these steps is likely to lead to problems down the road. You are unlikely to find synergy, even though you may have paid up front for the privilege of doing so. Take the case of BMW's acquisition of the British car company Rover. The German company paid over $1.3 billion for 80 percent of Rover's assets, it but ended up owning a hollow shell of a company. Before the acquisition, Rover had a tight alliance with Honda, which for years had supplied Rover with technology, parts, and management. Following BMW's acquisition, Honda pulled out of the arrangement altogether, taking with it these critical value blocks that had kept Rover alive for years. Had BMW looked more carefully into Rover's internal stack, the German company would have realized that the anticipated synergy would have come from tying up with Honda itself. As it turned out, BMW poured another $4 billion into the British operation before pulling out and selling the remaining assets for a song to a private equity firm. (BMW did retain the Mini Cooper brand name and basic design, which the automaker later turned into a profitable line of cars, made in Germany.)

As the example shows, combinations between value blocks may come in different forms. Full ownership and control of assets in one bundle is one such form. That is how BMW tried to build synergy with Rover. But as other examples in this chapter suggested, various forms of contracting may achieve similar aims. Honda's combination with Rover (which was more successful than BMW's) involved a minority stake in the British company and a series of supply and technology contracts. The next chapter dives deeper into how you can select the right form of deal for your company and goals.

Chapter 4

Second Law: Govern the Collaboration

T O REALIZE THE PROMISE OF JOINT VALUE, YOUR FIRM must ensure effective governance of each business combination. The value potential can easily be destroyed by poor governance. Worse, poor governance can also hurt the value of each party, such as when a joint-venture breakup ruins reputations or when time is lost sinking money into badly managed acquisitions. In other words, the first and second laws need to work together. In addition, the governance law affects the way value is shared—an aspect addressed by the third law. Good governance, therefore, is pivotal to your remix strategy.

The term *governance* here means something different from board-of-directors policies and corporate bylaws. Governance in this book means the way you manage the resources of the combination. We saw the whole spectrum of relationship choices in chapter 2. Where should you locate a combination for greatest effect? How should it be managed over time? As we saw, and will see in more detail here, each choice calls for a different way of managing the joint activities of the combination. What matters, again, are not the detailed terms and legal conditions of these structures, but the underlying approach to governing the combination.

Take Off Your Blinders

I've noticed over the years that managers have strong feelings—prejudices, really—about where they *want* to locate their organization on the relationship spectrum. This is a problem, as the strong opinion gives them blinders—just when they need to be open-minded. Consider the following example.

Some years back, while preparing to deliver a workshop on alliance strategy to a large US high-tech company, I received a last-minute call from the organizer. "Don't use the term *alliance*," she said nervously, "because our lawyers don't like it." She explained that they preferred the term *partnership* and asked if I could use that instead. It seemed like a minor semantic issue to me, so I replaced the terms in my presentation material. I didn't realize then how deep a chord this issue struck inside the company.

I began to see what was at stake during the workshop when participants were given a newly drafted sheet of thirteen rules set by the top of the company. With sections titled *Partnership "Big Rules"* and *Business Relationship "Style Guide,"* the document stated: "[The company] does not engage in 'alliances,' even though it recognizes that other companies do. 'Alliances' in [the company's] parlance are long-term, broad, open-ended, and ill-defined structures in which one party gives something without clear or agreed quid pro quo."

My interest was piqued beyond the scope of the assignment. And the more I studied this company, the more I realized that these rules were just part of a larger pattern. It's not as if the company did not do deals. The company did make deals, because it had to—and even the style guide recognized that "no company can supply all the value-added needed by end-users." But the rules show how much the company feared yielding control in its business relationships. Many companies are control freaks, an attitude that manifests itself differently in different companies. "If it is worth doing, we'll do it ourselves" is one such approach. Another is "our way or the highway." Control-obsessed companies often have rules for partnerships, eschewing equity investments or joint ventures or allowing only majority-owned joint ventures.

The problem is, in modern competition, such rules often are a self-imposed handicap. When you exclude from consideration a particular type of business combination—any type—you tie one hand behind your back before entering the ring. Better to compete with all the tools at your disposal. For every firm that swears off joint ventures, there are others that insist on fifty-fifty joint ventures and succeed famously with them. Like my client, companies often claim that their restrictive approaches are all about legal implications, but *their* lawyers might proscribe "partnerships" and prefer "alliances"! Does the label really make a difference?

How can you avoid putting on blinders that constrain your deal-making options? Begin by understanding those options. From there, you can put every deal in its proper place. We'll see how to do that in this chapter.

We'll also look at another issue, which is related to company biases such as the one just described. Alliances and partnerships are particularly tricky combinations to manage, for reasons we will see. Because of this difficulty, managers often have an aversion to these relationships and instead prefer the two ends of the spectrum— simple transactions and full acquisitions. Often, it's because the managers simply have more experience with transactions and acquisitions than with partnerships. At the same time, partnerships are increasingly common and needed. So, this chapter also includes tools that will help you design and manage alliances.

Three Relationship Models

To choose a particular type of combination, some companies use a variant of make-or-buy analysis, perhaps extended with an *ally* option. Even so, the companies often apply loose or idiosyncratic criteria for their choice, and as a result, governance quickly becomes a challenge.

Consider the choices Boeing made when establishing external relationships for building the Dreamliner 787. The company delegated to outside suppliers larger parts of the work than it had for earlier programs, ostensibly to save costs and ramp up production more quickly. At the same time, it challenged engineers to push the envelope of design and materials used to create a revolutionary, state-of-the-art aircraft.

It turned out that these objectives did not jibe—doing more new and harder things, and doing them cheaper and faster besides, is a tall order. Key suppliers did not invest sufficiently to take on all the new work, critical parts were not always ready when they were needed, and whole sections of the airplane at times literally did not fit together. Boeing turned things around by buying up important suppliers and ramping up its own plants to do more assembly work internally. But the successful maiden flight of the Dreamliner 787 took place almost two years behind schedule.

Excessive outsourcing is not always the problem—sometimes companies insist on doing internally what may be better left to outside parties. Sun Microsystems hung on to its internally developed Sparc hardware and Solaris software long after the Linux operating system and Intel architectures had become widespread (and cheaper). Early on, these assets did give Sun a performance edge. But tougher competition later did the company in.

And sometimes, the dogged pursuit of internal control leads to doomed acquisitions or mergers. With hindsight, Time Warner would have been better off contracting for the internet services of AOL or other parties instead of merging with AOL.

These examples of excessive dependence on control are perhaps a legacy of old ways of thinking. Over the last two to three decades, the communications and digital revolutions have made it easier and cheaper to coordinate activities without ownership control. Business process outsourcing is a prime example. Because we can now track so many processes digitally, companies can now outsource many activities to specialists and monitor the specialists' performance remotely. Similarly, information technology has made coordination among suppliers easier—at least for standard parts; less so for unique and complex parts like in aircraft manufacture.

At any rate, no doubt the top managers of Boeing, Time Warner, and Sun had their reasons for making the choices they did. But the outcomes beg the question: Did they use a comprehensive approach for evaluating potential business combinations? You can't anticipate every possible snag in any plan, but you can avoid obvious mistakes in designing your business combinations by doing it systematically.

To decide what kind of deal you need, think first about your strategy and, only after that, about the specifics of the deal. Many managers make the mistake of drilling down prematurely into an analysis of the pros and cons of various deal structures. They forget that these structures are there to serve the underlying logic of the combination—their form must follow the function that is needed to generate joint value.

With this in mind, consider the key features of the three relationship models introduced in chapter 2: trade, ally, and merge. An overview of the key features of these three models is in table 4-1. The table is by necessity generalized; in reality, your deals may have slightly different features or may be hybrids that lean one way or the other.

The Relationship Models in Global Air Travel

The airline industry offers a general example of how these models differ. Commercial relationships of various sorts are common among airlines because air travel often involves a passenger taking multiple flights on multiple airlines—especially for international travel. But the degree of cooperation between airlines will vary, depending on the form of their relationship.

TABLE 4-1

Management Tool

Three relationship models: trade, ally, and merge

	How joint value is created	How the relationship is governed	How value is shared
Trade	Coordination of activities through exchange of outputs from independent parties	Each party is responsible for its own decisions, which are based on price signals	Arm's-length sharing: terms of trade (mostly prices) set at the start, and parties' own costs determine profitability of transactions
Ally	Coordination of activities through exchange of outputs and resources among parties that share some interests	Parties influence each other's behavior through contractual agreements and management communication	Pay as you go: terms of trade and returns to resource sharing are adjusted over time through profit-sharing mechanisms
Merge	Coordination of activities through unified management and interests	The behaviors of the parties are shaped by control from a common owner and by intracompany policies	Pay now, profit later: acquisition price provides return to seller of an asset; buyer retains the rights to residual profits—and losses

Let's assume that a passenger wants to travel from Toledo, Ohio, to Stuttgart, Germany. He or she could fly United Airlines from Toledo to Chicago and continue on another United flight to Frankfurt. But then the passenger would have to switch to, say, Lufthansa to get to Stuttgart, because United is not licensed to fly between points within Germany. So, it makes sense to the airlines and to the passenger for United and Lufthansa to coordinate their services. They do this as part of Star Alliance, but let's imagine away this development for a moment and see what options they faced at the start.

Trade between airlines. The simplest way to coordinate the flights between the airlines is with an *interline agreement,* which looks like the trade model in table 4-1. This kind of agreement allows one airline (usually the first on the route) to sell and issue a ticket that also includes the other airline's part of the trip. There are no shared mileage plans or expectations of common levels of service, and importantly, no special efforts are made to schedule the flights so that the connection is seamless.

In this model, each airline does what it normally would do and the parties just trade between themselves for the ticketing services, the passenger services, and the fees. Production (or service provision) is separated and covered by contracts with set terms.

Alliances among airlines. One step up from the simplest trade model is the *code-sharing agreement*. In this model, the airlines do all that is done in interline agreements, plus more. The basic code-share agreement involves a sharing of flight numbers, hence the name. In our example, the most likely leg for code-sharing is the Chicago–Frankfurt leg, where United and Lufthansa essentially compete, each having two or three flights a day. The airlines will now coordinate their flight schedules more, because the code-share flight now appears on both schedules. And though the actual flight is still the responsibility of the operating carrier, passengers will assume that the marketing carrier is at least monitoring service levels, as the marketing airline's name is on the schedule.

A code-share agreement thus begins to look like our ally model as it incurs more coordination of production, some sharing of risk, and some tailoring of the product to serve both partners. But there is still room to generate additional joint value by cooperating more. Code sharing by itself is a stripped-down alliance—on the bottom left corner of the ally zone in our relationship spectrum (figure 2-1 in chapter 2). In fact, airlines alliances have gone much further, climbing all the way to the top right corner of the ally zone. Many of the relationship variants airlines have implemented are still alliances by our definition, but they involve progressively more cooperation, such as the following:

- Sharing mileage programs and allowing the use of miles earned on a partner program

- Sharing the use of lounges and service desks

- Locating gates near each other in major airports

- Sharing personnel and ground services

- Joint marketing under a common brand (e.g., Star Alliance, in this case)

- Joint purchase of supplies and fuel

- Joint purchases of aircraft

- Equity investments in each other or together in sister airlines

Actual airline alliances have involved a mix of all these features, and more. They have also grouped these alliances in large multiparty constellations, as we saw, raising additional issues of governance and strategy that we will discuss in later chapters.

Though these alliance deals have been complex and largely successful, they too proved to be limited in their ability to generate certain kinds of joint value. For example, airline fleets and route structures were unlikely to be trimmed or rationalized in an alliance, as the structures usually made it hard to share the benefits of cutting back on seats. Similarly, because alliances were limited in the incentives they offered to partners to make major commitments, a full integration of services and branding was unlikely with loose arrangements.

Mergers among airlines. To avoid some of the disadvantages of alliances, many companies consider going one step further in cooperation to a full merger. They do so to gain unified control over the joint operations, which should allow for deeper integration and investment commitments and the ability to manage or limit rivalry. But compared with an alliance, a merger cannot easily focus on only one narrow slice of the business—United and Lufthansa cannot just merge their Toledo-to-Stuttgart business in a normal merger. A merger is also often more costly up front and usually harder to reverse than an alliance. What's more, the risks that arise during integration are often not shared equally.

So, the global airlines sought deeper alliances on specific routes. But an alliance that managed capacity and pricing on competing routes risked being ruled anticompetitive by the US and European Union authorities. Consequently, the airlines applied for antitrust immunity to create what they termed a "joint venture" that could share profits on these routes. The carriers asked the authorities to sanction this kind of cooperation. United and Lufthansa received immunity on the argument that there remained sufficient competition from other airlines flying trans-Atlantic routes that were close substitutes to the Chicago–Frankfurt route. Antitrust immunity, in effect, allowed the alliance to operate much like a merger, at least for specific routes. United and Lufthansa were not the first to receive this immunity, and by now, all the major airline groupings have antitrust immunity in place among some of their members.

This solution lies at the margin between the ally and merge zones of the relationship spectrum. The alliance structures here look and behave very much like mergers. Conversely, some mergers can allow the units to remain fairly independent and thus behave almost like companies in an internal alliance. At the lower end of our spectrum, the same situation arises in deals that are on the margin between trade and ally. The bare-bones alliances there (e.g., pure code-sharing) behave almost like simpler, arm's-length trade relationships. And by the same token, some trade relationships may involve repeated contracting that makes them behave like alliances.

Of course, airlines also do whole-scale mergers when the benefits of doing so cut across many routes—and regulations allow it. Airline regulations still disallow mergers between airlines from different nationalities, but mergers are possible between US airlines or between European ones, if approved by antitrust authorities. In pursuit of scale advantages in their national markets, therefore, Delta merged with Northwest, United merged with Continental, American with US Airways, Lufthansa with Swiss Air, and KLM with Air France—the last of these in a complex arrangement that maintains some national differentiation.

How the Pursuit of Joint Value
Shapes Governance

For the purposes of discussion, the three zones shown on the relationship spectrum (and the relationship models they suggest) are useful. In reality, though, the choices for business combinations really lie on a continuum along which there are few, if any, breaks. Often, whether you call something an alliance or a market transaction is a matter of degree. Some alliances approximate acquisitions in their tight structure, and some acquisitions are so loosely integrated that they feel more like alliances.

Placing a prospective combination too early into one or another zone is therefore often a mistake. Many companies fall into this trap, especially when they assign different kinds of deals to different management or staff units. You are better off thinking more holistically about the design and recognizing that the choices lie on a sliding scale, with various factors pushing the design up or down the scale. Some factors will argue for a tighter combination, in the direction of merger; other factors will argue for a looser combination. Your best solution may be a compromise between these forces or might have features from both ends, with some aspects being tightly linked and others, more loosely. The key to these decisions, of course, is to consider the impact of governance on the process of creating joint value.

The main influences on governance choice for a combination are shown in figure 4-1. You can think of each of these as turning the dial up or down toward a merger or a trade. Depending on the balance of these conditions, the best model for the deal might end up being in between (ally), or on one or the other end of the spectrum. For example, when multiple value blocks are needed from various specialty firms, governance should tend toward the left of the scale (first arrow from top). However, if the parties need to invest in specific assets, governance should tend toward the right of the scale (fourth arrow down). The final choice depends on such trade-offs along the variables shown in the figure.

FIGURE 4-1

How joint value shapes governance

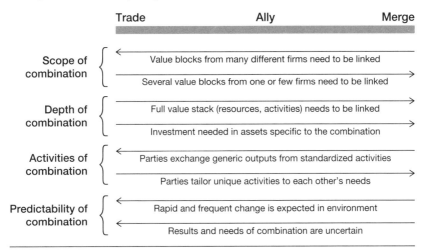

| Trade | Ally | Merge |

Scope of combination
- ← Value blocks from many different firms need to be linked
- Several value blocks from one or few firms need to be linked →

Depth of combination
- Full value stack (resources, activities) needs to be linked →
- Investment needed in assets specific to the combination →

Activities of combination
- ← Parties exchange generic outputs from standardized activities
- Parties tailor unique activities to each other's needs →

Predictability of combination
- ← Rapid and frequent change is expected in environment
- ← Results and needs of combination are uncertain

Scope of the combination. When the joint-value strategy relies on inputs from numerous specialists, then looser, focused alliances may be better than tighter, broader forms of combination like mergers, because the focused links will give you the flexibility to collaborate with different specialists. Think of the alliances springing up around the prospect of an internet of things. In the health-care industry, for example, the makers of smart, connected devices such as heart monitors are striking multiple alliances with data analytics companies, mobile software developers, network service providers, and, of course, hospitals and doctor's offices. At the start, these are loose alliances because most players need to be connected to multiple other players, and they want to retain the flexibility to respond to changes in the emerging industry. Over time, these internet-of-things alliances may well become deeper and more selective.

A similar outcome—targeted alliances rather than tight mergers—is called for when the scope of the combination is narrow, that is, the combination links only parts of the businesses of each party. This is a classic reason behind many large-company alliances. Apple and IBM decided to collaborate to develop mobile solutions for the corporate market. Though it may well grow, this prospective business is still a narrow slice of each company's portfolio. Plus, creating joint value will require linking specific parts of each company's value stacks—IBM's corporate sales and consulting activities and Apple's mobile technology capabilities and products. Their new alliance is a targeted attempt to address that specific opportunity.

Depth of the combination. But if the combination needs to link several building blocks up and down each company's value stack, then a tighter, deeper combination is better than a loose one. Automobile company combinations often are of this type. When Renault joined up with Nissan, and, more recently, when Fiat invested in Chrysler, the partners in each case planned to integrate car design, manufacture, and sales, all across the value chain. They also needed to get the best out of the design capabilities, brand equity, and plant locations of each partner—this called for collaboration up and down their value stacks. The alliance forms they chose were joint ventures, that is, they were close to the merger end of the scale.

A tight alliance—or merger—is even more likely when creating joint value requires investment in specific assets. As noted earlier, these are assets that are more valuable when dedicated to a relationship than they would be if the relationship were to dissolve. A classic example of this is bauxite refining plants. These large investments are usually located adjacent to aluminum ore mines because the ore is costly to transport in its unprocessed form. Furthermore, each refinery is optimized to the characteristics of the ore at its location. In other words, these refinery assets are specific to the relationship with the mine operator. As a result, these plants are almost always owned by the mine owner and the aluminum company that will take the output for export. Without ownership control, the refinery owner may fear being "held up" by the mine operator and having no recourse, or the reverse.

Activities of the combination. Similarly, the nature of the activities involved in creating joint value—whether they are generic or tailored—should influence the choice of governance form. Commodity products, of course, need not be traded through alliances at all—there are open markets for them. But there are no such markets for specialized components, such as in the aerospace industry. This is one reason why Boeing and Airbus manage their suppliers tightly. Carmakers face this issue too, but some automobile components are not highly tailored, so their relationships with the suppliers of these parts can be closer to the trade end of the scale. An interesting example is tires—they are generic today, and any tire will work on any car. But early in the history of the car industry, tires were made for and sold with specific cars. That is one reason why Ford and Firestone struck a tight alliance in the early 1900s. More recently— after tires became generic products—that collaboration fell apart when product failures led each partner to blame the other.

Predictability of the combination. The last major influence on governance of collaboration is the degree of change and uncertainty in and surrounding the combination. We just looked at the importance of flexibility in a dynamic environment in the example of the internet of things. In addition, sometimes it simply is not clear at the start of collaboration precisely how joint value will be created. These conditions call for combinations that are flexible, rather than tight, mergers.

The collaboration of Chevron and forestry company Weyerhaeuser in biofuels illustrates this point, as well as several of the other factors in figure 4-1. In the mid-2000s, several US states set new regulations calling for an increased use of ethanol in gasoline. These biofuel mandates meant that the businesses of Chevron and Weyerhaeuser instantly became complementary. The companies expected to produce "second-generation" ethanol from the cellulose in grasses and other plants. The emerging value chain would likely include growing and harvesting plant material, which was Weyerhaeuser's expertise. At the other end of the value chain, Chevron's refineries would blend the ethanol with gasoline.

But there was a critical step in the middle of the value chain that neither partner mastered—the processing of cellulosic material in so-called bio-refineries.

The uncertainty involved in the market and in the technology turned the dials in figure 4-1 toward a small joint venture that could be dissolved if things did not pan out. Furthermore, this joint venture then entered into an alliance with KiOR, a bio-refinery start-up that received funding from Bill Gates and Silicon Valley venture capitalist Vinod Khosla. But KiOR's technology did not succeed, and market conditions turned against the venture when oil prices fell dramatically. KiOR filed for bankruptcy just a few years after its deal with Chevron and Weyerhaeuser and its IPO. For Chevron and Weyerhaeuser, the alliance had been an experiment rather than a major commitment. This form of governance was appropriate for a combination that involved a lot of uncertainty in technology and markets.

Regulatory constraints. A caveat is in order: this discussion suggests best choices in governance assuming you *have* a choice! Some combinations are mandated or appear to be so. For years, the only way for a foreign company to enter China, India, and many other emerging markets was through a joint venture; in many industries in these countries, this is still the case. Even in industrialized countries, industries like airlines and defense are still closely guarded from outside investors. So, the wholly owned option (akin to a merger in this scheme) may simply not be available in some situations. That's not the only way your options might be constrained. Pharmaceutical companies seeking an exclusive license for a promising new drug from a biotech start-up are often told that only an alliance or acquisition will give them access to the prize.

Even when your choice seems constrained, however, you need to understand the joint-value logic behind the combination. Restrictive governments have been known to bargain away their barriers when faced with compelling reasons why a foreign firm needs greater control than the standard law allows. And even start-ups will sell their jewels at the right price. Alternatively, knowing what you need in the ideal case will help you decide when to walk away in response to constrained options. IBM famously exited the Indian market in the 1970s when forced to take on a local partner; at the time, IBM's decision made sense, given the company's strategy of global integration and India's still-struggling modern economy.

Whether constrained or free, the choice of when to ally is particularly tricky for many managers—they are usually most familiar with the two ends of the relationship spectrum, not with the middle zone. Later in this chapter, we will examine when it's best to govern a transaction by an alliance instead of a simple trade arrangement.

A Closer Look at Alliance Governance

You see now how the relationship spectrum works—the conditions underlying a deal suggest which governance form is best suited to the task. But we have so far treated the three relationship models more or less as equivalent choices. It turns out that the middle zone—alliances—presents special problems and is the least understood by most managers.

To succeed with business combinations, managers should be equally comfortable working with any governance form on the spectrum, including alliances. Traditional management techniques are geared to the two ends of the spectrum—the trade-type contracts on one end and the internal control of full integration on the other end. If you understand the middle, you can see clearly how it differs from the two ends.

Recall Scott McNealy's tweet in chapter 2: "Favorite partnership for me is a purchase order." The problem with this statement is that a purchase order is most decidedly *not* an alliance at all. It is a contract for a simple transaction, which we placed on the bottom left corner of the relationship spectrum in that chapter.

The most likely reason why McNealy was skeptical of alliances is this: behind every alliance lurks an *incomplete contract*. That is a technical term in economics that some lawyers may not like to hear. Simply put, it means that the agreement between the parties does not cover all contingencies, all issues, or all possible states of the world. Such "gaps" are common, but not because the lawyers were lazy or incompetent. In complex tasks, it is simply hard to specify all these things. (The sidebar "The Theory Behind Every Alliance" provides further background on this theory.)

The Theory Behind Every Alliance

A little theory goes a long way. The economic theory behind alliance governance is called *transaction cost economics*. Ronald Coase and Oliver Williamson received Nobel Prizes in economics for this line of thinking. The theory holds that the transaction costs between economic units are shaped by the nature of the interaction between them.

According to this theory, transaction costs are not operational costs like commission fees or transportation costs. Instead, costs stem from the lack of clarity and enforceability of the terms of the interaction and the dependence of each unit on the interaction. Let's look at some sources of incompleteness in contracts.

Negotiating a Transaction

- Time or other constraints on due diligence may limit the information available to negotiators.

- Changing technology and markets may make it difficult to foresee future contingencies.

- Uncertainty in project requirements may make it difficult to specify all costs and benefits.

Monitoring an Ongoing Transaction

- Companies have information and conduct actions that are hidden, intentionally or not.

To govern an alliance successfully, then, you need to manage these gaps. When faced with open-ended situations, however, traditional management techniques call for command and control—to respond quickly and decisively to new conditions. But this approach, too, is missing from an alliance. In fact, every alliance is marked by some type of shared control. It may be a formal joint venture with shared ownership or a looser arrangement whereby

- The value of some inputs or outputs may be difficult to measure or quantify.

- Links to other projects make it hard to isolate costs and benefits of the transaction.

Enforcing an Agreement

- Weak intellectual-property regimes may prevent a firm from resorting to courts.

- One partner may find it hard or costly to enforce partner agreements without actually threatening a breakup.

- Dependence on a transaction may lead to a risk of being held up on profit sharing.

As the economic theory explains, when managers spot these sorts of problems on the horizon, a deal that potentially will create value may not get done because the contract is bound to be incomplete. Since a contract cannot cover all contingencies or specify all terms unambiguously, it would be subject to the risks of costly litigation or opportunistic behavior on the part of a partner.

As a result, partners in an alliance must consciously manage the gaps in their contracts. And it pays to design the alliance correctly in the first place—minimizing potential conflicts and maximizing the incentives for collaboration. Tools in this chapter show how to do that.

one party controls certain parts of the joint project and the other party controls others. So, each partner's control in these combinations is also incomplete. No wonder inexperienced managers consider this tricky territory!

A final piece of the alliance puzzle is this: What keeps these alliances together if both the contractual ties and the ownership ties are in a fundamental sense incomplete? The answer, in theory and in practice, is the promise of future joint gains. Game theorists call this potential the *shadow of the future*. Managers may refer to it as the *relational value* of the alliance. Because of this promise of future gains, the parties in alliances have an incentive to resolve issues that were not foreseen in the contract and that are not within the clear decision authority of either party. To do this work, smart alliance practitioners usually create governance structures and processes up front. Technically, these kinds of deals are referred to as *relational contracts*.

The Soul of Every Alliance

It is important to define *alliance* explicitly, because the definition shapes how you manage deals in the middle zone of the relationship spectrum. Economic theory plus management practice can be boiled down into this specific definition of an alliance:

> An *alliance* is . . .
>
> . . . an organizational mechanism
>
> . . . that uses shared control to govern
>
> . . . an incomplete contract
>
> . . . between independent parties, and
>
> . . . that is sustained by relational value.

Read as one sentence, it's a mouthful. But each of the five parts of the statement should be clear by now. First, an alliance is a way to administer a business combination, whether with formal corporate structures, looser management processes, or both. Second, none of the parties to the alliance has full control over decisions, or else the deal would be called a merger. Third, the joint work done by the alliance is not fully specified in the formal agreement. Through no fault of the lawyers, the alliance will face important open-ended questions, decisions on issues not foreseen at contract signing, and so on. If it were not for these open ends, the agreement between the parties would be called a trade by our terminology. Fourth, the parties each stand alone, in that they are not joined by ownership. Finally, this messy deal structure hangs together because the parties expect to benefit from the relationship now and in the future.

Figure 4-2 is a visual representation of an alliance.

The Rise and Fall of a Model Partnership

The decades-long alliance between Hewlett-Packard (HP) and Oracle is a great example of an alliance that worked with an incomplete contract and a clear promise of future gains for both parties and that fell apart when the promise of gains disappeared. For over two decades, HP and Oracle had what many considered an

FIGURE 4-2

An alliance as a way to manage open-ended agreements

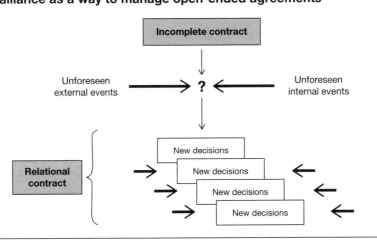

ideal partnership. Then the two companies became embroiled in a serious spat that resulted in millions in court costs.

Oracle and HP were traditionally in highly complementary businesses. Simply put, HP made hardware and Oracle made software. There was little direct overlap in what they did—the hardware business depended on the software business, and vice versa. Recognizing this ideal scenario for a partnership, Oracle and HP developed a deep alliance, with organizational processes that coordinated their efforts in R&D, production, sales, and service.

The logic of the partnership began to change when Oracle acquired Sun Microsystems—a longtime competitor to HP in the hardware field. The acquisition was Oracle's first major entry into hardware. Around this time, HP itself had begun to edge into software and services, with its own acquisitions of EDS and Autonomy.

The bombshell exploded when Oracle announced that it would stop supporting HP computers with new versions of its popular database software. Oracle claimed that it had the freedom to act in this way, as nothing in its partnership with HP specified that Oracle would support all future generations of HP hardware— such a future commitment had been one of the gaps in their agreement. The companies had not signed a formal contract that specifically ensured this ongoing support. Why not remains a bit of a mystery.

HP sued Oracle for breach of an implicit contract, as the practice between the partners had always been that Oracle would support HP machines with software updates. In sum, the companies had a relational contract, HP argued. In a surprise to analysts, the courts upheld HP's claim. Still, HP had won a Pyrrhic victory, as the relationship with Oracle—on which the hardware maker had previously depended—was clearly shattered.

Lessons from a Broken Alliance

Companies using partnerships can learn both from the success of the HP-Oracle partnership in its heyday and from its decline. In fact, many of the same partnership success factors present in the first phase of the Oracle-HP relationship were absent in its latest phase.

Don't just trust "trust." Personal trust is indeed good for communicating openly and establishing smooth working relationships. In the good years, Oracle and HP had such relationships at the highest levels. But then circumstances changed.

You cannot rely on personal relationships to maintain a major business cooperation through the years, especially if your strategic interests have diverged. This conclusion is confirmed by the history of many other alliances. People leave. Leadership changes. A personal commitment is never the same as a corporate commitment, at least not in large organizations. Corporations are not people—they are complex organizations that should follow the interests of their stakeholders, not the personal affections of their executives.

Use contracts when you can, even within a partnership. At the root of the problem facing HP and Oracle was a gap in their agreement—a gap that could well have been covered by a contract. The idea that good alliances survive on handshakes is a myth, and a dangerous one at that.

Years ago, I asked the American director of a highly successful US-Japanese joint venture how often he looked at the contracts between the partners. His answer startled me: "Every day." He explained that every day, his company was conscious of the roles, responsibilities, and constraints in these contracts. And each time that these roles changed in substance, there were additional contracts signed to confirm the mutual understanding. These trusting partners took their contracts seriously.

The fact that every alliance is based on an incomplete contract does not absolve the lawyers from trying to close gaps when they can. The alliance agreement is left open-ended—not out of complacency or laziness—but because attempting to close all the gaps will either be exceedingly costly, time-consuming, or misleading.

Use good partnership management to govern the gaps. Even with well-intentioned effort, however, partnership agreements will usually still have some gaps. Some items will have been left vague, perhaps because the parties could not foresee what issues might arise. They agreed to agree later, even on questions that they did not know they would face. To manage such gaps, the parties need the right communication channels, decision protocols, and leadership.

Much has been written on the mechanics of alliance management. Ironically, HP was often touted by observers as one of the models of best practices in alliance management. In a way, the firm probably was—at least in the first phase of its relationship with Oracle. HP had dedicated alliance teams, assigned champions, books and websites with guidelines, and some valuable success cases to show for the alliance.

But in hindsight, these HP alliance practices were ideal for the steady state but inadequate for addressing radical change in strategies. All management processes and routines probably suffer from this weakness. In the HP-Oracle case, both partners were changing their underlying business strategies, quite apart from the personnel changes at the top.

Focus more on the strategy behind the deal than on the specifics of the deal itself. This last lesson underlies them all: because partnerships are sustained by a shadow of the future that promises benefits from the relationship, any change in circumstance that affects the business strategy of one or another party may jeopardize the partnership.

The strategy behind the deal, in other words, has multiple elements that extend beyond the mechanics of the deal. Among these elements are the very goals of the alliance, the choice of partner, the relationships between the alliance and each partner's other businesses, the interactions the partners have outside of the alliance itself, and each partner's backup strategies. A simple play on words here becomes serious: the mechanics of each *strategic alliance* are less important than the comprehensive *alliance strategy* behind the deals. To avoid this pitfall, always flip the terms when you see the phrase "strategic alliance."

Tools for Alliance Design

The preceding lessons and the transaction-cost theory discussed earlier lead directly to three tools that will help you design and manage alliances. To succeed with alliances, you must pay attention to three aspects right up front: (1) knowing when to use an alliance instead of a more complete contract such as a vendor relationship; (2) selecting a partner with which you can produce maximum joint value, govern effectively, and share returns; and (3) creating a structure that facilitates cooperation between you and your independent partners.

One large American telecom company underestimated the task of designing and managing an alliance and suffered the consequences. It needed a billing system for an international wireless service. It ruled out buying an existing software package from a vendor, thinking that a customized billing system would give it an edge in the market. This analysis then led—all too quickly—to the choice of a partnership with a small software company. The goal of the partnership was to develop a cutting-edge software package in time for a launch-date commitment made to a foreign host government.

The story of what went wrong with the design and management of this partnership is the stuff of juicy business school cases. Pretty much everything that could go wrong did. As a result, the product was not completed on time and the telecom company had to resort to incorporating an off-the-shelf product for the promised launch. With hindsight, the company would have been better off had it taken more seriously the options of buying an existing product from a vendor. Alternatively, if the telecom indeed had its mind set on a partnership, the company should have understood more clearly what was involved. Setting up an alliance and managing it as if it were a simple vendor transaction, as this company did, proved to be the worst of both worlds.

You need to have a reasoned approach to deciding when and why to form an alliance and to understanding the trickiest parts in that alliance. Aside from the general advice to flesh out the options before you decide, practice and theory suggests some more specific principles to follow. We'll look at three key questions.

Do You Need a Partner or a Vendor?

The first step in deciding if an alliance is the best governance model for your combination is to compare it against its two broad alternatives of trade or merge. As we saw, this choice is not a tactical one to be left to the lawyers to figure out—it is a strategic decision critical to creating value in your combination.

Earlier in this chapter, we focused on how the joint-value task should drive your choice of models in the relationship spectrum (figure 4-1). Armed now with a better theory of what an alliance is, you can now draw the dividing line between a trade transaction and an alliance—a choice commonly thought of as one between a vendor relationship and a partnership. It is this choice that the American telecom company failed to make properly.

Because an alliance is a way to govern the inevitable gaps that exist in many contracts, you should use it when those gaps indeed are inevitable. If, however, you can close the gaps with reasonable contract language, then a vendor transaction might do just fine. As noted, these gaps revolve around problems in negotiating, monitoring, or enforcing an agreement.

The guidelines in table 4-2 are derived from the transaction-cost theory discussed earlier and are supported by much practical evidence. As you did earlier in this chapter, think of each row in the table as a dial that shifts your choice of the best business relationship to one or the other column. For example, one condition in your business might call for a vendor transaction, and another condition for a partnership. You decide what to do under such mixed conditions according to which conditions are the most

TABLE 4-2

Choosing between a vendor and a partner relationship

Condition	Vendor: complete contract may be possible and effective	Partner: well-managed, open-ended contract is likely needed
Technology	Mature, stable	New, rapidly changing
Prices, costs	Known, good forecasts	Uncertain, volatile
Customer requirements	Detailed specifications can be formulated	Detailed specifications still unknown or likely to change
Competitive environment	Stable markets, commodity-like	Dynamic markets, differentiated
Task requirements	Well understood, predictable	Uncertain, to be determined
Investment needed	Generic assets, equally valuable without the deal	Specific assets, most valuable in the deal
Dependence on this relationship	Low; many possible counterparts	High; few other potential partners

salient. Also, mixed conditions suggest that some parts of the alliance agreement might be clearly specified in contracts, while other parts remain open. As a result, the analysis from table 4-2 will tell you which aspects of a combination may be the most contentious and deserve added management attention.

What Makes a Good Partner?

The choice of a partner is particularly important and complex in an alliance—more so than in trade and merger deals. Unlike the situation in those other kinds of deals, you will have to live with your partner after the alliance deal is signed. In fact, the success of the alliance depends on how well you and your partner can work together. Recall that in a merger, the partner in effect disappears when you buy it out. And in most trade transactions, the partner itself matters less than the product or service and, of course, the contractual terms of the transaction.

Even so, many companies all too often choose a partner prematurely. In one company—one with a multibillion-dollar business and employing many PhDs—the origin of most partnerships led back to someone's knowing someone who knew someone who worked for the partner. Once the initial contacts were made between these "friends," partnership talks frequently got serious without anyone stopping to ask if indeed this matchup was better than another one. Questions like this may have upset corporate friendships, of course. But you owe it to yourself and to your shareholders to ask these tough questions.

Using the three laws of business combinations, we can develop a more comprehensive approach (table 4-3). Like the other tools in this book, table 4-3 is a starting point for evaluating your potential partner; your actual decisions will also depend on legal, financial, organizational, and other circumstances. While these circumstances may be complex, the principles behind a good decision are relatively simple. First, different partners bring different resources to the table, and thus different company pairs might

---

Management Tool

TABLE 4-3

Assessing partner fit

Consideration (based on the three laws of business combinations)	How partner compares to your firm	Fit with potential partners		
		A	B	C
What is the potential for joint value? (first law)	Complementary capabilities: each party has what the other needs			
Can we work together to realize this potential? (second law)	Compatible attitudes and broad strategy: these don't need to be identical, but they must not conflict			
	Common vision for project: there is agreement on goals for the collaboration itself			
	Limited competing interests: direct and indirect conflicts are minimal or contained			
What will be the returns to each party? (third law)	An acceptable balance of returns: needed to provide incentives for commitment from both sides			

yield different potential for joint value. Second, don't just focus on this plus side of the equation. Even partners who have much to offer each other may find it hard to work together, for one reason or another. They may have incompatible strategies, may differ on the goals for the joint project, or may have too many competing interests. Third, the potential partners may not agree on the balance of power and share of gains due to each. In other words, to select your alliance partner, you need to follow all the three laws of business combinations.

Keep in mind that for each criterion shown in table 4-3, one partner may seem a better fit than another, and these rankings may well vary by criterion. For example, a partner with great complementary capabilities (the first criterion), may not have compatible strategies (the second criterion) or may have competing interests (the fourth). To select a partner, then, you need to weigh the trade-offs among these criteria.

This approach to partner fit helps explain why IBM and Apple failed in their alliances in the 1990s and why they have a better chance now with their recently launched mobile apps alliance. In their first try, the two firms tried to work together on a common microprocessor platform (the PowerPC), a collaboration that also included Motorola. IBM and Apple also tried to work together on a new approach to software design, and they aimed to sell some things jointly—specifically, to bring Apple technology into the enterprise. With the exception of the microprocessor plan, the objectives in the new alliance are not much different—joint development of mobile apps and bringing Apple's mobile technology into the enterprise. The jointly developed corporate solutions would be guided by IBM's global services arm and tap into IBM's data analytics software and cloud infrastructure.

Why did this attempt at an alliance fail in the 1990s? For one reason, the companies were still direct competitors. Not a decade before, Apple's famous "1984" Super Bowl ad had proudly proclaimed that the Macintosh would shatter the IBM world, portrayed as Big Brother. By the time of the first alliance between Apple and IBM, the rhetoric had died down, but that was partly because IBM's own business was down, in no small measure because of the microcomputer revolution. Helping Apple enter the enterprise? It sounded like a pipe dream from the start. Working together to create a new microprocessor platform? That strategy had a higher chance of success because both companies faced Microsoft and Intel as their rivals. But that early Apple-IBM alliance failed, in part because Apple itself moved on to Intel.

Why do IBM and Apple have a better chance today? By now, IBM has changed its business dramatically, and so has Apple. IBM no longer makes personal computers (it sold the business to Lenovo), and it is no longer primarily a hardware company. IBM aims to put together whole packages of services and equipment to corporations and to grow into the hot new fields of data analytics and software as a service. Increasingly, doing these things means doing them on *mobile devices*—Apple's new strength. In that field, IBM has had no presence at all; in fact, IBM's lack of mobile experience may still be what holds back this alliance. Still, if IBM is willing to guide Apple to focus on what corporate clients need, and if Apple is able to develop the mobile software to fulfill those needs, then this could be a good match. Early results suggest that the two firms are indeed on a path to developing joint value.

In short, the complementary capabilities of IBM and Apple are there today but were also there in the past, when the partnership failed. What is different this second time around, is that the companies' goals are more compatible and their rivalry is much more limited. And what about the balance of power between the two? We don't know much about that yet. Thus, this criterion related to the third law of business combinations can still make or break the new alliance.

How Do You Enable Joint Decision Making?

In addition to selecting the right model and partner, you also need to structure the alliance carefully. The joke is that when you have seen one alliance, you have seen one alliance. There are infinite variations of terms, decision structures, and so on. All have one thing in common—the structure needs to facilitate joint decision making even when no side has full control. As we saw in chapter 2, the need for joint decision making was the signature feature of deals in the middle zone of the relationship spectrum. The concept of contractual gaps makes this idea more precise. The structure and management of your partnership need to help you make joint decisions about open-ended issues—including decisions you did not even think you would be facing. The success of your combination depends on the alliance's ability to make good joint decisions.

Successful joint decision making takes many forms. Sometimes, it is just as it sounds—the partners get their heads together to solve the problems they face and come to decisions together. One US-Japanese joint venture that I worked with had periodic "codestiny" meetings of the CEOs. In these meetings, the executives identified strategic issues and developed broad plans. The meetings were then followed by lots of interaction at lower levels of the organizations, to work out details and implement the plans. To really make the plans work, the partners exchanged personnel to learn from each other and to facilitate communication. Formally, the joint venture board voted on key decisions, but joint decision making in this partnership was much more than a board decision.

Sometimes joint decision making means allocating roles and responsibilities clearly and agreeing to let each side take charge of what it does best. Corning took this approach with its joint venture with Samsung. Soon after the first investments were made in glass factories in South Korea, it became clear that Corning could not—and should not—manage those local operations. So the American firm left factory management, labor relations, and local supplier relations to Samsung. At the same time, Corning retained ultimate control over technology decisions, and the two parties had to agree on annual plans and investments.

The structure of an alliance includes both the "hard" architecture of the combination and the "soft" management processes and routines around how joint decisions are made. These decision-making systems won't work if the partners are mismatched from the outset or if the very rationale for the alliance is misguided. But given that these two criteria are met, we can identify some of the practices of successful alliances (table 4-4). The setup of the alliance and its management processes determine whether the parties will be able to work together throughout the life of the alliance. The initial setup must align the incentives of the parties, enable joint decision making, help with conflict resolution, and have enough flexibility to allow the partnership to adjust to new conditions. Subsequent management can then build on this foundation.

> **Management Tool**

TABLE 4-4

Designing and managing alliances

Alliance Design

- **Provide incentives for collaboration at all key levels and functions.** Collaboration with an outside party is not natural for many employees. Salespeople, engineers, and managers of business units need to receive tangible benefits from working with the external party.
- **Define what is in and what is out of the alliance.** Rivalry between partners may sometimes exist, but it will hurt collaboration if competition is not kept out of the scope of the collaboration. This strategy demands excellent contract design, as well as careful thinking about strategic direction.

Alliance Operations

- **Define partner roles.** A division of labor, and sometimes a division of decision-making authority, can focus each partner on what it does best. For example, one partner might run local factories in a joint venture, but both partners will share planning and investment decisions.
- **Create processes for making joint decisions.** The open-ended contracts that are typical of alliances rely on excellent decision processes in the alliance itself and between the parent companies. For joint ventures, these processes are defined in corporate bylaws. In other alliances, you may have agreements on how decisions will be made and what issues will get escalated.

Relationship Management

- **Manage the joint business as well as the relationship itself.** The two tracks, or roles, may demand different skills and personnel. Distinguish between the technical success of an alliance and the health of the relationship itself.
- **Build and maintain trust on purpose.** Negotiate good contracts, deepen personal contacts, and act reliably and with reciprocity. Yes, these practices are easier said than done, but trust does not appear magically; it must be built and nurtured with concrete management tools.
- **Allocate sufficient resources to alliance management.** None of the above practices can be done on the cheap. Yet, under-resourcing alliance management is the single most common mistake that even large and rich companies make.

The practices listed in table 4-4 are for the most part self-explanatory. But they are often overlooked. The last guideline is the one most commonly violated. Companies often give alliance management short shrift. Ironically, they do so at great long-run costs. One reason for this mistake is that companies may see alliances as a way to "outsource" decisions and operations to a partner, who, perhaps, knows more about the business. But even when you outsource a task in the classic sense, you face a new responsibility to govern that task properly. The burden of manufacturing a part or running a call center, of course, is shifted outside the company, but responsibility for managing the supplier and for ensuring customer satisfaction doesn't budge. Denying this reality amounts to governance myopia.

A poorly governed alliance can cost the company dearly. Poor governance can hurt the immediate bottom line or the company's reputation, which can be just as important in the long run. Pharmaceutical companies have taken the concern with reputation one step further. For most of them, good relationships with innovative biotechnology firms can be a key source of new drugs. In many of these firms, fully half of their pipeline of new drugs now comes from collaboration with external parties—often smaller companies and start-ups. As a result, the pharma companies have vied with each other to be seen as "partner of choice," so as to attract the most promising partners to their network. Eli Lilly, for example, created an extensive alliance management organization within the company and trained its professionals how to manage these sensitive external relationships. This organization introduced processes and practices that helped Eli Lilly communicate better with its partners and resolve conflicts more rapidly. As a result, the company developed a reputation for good alliance management, and its collaborations yielded a number of important products.

Like Eli Lilly, you do not need to fear the middle zone of the relationship spectrum if you are well prepared for managing these kinds of combinations. Reducing managerial bias for one type or another across the spectrum will help you put the right governance in place for the opportunity at hand. Good governance will help you manage joint activities more effectively and produce the value that the combination promised. The first and second law of combinations, in other words, can be met successfully. What about the third? How will this joint value be shared? You know that how you share value in a partnership can make or break a deal. Tackling this issue is often not easy or may seem impolite in the context of a cooperative relationship. The next chapter examines how to think of value sharing and what you can do to avoid winding up holding the short end of the stick.

Chapter 5

Third Law: Share the Value Created

WHEN YOU FOLLOW THE FIRST TWO LAWS OF BUSIness combinations, you enter into a relationship that generates new value. But one key to success may still be missing. The relationship combines resources from different owners; that is, some of the resources are owned by your firm, and some are from external parties. None of these resources—neither yours nor theirs—come for free. Each set of resources in the bundle will demand a return, a profit, or a payment. Otherwise, the owners of the resources would not allocate them to the new combination.

Sharing the value produced, therefore, is not just a matter of collecting on a successful strategy. It is a fundamental requirement that applies to all parties in a combination and hence forms the third law in the triad. If a party does not receive a rewarding return on its contributions—that is, if the third law is violated—the party is likely to withdraw from the joint effort, and the combination will fail. Just as governance was the linchpin in making joint value real, value sharing is critical to making governance workable.

An early warning is in order. Research on value sharing is ongoing, and managers with experience in profit-sharing mechanisms are always hesitant to talk about it. For one, the allocation of value in a deal is hard to measure because there are often multiple channels for earnings, from profit shares to transfer prices. Plus, these mechanisms are often among the best-kept secrets of a deal. In acquisitions by and of public companies, the prices paid are known, but in just about any other kind of combination, the terms of the deal are seldom publicized.

Still, we have enough evidence and theory to sketch the pattern of how value is shared. These patterns suggest important guidelines for how to manage combinations so that you and your partner can collect what both of you earn.

We will start by clarifying key terms and explaining why value sharing is tricky and fluid in business combinations. The chapter then takes a closer look at co-opetition, a new-economy term used to describe the mixing of competition and collaboration. After that, we will see how partners sometimes try to shift their position at the bargaining table during the life of an alliance. Finally, the chapter examines guidelines for managing your share.

Rivalry Remains, Despite Collaboration

At the root of sharing value in combinations lies the dilemma of how the parties compete for a piece of the pie while also collaborating to create that pie. This dilemma is, of course, a general problem in all negotiations.

At a recent conference—or "un-conference," as the organizers preferred to call it—I had a spirited debate with a musician on how to balance competition and collaboration in all sorts of combinations. At least that's what we started talking about. We soon found ourselves arguing over analogies from sports teams to jazz quartets, trying to find lessons in how each model handled this dilemma.

The sports analogy, of course, is well known. A team bundles together the best talent it can acquire and then pays that talent to compete with other bundles of talent to win a championship. Inside each team there is usually some competition, too, as players vie for a spot on the roster. Is business collaboration like sports?

Then there's the jazz analogy, also well known. The emphasis here is on mutual appreciation of talent, not on jockeying for position. Players will follow each other's lead, even when there are no clear leaders; they will trust each other's innovative riffs and ultimately make music together that defies competitive ranking, let alone championship wins. Is *this* what business collaboration is like?

The truth is that both of these analogies are stereotypes. In reality, sports teams win in no small part because of the chemistry among their players. In 2012, the last-place Boston Red Sox traded away many of their stars on the theory that these players had become clubhouse toxins. With a new team culture, Boston won the World Series in 2013. Conversely, the success of many major music groups is in part due to competition among players. The Beatles are famous for the friction between John Lennon and Paul McCartney, as well as for the group's early rivalry with the Beach Boys.

Calouste Gulbenkian, the early-twentieth-century oil entrepreneur, had a more realistic analogy for business partnerships than either the world of sports or music. "Oilmen are like cats," he said. "You can't tell from the sounds they make whether they are fighting or making love." He knew what he was talking about—he was responsible for engineering the global merger between Shell Transport and Trading and Royal Dutch Petroleum, as well as bringing together the central players who went on to develop the oil fields in what is today Iraq. In return, he kept a famous 5 percent stake in the Middle East ventures that by his death in the 1950s was estimated to be worth over half a billion dollars.

The twentieth century's hardball bargaining in the Middle East oil patch probably *did* sound like fighting cats, and maybe that's not an extreme to emulate, but at least people were putting their cards on the table. Compare that style of negotiation with the genteel discussion suggested in many of today's books on deal making. Roger Fisher and William Ury's long-lived best seller *Getting to YES,* for example, was one of the first books to draw a sharp distinction between what the authors call "integrative" and "distributive" bargaining. Integrative bargaining seeks to create joint value, and distributive seeks to split up the pie among players. They apparently wrote the book as an antidote to what they saw as the win-lose mind-set of distributive bargaining; they go to great lengths to explain how win-win negotiations can turn erstwhile opponents into problem solvers that together create new value.

Fisher and Ury make many good points. As a result, however, the win-win mantra is now so deeply ingrained in general business culture that prospective partners are often unwilling to even address the value-sharing part of their deal, lest it spoil the courtship or the honeymoon. One manager at a top industrial firm, for example, was reluctant to sign on to a formal partnership with a customer because the customer wanted to know in advance exactly what sort of discounts they would realize after the partnership was formed. In another case, the senior managers at a large telecom company told their lawyers to drop the tough penalties for nonperformance in a contract under negotiation, in an effort to show trust in the company's new, smaller partner. Maybe such skipping of legal details can sometimes work, but it didn't here—the smaller partner did not perform, the large company had no recourse, trust was broken, and the very idea of innovative partnerships was soiled in the large company's culture.

Sure, you want to beware of extreme hardball. But who doesn't want to get paid for their work? And it's essential to every partnership that the value created jointly is also shared among members. What's more, the terms of this sharing are critically important. How value is shared can entice members to work together, create incentives for them to invest in the partnership, and sustain the partnership over the long run. Or the terms of value sharing can fail to do all of that—poor value-sharing terms cause shirking, underinvestment, and instability. That is why this aspect of business combinations—the "what's in it for me?" aspect, to put it crudely—shouldn't be taboo, but instead should be addressed early with honesty and care.

Why Collecting Your Earnings Is Tricky

In discussing the terms of value sharing with your partners, you need to start by using the right words, so that the people you're negotiating with understand what you're proposing. One of the root problems with many discussions of value sharing today is that the terminology that business strategists use is often loaded and misleading.

For example, the classic term *distributive bargaining* connotes a win-lose or zero-sum activity. That's not a helpful image; no wonder that *Getting to YES* emphasizes the opposite. Nor does the term truly describe the results of bargaining. The distribution of gains in a good partnership will actually leave everyone better off, as it enables the very effort that creates joint value. More importantly, the outcome of this distribution sets the incentives for cooperation. That is, partners are either motivated or demotivated to help each other. Therefore, the question of how value is shared may well be primary, not secondary, in your gaining commitment to a joint activity.

Other approaches in the strategy literature are similarly biased in unhelpful ways. Many modern textbooks, for example, talk separately about business strategies that "create" value and those that "claim" value. This approach might be a helpful distinction in theory. But in reality, neither of these terms can possibly tell a complete story. A deal that creates value will also have to divvy that value up. Similarly, the notion of claiming your share suggests a fixed entitlement (like "Pass Go and claim $200"), which is not realistic either.

Another term in the strategy literature, *value captured,* may better reflect the chess moves and power plays that can go into striking a deal, but often, people are reluctant to use this term. That's because capturing value is akin to grabbing something with powerful, fast movement and a subsequent determination not to let go; it doesn't sound very nice when you're trying to "make friends."

Earned Value

A more neutral (and more productive) way to talk about how value is shared starts with a cue from routine employment contracts, which, after all, also involve the distribution, claiming, and capturing of value. In employment, we tend to use the term *value earned*. In civilized societies, employees don't grab their pay; they earn it. Who could argue with each party's earning its share from a combination? The implication is that you work for the value, that you deserve it, and that you brought something to the table in exchange for it.

The concept of earned value has its own history (and flaws), of course. From Adam Smith on, economists have tried to explain how labor, capital, and other factors of production earn their share of the wealth they produce. The models of modern economists suggest that unlimited competition and other "perfect" market conditions mean that earnings reflect the marginal productivity of each factor. (Even Karl Marx—at root a classical economist—admitted that in a socialist state, each worker would earn "according to his contribution.") It surely seems respectable to earn your share when you cooperate with partners. But of course, the idealized conditions of these economic models don't often arise in reality. More often, negotiations are between a few players, each with varying characteristics and power, and market conditions are imperfect by the standards of the theory. So the relative power of the players will matter more in these situations, and not everyone will earn according to their marginal productivity (as Marx also recognized).

To understand how value is earned under these conditions, we need to take a step back and reconsider how value is created. The terms of value sharing depend critically on how joint value is created. In short, what you earn depends on your *value added.* This idea is borrowed from modern game theory. As business economists Barry Nalebuff and Adam Brandenburger explain, a player may "add value" to a combination if the player's actions or resources help enlarge the total pie available to all members of the combination. The amount by which this pie grows is called the value added of that player.

The value added of a player may depend on how important that player's contribution is to the common goal. If you are a key player on which the combination's value will stand or fall, your value added is higher than if you are a bit player who adds little to the totality. In the first case, you can earn more than in the second.

This valuable insight from game theory should be intuitively clear. Beyond that, however, the theory is notoriously complex and, even so, has a hard time reflecting reality, which is even messier. In the real world, there are usually many more players than in the simple models. It is hard or impossible to figure out just how much each party contributes, political power and regulations create nonmarket biases and constraints, and winnings are generated over time in an uncertain environment. As a result, members in a combination sometimes do earn more value than they add.

The earnings of Major League Baseball players offer an example. Baseball was always a game of numbers, and the *Moneyball* approach made it even more so. Baseball's big-data gurus today not only calculate the relative performance of a player compared with others, but also claim to be able to measure how much each player adds to a team's chances of winning. With some more statistical acrobatics, some analysts then try to calculate what a player adds to the profits of the team—the value added of that player. How do players' value added compare with their salaries? One analyst calculated that out of over three hundred major league players, almost one-quarter of the total earned more than the economic value they added to their team in a particular year.

These lucky ball players may be locked into multiyear contracts, so they will continue to collect more than their share. But that is not likely to happen in your business combinations. Your contracts do bind, but if the distribution of value in your partnership grows too far out of whack, the combination is doomed. We'll get back to this in a moment.

How Value Shares Are Determined

With the basic concepts and terminology understood, consider now the most important factors in determining the value split in a combination as it plays out over time:

- **Formal structure of a combination:** The business combination's structure shapes how value is claimed in a relationship and in courts of law. These structures, however, are the result of an earlier negotiation and may not be stable over time. They are also influenced by regulatory and other constraints.

- **Relative bargaining power:** Before and after a deal is struck, the relative bargaining power shapes how value is captured in a combination. Bargaining power has various sources, including those from outside the formal structure. The dynamics of how value is captured are not always explicit or the subject of open discussion between partners.

- **Contribution of each party to joint value:** Each party's value added is a fruitful way to discuss how to split joint gains. In practice, companies usually cannot measure accurately how this split ought to be done, but we can analyze the factors that influence it.

Because of these three factors, value sharing is always a dynamic game. Each factor matters, but its relative importance changes with time. Fortunes and outcomes can shift unexpectedly.

Consider the oil industry again. Gulbenkian's strategy for combining assets of oil companies and oil countries involved a cartel that limited competition among the players. This structure was stable until the decades after the Second World War. The big break in the prewar structure came when Aramco, a joint venture of what later became Texaco and Chevron, discovered the huge oil reserves of Saudi Arabia. The discovery led the Saudis to seek additional American partners with greater resources, which the Saudis found in Exxon and Mobil. As Aramco expanded, Gulbenkian's cartel fell apart. In effect, the discovery of oil in Saudi Arabia realigned the options available to all the industry's players and thus doomed the cartel's existing partnership.

Furthermore, over time, the power of the producing governments grew, in part because of the rising demand for oil in the West and in part because of the rise of resource nationalism in the oil countries themselves. Another contributing factor to the rising power of the oil countries was the diffusion of oil-producing technologies and the increasing rivalry among the companies to gain access to petroleum reserves.

As a result, how the benefits from Gulbenkian's combination were shared changed significantly. First, oil countries began to raise taxes and royalties, usually with the acquiescence of oil-consuming countries that could do little to stop this trend. Then, the governments increased their ownership in the joint ventures that exploited their natural resources, often leading to outright nationalization of oil exploration and production on their soils. When supply and demand conditions became particularly tight in the early 1970s and political conditions were ripe, the Organization of the Petroleum Exporting Countries (OPEC) cartel succeeded in raising the oil countries' take of total value even more. Since then, the balance of power has waxed and waned and varies by region and even by product.

Why Value Shares Always Change

For reasons just discussed, you may often have difficulty accurately predicting what you will earn from a combination. To make matters worse, these earnings often change over time, sometimes in unpredictable ways. And trades, alliances, and mergers are very different in this regard.

Timing of the value split. The chief difference between the value-sharing mechanisms in the three combination models is *when* the allocation is made. Because the success of any combination is always uncertain, this question of timing affects who carries the risk of performance. Simply put, in a merger, the target company is paid in full for the transfer of its assets, and it usually has no remaining interest in the outcome. The acquirer, on the other hand, now carries all the risk—if a premium was paid over market value, as is usual, then the acquirer must now work to realize an additional *joint value* that is greater than the premium. Many mergers go awry because of overpayment to the shareholders of the target company—in other words, premature payouts that exceeded the value created.

Risk is shared in a more balanced fashion in an alliance. The risk that joint value will not be realized is still there, but the earnings of both parties—not just one party—depend on this outcome. The payout mechanisms typical of alliances ensure this sharing of risk. In joint ventures, profits are explicitly shared according to ownership stakes; in many contractual alliances, earnings to one party are a share of, or a royalty or commission on, the earnings or the revenues of the other. In supplier alliances, the success of the supplier depends on the sales of the buyer, and vice versa. Most arrangements that could be classified as a trade will similarly have some shared payout, even if the terms of the trade are less flexible than in an alliance.

In reality, of course, business combinations rely on all of these mechanisms and more. For example, some mergers carry a contingent payment to shareholders of the target company, or these shareholders are paid in shares of the acquiring company. And in alliances, there may be up-front payments that fix some returns for one party or another. Even the valuation of assets brought into a joint venture is a source of prepayment, much like the valuation of assets in a merger.

Value sharing over time. Changes in value shares over time are the rule rather than the exception in alliances. Because these deals often involve several channels where value can be earned, the profit split is often a result of the progress of the joint business. Maybe one product category sells better than another or sales in one region are stronger than expected. If each party earns different amounts from each part of the business, the ultimate profit split will also vary.

Many business combinations have survived a long time with a symmetric 50-50 split of benefits, as well as with an asymmetric 70-30 or 30-70. What matters more to survival of the combination is the possibility of divergence from the profit split intended in the agreement. A deal that starts out as 50-50 and gradually veers to 70-30 is bound to generate friction, and if the parties fail to address the imbalance of results, the alliance can easily crack on this issue. To address the imbalance, you may need to redefine the value-share rule to generate more balanced results, or you may have to reset your expectations to accept the 70-30 split as the new normal.

What happens in such an imbalance is illustrated in figure 5-1. In scenario 1 (the dashed line), the value distribution stays close

FIGURE 5-1

Planned and actual value sharing

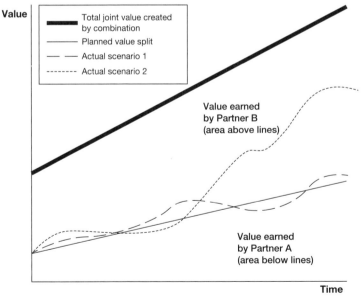

In this illustration, the planned value split has Partner B earning more than Partner A. In the actual scenario 1, the value earned by each partner varies over time but stays close to the plan, while in scenario 2 the split seems to deviate from the plan permanently.

to the plan (the thin solid line); such results can sustain the alliance, assuming some mutual forbearance—some give-and-take—in the short term, from year to year. In scenario 2 (the dotted line), the split deviates significantly from the plan. In this case, the parties would probably need to renegotiate the alliance to reset expectations between the partners. Under the new profit split of scenario 2, partner B may no longer consider the alliance attractive.

In an acquisition, the risk of changes in value is usually borne by the acquirer, because the target company has already been paid in full. In that case, only the changes in joint value (the thick solid line) matter.

Fuji Xerox, the master of flexibility. A prime example of how value shares change over time—and why an alliance often needs to be modified to reflect this—is the long-standing joint venture between Xerox and Fuji Photo Film. (Full disclosure: I cut my alliance teeth on this joint venture, which occupied a major part of my first book on the topic.)

The Fuji Xerox joint venture is over fifty years old and is still the most successful alliance on record between an American and a Japanese company. With revenues of more than $10 billion, Fuji Xerox is today a major player in the Xerox group. Earlier, when Xerox was on the ropes in the American market, the assets and capabilities of Fuji Xerox helped save the parent company—not once, but twice. In the 1980s, Fuji Xerox helped Xerox compete with machines designed and made in Japan. Later, in the 2000s, Xerox cashed out some of its ownership to bolster its finances at home. And through the decades, Fuji Xerox provided a steady stream of market intelligence, sourcing options, and successful design technology.

This outcome was totally unforeseen at the launch of the venture. At the time, Xerox intended to use the joint venture as a Japanese selling arm for its copiers made in the United States. From the start, this plan was scuttled. It turned out that Fuji Xerox rapidly learned to design and manufacture its own machines for sale in Japan and, eventually, in the Xerox home market too. The joint venture did this using Xerox technologies and brand, for which Fuji Xerox paid royalties. But these royalties themselves declined over time, as the Fuji Xerox capability grew and as competitors chipped away at Xerox's original monopoly in copiers and printers.

Over time, therefore, the joint value produced by the venture greatly exceeded the expectations of the founders—and was of a wholly different character. At the same time, Fuji Xerox steadily gained power inside the Xerox group, as the venture gained capabilities and succeeded in the marketplace with its own products. In the face of such unexpected outcomes, the value-sharing arrangements between the partners had to change. As long as there were future benefits to the relationship, both parties had an incentive to modify their agreements.

And so they did. Every new manufacturing contract, royalty, or marketing profit split was renegotiated within years, usually before the official terms were over. Royalties began to flow both ways. As Xerox retreated from certain markets, the joint venture gained territory—from its original home in Japan, to becoming responsible for the business in much of Asia. Ultimately, Xerox even sold half its 50 percent share in the venture to Fuji Photo Film, becoming a minority shareholder, albeit an important one because of the continuing collaboration on technology, branding, and sales.

What kept this alliance together, of course, was its relational value—the shadow of the future described in chapter 4. To the extent that the Xerox parties still had much to gain from future collaboration, they found ways to restructure the deal. Contrast that with the situation seen, paradoxically, in some *successful* alliances between small biotech start-ups and big pharmaceutical partners. After a collaboration yielded a successful drug approval, and all that was left was to market the product, some of these alliances ended up in court battles over how to divide the spoils of success. Allies in war, too, often break up when victory is secure.

How to Manage Co-opetition

In most complex alliances today, the factors shaping how value is shared are not as clear as in the Fuji Xerox case, and partners are not always as flexible as the Fuji Xerox parent companies were. The story of a recent biotech alliance shows how the core ideas developed here apply, even if the outcome was not as happy as it was for Fuji Xerox. This story also illustrates how competition is sometimes embroiled in cooperation and why business leaders need to manage this co-opetition carefully.

The Battle over Value Shares in a Medical-Device Alliance

Boston Scientific, a large medical equipment company, and Medinol, a small Israeli engineering start-up, had formed a ten-year deal to make and sell coronary stents. At the start, the combination of resources between these companies seemed ideal. Boston Scientific had been eager for a way to enter the lucrative market for stents, even though its own efforts to develop the technology had failed. Medinol did develop a unique technology, but was short on cash and had no way to reach the market.

The supply agreement between the companies covered many of the usual points and some unique provisions. For example, Medinol and Boston Scientific agreed that they would participate jointly in a development program for the future generation of stents, including exchanging development and manufacturing equipment, sharing intellectual property, and enjoying limited shared access to one another's offices. The supply agreement set a pricing scheme for the intermediate products (the bare stents) that were to be transferred from Medinol to Boston Scientific. The transfer price was set at 30 percent of the sales price of the complete stent systems sold by Boston Scientific.

Other provisions related to security of supply. For example, Medinol was to become Boston Scientific's primary source of stents for at least ten years. To meet that obligation, Medinol agreed to establish two production lines in Israel, for which Boston Scientific would supply the capital. In addition, however, another manufacturing line—called the "alternative line"—was to be installed by Medinol engineers at a Boston Scientific facility in Ireland at Boston Scientific's own expense. If Medinol failed to provide sufficient supplies, Boston Scientific could activate this production line; otherwise, the facility was to be mothballed.

And so they began. But almost from the start, the alliance experienced tensions that would ultimately tear the pair apart.

Distribution of profits. Medinol and Boston Scientific planned to profit mutually under a fixed formula; in this case, the division of profits was mostly determined by the transfer price of the stents made by Medinol. This division of costs, of course, is not equivalent to a division of profits. Rough calculations from available data suggest that Medinol made about $120 in profits per stent, while Boston Scientific made $98.

Was this a fair division of the joint value created? Often, questions such as these are answered by reference to what other options are available on the market. Here, that approach couldn't work. What, for example, would the Medinol-type product sell for if Boston Scientific were to purchase it elsewhere? In this case, there were no other potential suppliers. Conversely, what if Medinol had gone through a different commercialization partner? Again, there was no obvious alternative available to Medinol. In other words, there were no benchmarks for these unique products and services.

To economists, the problem faced by Medinol and Boston Scientific is akin to the classic case of a *bilateral monopoly*—one buyer facing one seller. In the words of economist Frederic Scherer, "the theory of bilateral monopoly is indeterminate with a vengeance." It is extremely difficult to figure out in theory or in practice how prices and profits should be set when a single buyer faces a single seller.

Dependence. Despite the early agreements about manufacturing capacity, supply challenges quickly became another source of tension. The partners seemed to be coping with strong demand for their product, following the terms of their agreement. But then, the US Department of Justice found something troubling as part of an unrelated investigation. Department officials discovered in Ireland yet another fully functional stent manufacturing plant that Boston Scientific had deliberately kept secret from its partner and even from many of its own executives.

The officials concluded that "the goal of this project was to establish a Boston Scientific stent manufacturing facility in Ireland that was hidden from Medinol." In effect, this hidden production line was a carbon copy of the "alternative line" that was allowed by the contract (and that remained mothballed). The aim of this secret project, according to court records, was to enable Boston Scientific to reverse-engineer Medinol's stent design and manufacturing process. By developing this technology, Boston Scientific would then be able to claim the next-generation stent as its own intellectual property.

When Medinol learned of this project, it sued Boston Scientific in US courts. Medinol founder Kobi Richter reportedly said that the American company wished to "put its hands on Medinol's impressive profit rates" and walk away from a ten-year supply agreement. Boston Scientific countersued. After an initial ruling went Medinol's way, the companies settled out of court, with Boston Scientific paying Medinol $750 million.

We will probably never know the full story behind the case of Boston Scientific and Medinol. But the failure of their partnership does reveal how competition between partners, or co-opetition, can affect every aspect of a collaboration's risks and returns. This kind of competition drives the battle over value shares. So, it is worth understanding its roots—and avoiding it if you can.

Variants of Co-opetition

When the term *co-opetition* was coined by Silicon Valley entrepreneurs, it described a situation in which firms would cooperate on early R&D or on technology standards while still competing in end-product markets. In this instance, and others, the partners would compete directly with each other in one arena while also cooperating in another, or at least attempting that. This kind of co-opetition does not work out too well. At the very least, it is constrained in the joint value it can create.

But co-opetition can work—if it is tamed. The history of Xerox and Fuji Photo Film again is a case in point. These two firms shared technology freely and cooperated on many fronts, but only because the competition between them was tightly circumscribed by territorial licensing contracts. "Good fences make good neighbors" was their motto. Another US-Japanese joint venture shows the other side of the coin. Honeywell and Yamatake had a long-lived alliance to make and sell building controls, but direct competition between the partners was managed solely by personal relationships, not strict contracts. Later, rivalry between the partners over lucrative markets in China eventually caused the partnership to fail.

In this classic version of co-opetition friction, therefore, the clash comes when products go to market. In Brandenburger and Nalebuff's more complex version of co-opetition (the word is also the title of their book), the friction occurs at any interface between suppliers and buyers, or among what the authors call "complementors." Thus, the term can describe everything from battles over shares in jointly created value to battles around mutual dependence, such as what happened with Boston Scientific and Medinol.

Tugs-of-war over profits, technology, and control. The returns to each partner in the stent case were closely tied to the intermediate product's transfer price, which quickly became a point of contention between the partners. A tug-of-war over profits is not uncommon, especially in alliances with mutual exclusivity. The total pie in such a partnership is not fixed, so the division of this pie is not strictly a zero-sum game, where one's gain comes at the other's loss. But in the short and even medium run, the profit distribution can well seem that way, especially if the scope of the partnership is narrowly defined.

Medinol's and Boston Scientific's battle over actual profits was echoed by another battle over potential profits. In this fast-changing biotech industry, market share and market power are often closely linked to innovations. Initially, both partners invested in their own R&D programs, but halfway into the work, they decided that the Medinol approach showed more promise. Still, the race to learn did not end there. Soon after the breakup of the alliance, Boston Scientific revived its own program and in the span of a few months found a solution to a problem that had been eluding the company. Medinol claimed that this solution came directly from its intellectual property.

This pattern of behavior is common for high-tech alliances. When technology advantages are central, partners often seek to push their own technology development and to maintain or gain control over intellectual property. Which party advances in this race, of course, has clear implications for the division of future profits. The availability of a new internal option can dramatically raise the bargaining power of one party in the next round of negotiations.

The battle over value in the medical stent alliance ultimately revolved around control, as do many other such battles. Not coincidentally, Boston Scientific's secret activities in Ireland were code-named—interchangeably—"Bringing a Better Deal" and "Project Independence."

The key driver of control, in this case and in others, is the existence of alternatives either inside or outside the alliance. The bargaining power of one party in a combination will usually increase with the number of alternatives available to it. This "optionality" creates negotiating power by offering an exit route, a benchmark price, a ceiling on concessions, a safety net to a risky deal, and so on. In negotiating terms, the best alternative to a negotiated agreement is generally improved if a company has such options. As a result, the battle over value sharing within a combination often revolves around creating such alternative options.

Front-Loading Co-opetition. One way to resolve the various forms of friction between alliance partners is through a merger. In fact, Boston Scientific tried several times to acquire Medinol, but the parties could not agree on a price.

Let's consider the potential advantages and disadvantages of such a merger. Certainly, a merger would change the relationships between the parties. Direct competition in the classic sense of co-opetition would be suppressed, or at least there would be a common owner to adjudicate any remaining conflicts between divisions. But in another sense, an acquisition would be the riskier move among the alternatives, at least for the acquiring company. The reason lies in the mechanism of value sharing. In an alliance, value is shared on a pay-as-you-go basis. In a merger, the sharing is front-loaded—one party (the target) receives its whole payment at the closing, whereas the other party (the acquirer) gets the residual right to all remaining value created.

As a result, the target gets a risk-free payment, and the acquirer holds all the risk in how much joint value will indeed be created. If the business tanks for any reason, the target does not suffer, but the acquirer can easily end up with a loss on its purchase. That is why larger mergers often end up in large write-offs for the acquirer down the road. In a classic alliance relationship, that outcome is less likely. If the joint effort in an alliance succeeds, both parties will have a chance at the winnings, though they may haggle over their shares of the winnings. If the joint effort fails, they will haggle over the losses, but no party is guaranteed any return up front. Risk is thus shared in alliances and is transferred wholesale from target to acquirer in mergers.

A merger would probably allow tighter governance of joint activities between two parties, especially if they otherwise would have competitive friction. That tighter governance might lead to greater joint value (that is why many economists would prescribe full integration in situations of bilateral monopoly). But a merger does not excuse the parties from fighting about how to share value. It just changes the location of the battle, which will now take place over the present value of future cash flows, as opposed to taking place in real time over the actual, periodic cash flows.

As a result, some of the very same analysis that is relevant to how value is shared in an alliance also applies to how value is shared at the point of acquisition. To the extent that a special advantage or another factor gives the edge to one party in an alliance, the same factor is also likely to give that party the edge in bargaining. In an alliance, a bargaining advantage translates into a larger share of value. In a merger, a bargaining advantage affects the price of the acquisition—moving it higher if the selling party has that advantage, and lower if the buyer has it.

What should you do if you face the prospect of co-opetition such as described? Follow the steps outlined in table 5-1 to ensure that you mix collaboration and competition only when necessary, and that you do so with proper caution.

Management Tool

TABLE 5-1

Taming co-opetition

- **Be realistic: see co-opetition for what it is.** All too often, the possibility of conflict between partners is not faced honestly when businesses are planning a partnership. Conflict is understandably a sensitive topic. But it needs to be addressed first in your own planning and then in conversations with your prospective partner.

- **Be cautious: avoid co-opetition, if you can.** With few exceptions, being in competition with your partner is not helpful for a combination. When the cost of competition appears high, you may do well to avoid the partner or even the alliance itself.

- **Be preemptive: squash co-opetition up front, if you can.** If you cannot avoid it—perhaps because competitive conditions leave you no choice—then you can try to squash the competition up front through a full merger or an asset swap that in effect puts all the competing assets under one roof.

- **Be smart: manage co-opetition, if you can't avoid it.** If a merger doesn't work—and, again, you could not avoid forming a combination with a competitor—then try to structure the alliance so as to minimize competition. For example, territorial boundaries (where legal) can keep the partners out of each other's way.

- **Be bold: in exceptional situations, ignore the above advice and jump in.** In some situations, competitors may indeed work together toward a common goal, such as strengthening the infrastructure or ecosystem of their industry. This kind of co-opetition does little to give one party the edge over the other, but may lift all boats.

How Partner Positioning Affects Value Shares

Because value sharing in alliances is subject to change, partners often try to influence the direction of that change. You can easily imagine how in an exclusive partnership, each side would try to maneuver the situation to gain bargaining power.

The Fragility of Exclusivity

The history of the Wintel relationship between Microsoft and Intel is full of examples of this kind of maneuvering. From the launch of the IBM PC, Intel and Microsoft were tied to each other; they were mutually dependent, even if perhaps not fully exclusive partners. Within a decade after that launch, the partnership had begun to yield huge profits, leading the partners to jockey for position in a classic fashion.

Through a series of moves, Intel tried to move into software territory itself and implicitly threatened to bypass Microsoft's operating system for some of the chip maker's functionality. Intel also developed chips for other operating systems aside from Microsoft's, most importantly Sun and, later, Apple. Microsoft, for its part, also tried to reduce its dependence on its main partner Intel. It developed Windows versions for advanced processors that competed with Intel in the PC domain and special versions of Windows that ran on mobile devices dominated by Intel's rivals.

Even in a hugely profitable partnership, therefore, mutual exclusivity is seldom comfortable and usually unstable. Another court battle, between Toys "R" Us and Amazon.com, proved this point. The two retailers signed a ten-year alliance contract with the intent of having Amazon.com sell toys supplied by Toys "R" Us. Within a couple of years, cracks began to appear between the parties. Toys "R" Us accused Amazon.com of allowing other toy sellers on its site through its marketplace. The toy retailer sued Amazon.com for violation of the exclusivity terms of the contract, and the collaboration ended.

The court found that the contract provisions on exclusivity were confusing, but the judge still ruled that Amazon.com had violated the intent of the agreement. "Long-term commitment in a world where the technology is advancing almost on a daily basis is difficult to maintain," concluded Judge Margaret McVeigh of the New Jersey Superior Court. "What constitutes an exclusive partnership continues to be a challenge not only for individuals who work on the partnership daily, but for business entities."

McVeigh's conclusion suggests that long-term, exclusive commitments are in some sense unnatural in business: industry and technological trends are bound to overcome them and make them crack. In high-tech industries, these trends move fast, and so ten-year agreements are bound to break up before their time. But even when events move slower, exclusive deals are likely to unravel.

Strategic intent is sometimes involved in the end of an exclusive relationship. If a company can tactfully restructure an alliance from exclusivity to one where its partners compete for its business, the company may well increase its share of value created without breaking up the combination. This delicate restructuring is one of the strategies in *partner positioning*—maneuvering your partnerships to influence the way value is shared in the grouping.

Apple used partner positioning to earn more value with its iPhone services. Before the iPhone launch, Apple tried to gain Verizon's support, but Verizon refused to commit to the network investments needed for the untried product. AT&T jumped at the opportunity of an exclusive alliance with Apple, in an effort to catch up with Verizon. The Apple-AT&T alliance remained rocky, partly because of the network investments that AT&T needed to make and no doubt also because of the high cash subsidies AT&T paid to Apple for every new subscriber. By the time this contract was up for renewal, the Apple iPhone was a proven killer product, and Verizon as well as T-Mobile lined up to adopt it. As a result, Apple maintained a strong bargaining position with the telecom providers, ensuring that it would receive continued product payments as the telecoms sold Apple products to subscribers.

Apple also succeeded in broadening its supplier relationships for the iPhone hardware itself. At the start, Samsung was Apple's main supplier for critical parts, from flash memory and processors to displays. Samsung had not yet entered the smartphone business in any significant way and so did not compete directly with Apple. The situation began to change when Samsung joined the rapidly expanding world of Android phones, promoted by Google. Samsung quickly gained ground in smartphones and, a few years later, emerged as Apple's main rival for market share, innovation, and, as so often happens with old allies, in court.

Apple and Samsung claimed still to be good partners on selected components in an echo of the old co-opetition cry of Silicon Valley. Amid this shift, though, Apple tried hard and gradually succeeded in reducing its dependence on Samsung, finding alternative suppliers of memory and displays in Sharp and other Chinese companies. But Samsung remained a prime source of high-end displays and processors for Apple, in part because of the long technical relationship and substantial investment that the two firms had with each other.

Throughout these episodes, Apple kept an eye on all the three laws of business combinations. Apple had to continue to support partners who were needed for the creation of joint value—it would be no good to totally alienate them. The company also had to maintain a working relationship with them; the lawsuit with Samsung and the friction with AT&T threatened Apple's relationships with these companies, but the strong mutual interests kept the parties together. Finally, Apple played its hand—and tried to improve its hand—to ensure that it would earn handsomely. To do so, it explicitly managed its position and its partners' positions in the combination.

Intel, the Master of Partner Positioning

Intel has been the master at partner positioning in the last few decades. The general story of how Intel came to dominate the microprocessor business is well known, but the implications for alliance strategy are worth extra attention. Intel succeeded in flipping its position in its partner network from dependence to dominance. Industry conditions and trends helped, but this move was driven in no small part by Intel's own strategy.

Let's back up a bit for some background information. At the launch of the PC, IBM insisted that Intel license the design of the Intel microprocessor to a long list of major semiconductor makers, as well as to IBM itself. As a result, Intel competed with these licensees to supply one buyer, IBM. In this configuration, Intel could not capture much of the value created by its combination with IBM and Microsoft, even though the product line was growing rapidly. By one estimate, Intel earned only 30 percent of the revenues and profits of IBM's microprocessor purchases, even though the chip maker owned the design of the chip.

Luckily for Intel, the industry was moving fast. Moreover, license deals for one generation of microprocessor did not carry over automatically to later generations. When the second generation of the Intel chip came out, Intel purposefully reduced the number of licensees to four, while launching an intense marketing and sales campaign dubbed "Checkmate." Any doubt that Intel knew what it was doing on the chessboard of alliance partnerships should have been erased by now. Intel would try to reposition the chess pieces to gain bargaining power with its partners.

This was a risky move, but luckily for Intel, the industry had evolved to generate more rivalry on the buyer side of the equation. Soon after the launch of the IBM PC, Compaq had succeeded in reverse-engineering the system, that is, Compaq learned how to make a PC that worked just like the IBM machine, using Intel-designed chips and the Microsoft operating system. Compaq's move gave rise to the proliferation of IBM PC clones, which created serious rivalry for IBM. The tables were being turned.

With the rise of the clones, Intel gained the bargaining power to refuse to license any other independent producers in later generations of its chips. Now in sole control of production and pricing, the company could triple its average selling price per chip. The rest is history. Intel maintained its dominance and sole position in one chip generation after the next, leading to a strong rise in profits and Intel's market value.

To visualize the change in position that Intel engineered, consider figure 5-2. It shows how the configuration of options available to one party in a combination influences the relative bargaining power of both parties. Imagine that Company A (circle) needs resources (squares). It decides to form an alliance with, or to acquire, Company B (whose resources are shown as the black square). In addition, however, the resources may also be available internally (the white square), from a second business deal with another company (whose resources are shown as the dark gray square), or from potential deals with other companies (the light gray square). The more of these options that Company A has, the stronger its bargaining position in sharing value with Company B. For an acquisition, the price of the deal will be affected by this bargaining power; for an alliance, the value-sharing arrangement will be affected.

In the early years, Intel occupied the position of Company B in its alliance with IBM, which occupied the position of Company A. In later years, the tables were turned and Intel was in the position of

Management Tool

FIGURE 5-2

Partner positioning in combinations

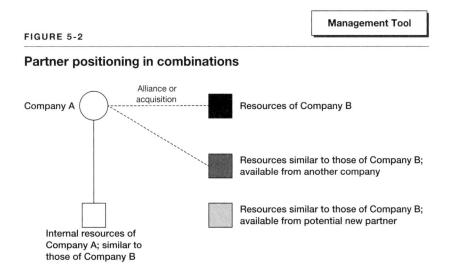

Company A

Alliance or acquisition

Resources of Company B

Resources similar to those of Company B; available from another company

Resources similar to those of Company B; available from potential new partner

Internal resources of Company A; similar to those of Company B

Company A to IBM's Company B. The profits accruing to IBM and to Intel followed suit—low for Intel at the start, and much higher later on.

In general, then, the more options you have to replace another party's contributions, the greater your bargaining power and, as a result, the more value you will earn. Conversely, the more replicable others' contributions are, the greater your bargaining power and, as a result, the more value you will earn. Conversely, the more replaceable *you* are in a combination, the lower your earning power.

Limits on Partner Positioning

Just as the growth of an industry can destroy the basis of exclusive deals, it can also limit the options for pursuing a strategy such as Intel's. As a result, while the Intel flip from dependence to dominance is attractive to many strategists, it may not be possible or may require additional acrobatics.

Two key ingredients made the Intel flip possible. First, *other* industry players, acting on their own interests, broke the IBM monopoly on the buyer side of the industry stack. The appearance of clones was critical, and surely, Intel helped make that happen. But their appearance did not happen just because of Intel's actions. Importantly, Microsoft, too, encouraged the rise of clones because it had retained the right to sell its operating system to third parties, beyond IBM.

Second, Intel had the technical and legal ability to change the terms of successive generations of its microprocessor. Added to the quick succession of these generations, this ability allowed Intel to change rules for sharing joint value without breaching its contracts. Licensing deals are not always structured in this way. In fact, the microprocessor industry itself learned from this experience, and later entrants often had to promise multigenerational licenses to encourage the adoption of the new companies' technology.

The British company ARM Holdings may now suffer from this fallout. The company became a darling of tech investors because its products were at the core of most smartphones. It was also a serious rival to Intel, because its chips run on low power—ideal for the mobile devices that were overtaking traditional personal computers. ARM's ability to challenge the chip-industry behemoth is a credit to the company and speaks to its tremendous success in technology development and business strategy. Intel was not an easy target, and many companies have failed over the years to unseat it.

But ARM has been less successful in earning a share of the profits it has generated than Intel was, in part because the British firm has not yet found a way to flip its partnership positioning as Intel did. ARM also started with a second-source strategy to encourage device makers to adopt its chip. In fact, it outdid Intel in this strategy—it soon had over four hundred licensees. Furthermore, many of its licensees not only had secured rights to successive generations of ARM products, but also had the right to design their own processors based on the ARM architecture. Generous licensing terms such as these were probably needed for the company to spread its technology fast and become the industry standard in mobile devices.

The ARM dilemma is echoed by the history of the Android operating system that runs on many of the ARM mobile devices. This software architecture, too, had to be practically given away by Google to break into the market dominated by Apple. Android devices in fact pay no royalties to Google for the use of the software. That strategy was wildly successful: Android devices exploded on the market and soon represented the largest share of mobile devices. But Android device makers notoriously compete fiercely with each other, and Google itself has so far failed to enter the mobile-device market with a dominant product.

Google clearly intends to gain from the proliferation of its operating system, but not by directly charging for its use. That cat is out of the bag, and a classic Intel flip would appear impossible at this stage. Instead, Google probably expects to profit from Android's links to other products it offers, like search, mapping, and other data services.

Still, profiting from adjacent or linked products is not a sure bet. A decade earlier, Sun made its Java software ubiquitous through a similar strategy: the firm gave the software away. Like Google, Sun stayed in charge of some design authority for the software, but the firm allowed other companies to build on the software and demanded no royalties in return. As a result, Java is today firmly embedded in three billion devices—from computers and smartphones to ATMs and parking meters—but Sun has earned not a penny on all that. After Oracle acquired Sun, there was some talk that the new owners might seek ways to extract value from their ownership of the Java designs. Still, a new strategy to do this did not appear. Oracle, Google, and ARM thus were constrained in shifting their positions in their partnerships.

An Approach to Managing Your Share of Value

The evidence and reasoning in this chapter confirm that the third law is no less important than the first two—without earning a sufficient share of value, no company would engage in a business combination. It's the bottom line, so to speak. But this third law grows out of the other two laws; there must enough total value created jointly so that its distribution leaves all parties with a sufficient return on their investment. Creating this total value, we have seen, depends on effective joint governance.

The trick to managing these linked forces lies in balancing competition as well as cooperation. At its roots, a business combination always involves managing competition. Managers and attorneys often prefer not to frame the matter this way, lest they infringe on antitrust rules. So, we often end up with overly benign expectations about cooperation, stripped of the competitive friction that is their reality. Or we hear misguided claims of partners engaging in cooperation and competition at once without diminishing either activity, as in co-opetition.

To manage competition and cooperation soberly and effectively, start by mapping precisely where each occurs—inside your combination or between your combination and external rivals. The value that ultimately accrues to your firm in a combination depends on competitive processes at these two levels, as shown in figure 5-3. The competition between your combination and its external rivals (horizontal axis) determines the total joint value created by the combination—the size of the pie, so to speak. Bargaining between your firm and your partners (vertical axis) then affects what share of that total pie you earn. To understand and manage your value-sharing relationships, keep an eye on both of these processes. The ultimate value that you earn is a product of these two

Management Tool

FIGURE 5-3

Determinants of how value is earned in combinations

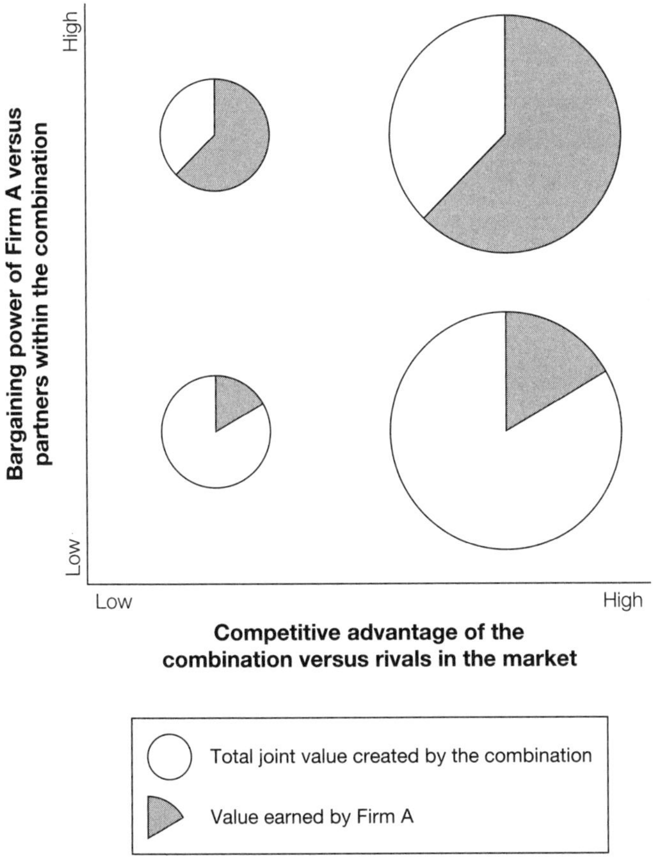
High
Low
Bargaining power of Firm A versus partners within the combination
Low
High
Competitive advantage of the combination versus rivals in the market
Total joint value created by the combination
Value earned by Firm A

processes—sometimes earning a smaller share of a larger pie will be a better return on your efforts than a larger share of a smaller pie.

To evaluate how these two forces affect your earnings, recognize first that joint value is created in competition with outsiders. This means that partners must band together to confront rivals outside their combination. As predicted by the first and second laws of business combinations, without a promising and well-governed combination, there will be no value to share at all. And how that value is shared will affect the effort and investment that each party is willing to contribute to the combination.

Second, understand how bargaining power inside the combination is shaped by the alternative combination options of each party. To see this, explore the patterns of who competes with whom and how intense this competition is. To uncover the patterns, ask these questions:

- **How much competition exists between your firm and the partner firm with which you intend to create new value?** Direct competition here spells trouble, as it can reduce the degree of cooperation, joint governance, and forbearance. You may find that reaching a stable agreement on value sharing is difficult under such conditions, but perhaps more important will be the cost to the value-creation strategy that lies at the very root of your combination. The recommendations in table 5-1 will help you strike this balance.

- **How much competition exists between your firm and other firms like yours that conceivably could also combine with your partner (or already have)?** Competition here generates bargaining alternatives that can be exploited by your partner firm to nudge the value-sharing formula in its favor.

- **How much competition exists between your partner and other firms like it, which conceivably could also combine with your firm (or already have)?** This is, of course, the mirror image of the preceding question, but it is worth calling it out. Competition here gives you options that help you move value in your favor.

Finally, take into account that, over time, external trends in the entire industry can influence the competitive patterns within your combination such as by creating more combination alternatives for you or your partners. We have seen how the number of players in an industry might grow over time and thus might affect partner positioning. Exclusive arrangements, for example, often crack when external trends give birth to new alternatives for one side or the other. In a sense, the internal partner positioning is forced to keep track of external patterns of rivalry, or the combination is likely to break.

* * *

Business combinations can shape the pattern of competition in industries, as we have seen. In the microprocessor industry, generous licensors created scores of competitors. The intense competition then made it difficult for these very licensors to gain a sufficient share of the value they created.

Business combinations today are reshaping rivalry in different ways and with different consequences. As Joseph Schumpeter predicted, a new combination can shock an industry and challenge the normal routine of the remaining firms. Often, rival firms will then have to form their own new combinations to meet the threat. Before you know it, the industry is overrun by mergers, acquisitions, and alliances. It may look like a fad. But the transformation is real—groups begin to compete against groups.

How do you survive and thrive in this new world? You'll need all the insight and tools offered so far, and more. We'll see that in part three of the book.

Part Three

How Remix Strategy Changes the Way You Compete

WHEN ASSETS ARE REMIXED IN THE WAYS DESCRIBED so far, new units of competition are formed. In the nineteenth century, an earlier business remix gave rise to the modern corporation that was driven by the benefits of scale and scope. Later, the same process led to business trusts and cartels that came to rule certain markets. In the last decades, remixing has given rise to groups of allied firms—the constellations introduced briefly in chapter 2. In many industries, competition has become a battle of group against group, not firm against firm.

In this world of group versus group, the three laws of business combinations are still valid—and even operate on a grander scale. Inside a constellation, every alliance or combination needs to fulfill the laws. Further, the group as a whole has to create joint value, must be governed effectively, and must share value in a way that is rewarding to members. The next chapter explains how to apply the laws to these new competitive groupings.

The final chapter steps back to show how the thinking in this book gives a fresh perspective on core issues in strategy. I am convinced that understanding remix strategy will help you think differently and make better strategic decisions.

Chapter 6

The Three Laws in Multipartner Groups

WITH THE THREE LAWS OF BUSINESS COMBINATIONS under your belt, you will see the world differently. Everywhere you look, you will see business combinations. This is not an illusion. You probably already have many business relationships, and you will still need more. Competition in many businesses has become a battle of group versus group. To succeed in this world, you will need to manage well not just one combination, but a whole portfolio of deals.

This chapter will explain how to do just that. Managing multipartner groups is both simpler and harder than it sounds. Simpler, because the same laws that you now understand well also apply to groups. Harder, because applying these laws to many deals at once can challenge the best strategists and managers.

All three laws will be discussed in this chapter in the same sequence as in part two. We will start again by defining key terms. After that, we will examine, in turn, how joint value is created in groups, how groups are governed, and how value is shared in groups. The management tools in this chapter follow from the analysis and evidence, as they did in part two.

Competition between Bundles of Assets

Economists aren't generally big on colorful metaphors. Even so, one particularly vivid metaphor is well known in the profession, courtesy of Nobel Prize winner Ronald Coase. In his famous 1937 essay "The Nature of the Firm," Coase reminded us that firms are like "islands of conscious power in this ocean of unconscious cooperation, like lumps of butter coagulating in a pail of buttermilk."

Coase developed a theory to help solidify that image of the firm, so to speak. But it turns out that today, the firm itself may well be the wrong unit of analysis. Edith Penrose, the mother of the resource-based theory of the firm, had a hunch about this in 1959: "For an analysis of economic power, there is no doubt that the industrial firm is not the most relevant unit," she wrote. But she reasoned that trying to define the firm "according to power groupings would produce too amorphous a concept to handle."

Today, you urgently need to come to grips with these amorphous "power groupings." Chapter 2 defined these groupings as constellations—your portfolio or network of partners—and sketched how to think about their structures. As reiterated throughout this book, you cannot understand or manage your business to its full potential without understanding and managing your constellation.

Examples of competition between groups of firms can be found in just about any industry:

- Apple's smartphone success depends on its relationships with suppliers for critical components such as processors, memory, and screens and on relationships with telecom providers, app developers, and content producers.

- Android competes against this Apple grouping by using an even more extensive network that includes multiple vendors of complete handsets (a part that Apple keeps to itself) and a consortium for open-source software.

- Airlines depend on coordination and marketing relationships with other airlines outside their home regions and on organizations that manage key groupings such as Star, oneworld, and SkyTeam.

- Boeing and Airbus both depend on a huge network of suppliers for major components and subsystems (as do automobile companies), while Airbus is itself a consortium of multiple European companies.

- Coke and Pepsi depend on an extensive network of bottlers to package and deliver their products and use both ownership stakes and long-term contracts to encourage their bottlers to implement their marketing strategies.

- Pharmaceutical companies depend on joint research with universities and biotech start-ups, and most of the large companies in the industry devote substantial resources to managing their portfolio of partners and attracting new ones.

- Petroleum firms depend on external parties for everything from drilling to transport, refining, and marketing, as became clear to all when BP and its subcontractors tangled over who was to blame for the disastrous Macondo oil-well blowout in the Gulf of Mexico.

- Zara, Nike, and most other leading fashion brands depend on fast response and quality production from shops in multiple countries—and increasingly are held responsible for the labor standards at these shops.

And the list goes on. Success in all these situations depends on the resources, strategies, and governance of the group as a whole. You too will need to use the three laws to manage a constellation of partners. We'll see now how the concepts from part two can be extended to this new world.

What Is a Constellation?

Simply put, a constellation is a group of firms linked together by alliances. Alliances, as we saw, can be hard to define concretely, because they come in so many forms and the line separating what is and is not an alliance is blurry. Even so, some theory and many examples helped us focus on the essential features that define an alliance.

As described in chapter 4, an alliance is an organizational mechanism that uses shared control to govern an incomplete contract between independent parties and is sustained by relational value. The definition is a mouthful, but every element in the definition is important.

Now we need to raise the ante, analytically, because constellations typically involve multiple alliances. Alliances are the glue that holds together the firms in a constellation (see figure 6-1). These alliances can be of various types, from loose to tight, as discussed before. As the figure shows, there may be alliances between some firms in the constellation and not others. As I use the term, a constellation does not require that all firms be linked to each

FIGURE 6-1

Components of a constellation

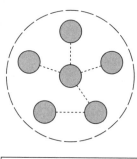

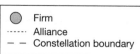

● Firm
······ Alliance
− − Constellation boundary

other or belong to a common organization. All of these possibilities help determine how the constellation is structured and governed, but they are variables, not prerequisites in our definition. Finally, the figure shows six firms, but a constellation can consist of just a pair or a trio of firms, or it can include scores of firms. The number of firms, again, is a variable, not a defining feature of the concept.

Constellations and Ecosystems

The definition of a constellation is different from the idea of a business ecosystem introduced by James Moore. As commonly used today, the term *ecosystem* refers to a broader and looser collection of players than the constellations discussed in this book. The ecosystem of a business consists of all its suppliers and buyers, plus the other firms that provide complementary products and services. A new smartphone model, for example, needs to have apps, accessories, and online services that help flesh out its potential; those ancillary elements form the ecosystem for that new model. More broadly, all smartphones benefit from having advanced telecom services available nationwide, so those services form part of the ecosystem for the entire smartphone industry.

This ecosystem metaphor gives insight, but it can be made more useful to management. For one, understanding the concept of an ecosystem does not by itself provide a way to think about the concrete organizational relationships between the firms in the system. In practice, just recruiting players to join an ecosystem does not guarantee the success of the group. In fact, these firms are often not a group at all, but a collection of independent entities with some commonalities and minimal organizational links. Many of the firms in a typical ecosystem are related to each other by simple trade transactions, not by alliances or mergers. Because a constellation is a set of firms linked through concrete alliances, it has ways to create and share value, as we will see in this chapter. To create value with the three laws, we need to think about constellations as more than loose collections of firms.

The ecosystem idea also becomes more useful if we consider how one grouping competes with another. Analysts using the ecosystem metaphor don't often emphasize this competition between groupings, which is the reality today. The Apple iPhone grouping competes directly with Google's Android grouping on everything from hardware design to apps, telecom services, and pricing. This kind of competition, again, is managed through alliances and business combinations—partners are recruited to join one group over another, groups compete over how well they govern their assets, and so on. We will see in this chapter how constellations use such mechanisms to compete with each other.

Joint Value Potential in Constellations

Constellation strategy revolves around creating the organizational structures that generate group synergies. These synergies, in turn, come from the natural complementarities between members of the group. The members may depend on each other for inputs, share markets and standards, or be part of a broader system in which each member plays a role. In chapter 3, we identified markets, chains, and stacks as three schemes that reflect the most common types of complementarity in business systems. The joint value in business combinations, we saw, stems from improving the way these natural complementarities are managed.

The same is true for constellations. Groupings of allied firms may arise in business systems of various sorts, and so their goals will differ—from horizontal cooperation in markets, to vertical coordination in supplier relations in chains, to integrating the various elements in a stack. Most constellations are hybrids of these forms, but we will analyze each of these as a pure form. Whatever the goals of a constellation, it will need to organize itself to bring out the potential of the combination. As before, the requirements of creating joint value shape how the constellation is best governed.

Let's look in turn at how joint value is created in the different types of constellations that arise from complementarities in markets, chains, and stacks.

Reaching and Combining Markets

A common type of company grouping is horizontal. That is, the members are competitors to some extent and operate in the same general market or stage of production in the industry's value chain. Sometimes the members sell the same product in the same market; more commonly, they sell similar products in different geographic or technical niches in the market. Examples are airline companies that sell the same types of travel services in one global market (or in regional markets) and computer companies that sell similar equipment to different niches of corporate users and home users. These *horizontal constellations* create value by the same principles of simpler horizontal combinations discussed in chapter 3, only here, the joint value depends on bundling assets from many more players.

A horizontal constellation always involves the suppression of competition to some degree; at the very least, it "manages" the competition that would have existed between its members. Can this arrangement ever be good for society? Without getting into the technicalities of welfare analysis, the answer from economists and antitrust authorities is generally yes—if the joint value created by the combination exceeds the costs of a (slight) reduction in competition among member firms. (See the sidebar "A Note on Anticompetitive Cartels.")

That joint value in a horizontal constellation can come about through a number of processes. For example, the constellation's members can share costs, invest in common infrastructure, increase production scale by consolidating capacity, and otherwise generate savings or greater investment from the increased scale that comes from acting as a group. That's the intent of the STARS alliance, a constellation of seven independent nuclear

A Note on Anticompetitive Cartels

Horizontal constellations are, of course, tricky from an antitrust point of view. In its *Antitrust Guidelines for Collaborations Among Competitors*, the US Department of Justice does admit that "in order to compete in modern markets, competitors sometimes need to collaborate . . . Such collaborations often are not only benign but procompetitive." Nevertheless, the guidelines continue, certain agreements that are highly likely to harm competition and have no procompetitive benefits may be ruled as "per se unlawful." All other agreements will be reviewed under the "rule of reason, which involves a factual inquiry into an agreement's overall competitive effect."

I am not giving advice here on which kinds of horizontal constellations violate antitrust regulations—that is for lawyers and the authorities to evaluate. But it helps to understand this issue, because my definition of a horizontal constellation does not depend on this evaluation. Illegal cartels can also be considered horizontal constellations, just as much as the "procompetitive collaborations" envisioned by the US Justice Department. And many horizontal constellations will lie in a gray zone. What's important for managers developing strategy is the underlying economic logic. Some airline constellations, for example, have received antitrust immunity from US and European authorities, while others have not; the decision usually depends on whether the constellation is perceived to enhance competition on the routes in question or not.

power facilities in the United States (not to be confused with the Star Alliance of airlines). In its review of this constellation, the US Justice Department related approvingly how STARS proposed to share personnel, parts, equipment, tools, and expertise and to coordinate planning and operating activities. The department also predicted that there would likely be little reduction of competition in input and output markets. It concluded that "to the extent that

Horizontal constellations that have only deleterious effects on competition, of course, can hardly be said to create value in the way we've talked about it in this book. By solely or severely reducing competition, these cartel-type constellations tend to reduce output and raise prices, without generating benefits such as increased innovation. Consider two constellations that dominated the world market for potash, a valuable agricultural fertilizer. Producers from Russia and Belarus teamed up in one constellation, and two Canadian producers joined in another. In each case, the producers sold their output through joint sales organizations. As these constellations coordinated output, potash prices rose from about $100 per ton in the early 2000s to over $400. The cartel structure began to come apart when the Russian producer threatened to leave its constellation, perhaps in an effort to punish a partner suspected of selling below the agreed-upon prices.

No new joint value was created by these horizontal constellations in potash and by the cooperation between them. The main "benefit" of these strategies was to increase the market power of the member firms. As a result, value was extracted from farmers all over the world, and food production and consumption in Africa and Asia may well have suffered from the high cartel prices. These cases serve as a caveat to our analysis. Business combinations that are purely anticompetitive, without procompetitive benefits, cannot be thought of as creating joint value. They merely redistribute value among economic players, often at a cost to the welfare of society.

the proposed cooperative activities increase efficiencies that result in lower costs, increased output (such as reductions in nuclear reactor outages that result in less downtime), or increased safety, the proposed conduct could have a pro-competitive effect."

The benefits of scale can be significant, but they don't come easily if the constellation isn't organized to capture them. Constellations made up of several medium-sized firms organized as a loose consortium, for example, often have a hard time reaping the benefits of scale. Without strong financial incentives to act jointly, constellation members in these structures often resist yielding control of their own purchasing and investment decisions. Similarly, it is often hard to rationalize capacity or allocate exclusive roles among members that are only loosely connected. In the end, to gain scale advantages, horizontal constellations often pursue tighter structures such as joint ventures with members as owners or partial mergers of members.

Another strategy of horizontal constellations is to share common costs across a broader scope of products or markets. This kind of strategy is often driven by one central firm rather than by a collection of competitors. The central firm may use a constellation of partners to operate in multiple geographic or niche markets or to adapt its products to multiple sets of buyers.

Corning International offers a good example. In the 1950s and 1960s, the company expanded abroad by forming joint ventures with local players that often managed national or regional factories for traditional glass products. Corning controlled the core technology of the factories and, often, their branding. In later years, Corning bought out many of its partners or sold units to consolidate the operations of these far-flung plants. At the same time, however, Corning began to form new alliances (usually, joint ventures) with partners who helped the company enter a variety of vertical markets—television glass, fiber optics, laboratory glass, and so on. Corning itself maintained control and continued to invest in the core glass-making technology. In this model, the partners were the leading firms in the various applications and often had complementary businesses, such as Samsung in televisions and Siemens in telecommunication. Over time, this strategy, too, evolved, and Corning bought out many partners, leaving itself in full control of a broader set of products.

Horizontal constellations may also generate network effects that raise benefits for consumers, even when the added scale of the group doesn't lower costs of production. The airlines seeking antitrust immunity from US and European authorities were motivated in part by the potential of network effects. A wider and better-connected network of fights, the carriers argued, justifies some reduction in competition among members.

Network effects are also central to the horizontal constellations that dominate the credit card business. Both Visa and MasterCard started in the 1960s as networks that were limited in size and controlled by one or a few banks. Visa, originally controlled by Bank of America, realized early on that with more member banks, it could expand its network of credit-card issuers and vendors. MasterCard followed suit by expanding its membership beyond the original handful of founding banks. The strategy of these constellations was based on classic network effects. The value to each vendor would rise with the number of credit-card holders, and the value of holding a card rose with the number of vendors accepting the card. What's more, a multiplicity of banks was useful for encouraging the growth of these vendor and consumer networks. For much of their history (until both credit-card companies went public), Visa and MasterCard were each at the center of a large constellation of member banks, with MasterCard actually being owned by its members.

At another extreme, some horizontal constellations consist of partners who are expressly *not* connected to each other, or at least partners for which the success of one party does not depend on that of another. The portfolios of biotech alliances that large pharmaceutical companies maintain offer a typical example. The central companies in these constellations seek to reduce their R&D risk by investing in diverse bets and options. Just as in financial portfolio diversification, the core idea here is to make investments with returns that are unrelated and uncorrelated.

This model is common in R&D outside the pharmaceutical industry, too. Every major oil company in the 2000s developed a diversified portfolio of R&D alliances in renewable energy. Their clean-energy projects ranged from ethanol to solar and wind and included partners as diverse as universities, national labs, and start-ups. Within some of the energy alternatives, the typical major oil company may also have placed several bets, such as on various feedstocks for biofuels. Aside from diversifying risk among these uncertain projects, this broad range of investments also enhanced the oil companies' options for the future. If one approach takes off, the reasoning went, it could be pursued and other avenues could be closed down. To maintain flexibility, and because the partners' activities were not directly related, the structure of these constellations was typically loose. The central companies typically managed the partners as portfolios, with little or no joint decision making and few connections between peripheral members.

Coordinating Supply Chains

Joint value can also come from combinations of firms in a chain, that is, firms that are not selling in the same market, but that sell to each other. Chapter 3 discussed the case of simpler combinations between two players. In many industries, buyers and suppliers work together closely or invest in long-term relationships, a situation compelling them to behave somewhat as a group. These groupings are usually organized around a central firm that manages the constellation—say, the final assembler at the end of the automotive production chain. (The supply network can actually be drawn from any point of view, including that of a supplier in the middle of a chain. Thus, both forward and backward links can be part of the vertical constellation around a firm, and the shape of a constellation is in the eye of the beholder.)

These vertical constellations do not involve all the external transactions of the central firm, but only those that are managed through combinations, as defined in chapter 2. Picture a cloud of firms around a central firm, with the partners arranged in concentric rings. Close-in partnerships in this scheme are tight alliances, and those farther out are looser relationships. Competing firms will differ on where they place the boundaries of their constellation. Some firms will do more work in-house than their competitors will, with only limited dependence on outside parties. Others will use outside suppliers and channels more often, but even these outside alliances will differ on whether the central firm considers the outside parties as arm's-length vendors or alliance partners.

Automobile manufacturers provide examples of all these approaches. Traditionally, Detroit's automakers kept much of their manufacturing in-house, but over time, they relegated more and more components and subsystems to outside suppliers, often using multiple competing suppliers for each part. Whether they treated these suppliers as vendors or partners (a distinction discussed in chapter 4) differed widely. Toyota famously treated its suppliers as part of its family and often owned stakes in them. Following this model, Chrysler pursued a strategy of close partnerships too, which helped it develop new products more efficiently. Interestingly, when Daimler acquired Chrysler, the German parent company replaced the American unit's supplier partnership model with vendor relations that were managed strictly by the numbers. Daimler claimed that, compared to strict vendor management, the Chrysler partnership model increased the cost of some components by as much as a third.

As this history shows, great debate has gone into the question of the optimal scope of a supplier constellation. Should you have a few tight partners or many looser vendor relationships, or should you do more of the work in-house? This question reflects a similar question from chapter 4—should you have tight or loose governance in a combination? And as before, the answer is, it depends. The laws that determine how best to organize a particular combination also help you decide on the scope of a vertical constellation.

Constellation design must balance specialization and integration. For a constellation, the governance question is best seen as the result of two forces—benefits of integration among components and benefits of specialization in the production of the components, as shown in figure 6-2.

Let's consider the horizontal axis in the figure first. The benefits of specialization, Adam Smith recognized, come in part from scale. The division of labor, he said famously, depends on the extent of the market. When markets are small, products will be produced on a small scale and producers will benefit little from outsourcing to others because external parties themselves lack scale to invest in specialized skills. Larger markets allow for specialization.

Management Tool

FIGURE 6-2

How joint value shapes constellations

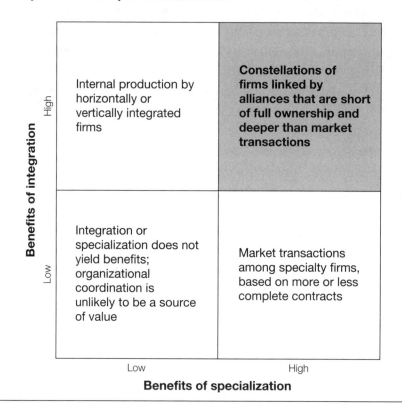

Benefits of integration

High

Internal production by horizontally or vertically integrated firms

Constellations of firms linked by alliances that are short of full ownership and deeper than market transactions

Low

Integration or specialization does not yield benefits; organizational coordination is unlikely to be a source of value

Market transactions among specialty firms, based on more or less complete contracts

Low   High

Benefits of specialization

This is one reason why start-up firms in new, niche industries often have to do more in-house than mature firms in well-established industries. There are simply fewer efficient external producers in niche industries compared to what exists in larger, mature industries. The relationship between specialization and scale partly explains why Tesla makes more of its components in-house than General Motors does. At the same time, Tesla believes that there are benefits to tight integration of its components, which is another reason for it to keep more component production in house. At the extreme, if specialization were all that mattered to productivity, and integration were not important, then separate firms would trade with each other with little need for constellations of partnerships or, much less, integrated firms.

The vertical axis in the figure measures those benefits of integration among components that Tesla and many other start-ups think are important. This axis measures the fit between components, their compatibility in operation, or the degree to which the design and production of each component needs to be timed or otherwise coordinated with those of other components.

The balance of these two economic forces—the benefits of integration and of specialization—determines the best way to organize a bundle of complementary resources. As is the case for single combinations, these forces are rooted in the source of joint value. Under certain conditions, a constellation of partners is likely to be the best way to create joint value—specifically, when both integration and specialization offer advantages (the gray quadrant of the figure). At other times, integrated firms are better choices (the top left quadrant), or independent specialty firms trading with each other (the lower right quadrant). When neither integration nor specialization offers benefits, then the way a bundle of assets is organized is unlikely to matter much to value creation (the lower left quadrant).

Boeing learned the hard way about the benefit of integration in its Dreamliner 787 project. As noted earlier, when Boeing embarked on this complex new airplane design, the firm had decided to outsource more production to suppliers than usual. The project suffered delays and cost Boeing billions. Part of the problem, Boeing found early on, was that the work of the suppliers needed to be coordinated much more than had been planned. At first, parts would arrive and not even fit physically with other parts. Later, suppliers turned out to be slow in investing, in scaling up production, or in fixing errors. The organizational solution for Boeing was to develop much closer relationships with key suppliers—often investing capital in them, sharing personnel, or bringing more of their production in-house. In terms of figure 6-2, Boeing started by operating in the bottom half of the matrix and found that many critical operations had to be moved to the top half—either by integrating them (top left) or by forming a tighter constellation with the specialty firms (top right).

As another example, if the benefit of integration is high and that of specialized production is low, you can expect firms to rely on internal operations for their components (the upper left quadrant of figure 6-2). That's part of the rationale behind Apple's tight control of software and hardware designs for all its product lines. Apple believes that to offer users the seamless, minimalist, and sophisticated experience it aims for, the company needs to control the design of all the key parts of the system. Apple still outsources the manufacturing of key components like chips and screens, and even final assembly, because there are great benefits to specialization in those stages. But even there, Apple works closely with the manufacturing partners in its constellation.

Industry evolution shifts the balance. The shape of the vertical constellation often changes as an industry evolves. Market expansion will tend to increase the room for specialization and so help move firms from the internal production model to a constellation of suppliers. Maturation of an industry also has this general effect, partly because it encourages specialization and partly because the way components are integrated becomes standardized over time. This standardization leads to modularization, whereby specialists can focus on different modules or subsystems without being too concerned about design choices in other modules. The matured, standardized interface between modules ensures that the subsystems fit together.

Industry evolution has taken place in computers and autos, as noted, and in pharmaceuticals. A few decades ago, pharmaceutical firms did much more R&D, testing, and production internally. The rise of biotech firms encouraged the rise of alliances and licensing between them and the big pharmaceutical firms. In addition, the pharmaceutical giants learned to outsource clinical trial work, drug manufacturing, and even sales activities. In each case, focused, large-scale specialty firms developed and used standardized methods in their work.

But industries don't always move from tight constellations to looser ones. Coke and Pepsi, for example, relied traditionally on independent bottlers to package and distribute their beverages. In the last decade or so, though, these two beverage giants have been buying up bottling interests to gain tighter control over this stage of the industry value chain. The expectation was that better integration between bottlers and the parent company would help Coke and Pepsi execute strategies that were increasingly more integrated across markets. Media companies, too, are moving toward greater integration in some fields, such as between distributors and content producers. Comcast's purchase of NBC is an example, as is the alliance of studios that launched Hulu. In these cases, greater integration created joint value.

Shaping and Growing Ecosystems

Constellations among firms in a stack can arise more or less spontaneously, or from the conscious action by one or more of the firms. Spontaneous collaboration of this sort is one version of James Moore's business ecosystem concept. To continue the biological analogy just a bit further, ecosystems in nature are usually spontaneous creations. Natural ecosystems may be shaped by a central natural event, such as climate conditions or island formation, but the different species that coevolve in that ecosystem do not really behave collectively or share common goals and decisions.

Business ecosystems, on the other hand, are always shaped largely by the conscious goals, planning, and actions of firms. There may be more or less coordination, as suggested by the examples above. But when coordination is needed, an explicit constellation can act as the organizational scaffolding of the business ecosystem. The linkages between the firms can spark the growth of the ecosystem, shape how joint decisions are governed, and determine how value is distributed among members.

You can use three strategies for building this organizational scaffolding: (1) creating platforms; (2) orchestrating cooperation; and (3) integrating systems. The three strategies give rise to different types of constellations in a stack, driven by various degrees of planning and spontaneous coordination.

Creating platforms for other businesses. A spontaneous, yet powerful, business ecosystem can grow from a platform created by a central firm. In this way, Apple and, later, Google set the table for mobile apps by creating the core technologies and common marketplaces for independent app developers. The business mushroomed naturally from there; new applications, creative content, programming tools, distribution mechanisms, and other elements developed rapidly. The web of players arose spontaneously, but only after the central firms created the scaffolding for this growth. A similar story can be told about the rise of the music industry in the 1900s, where recording technology gave rise to a spontaneous ecosystem of song writers, lyricists, musicians, and singers—an ecosystem that coincided with the Tin Pan Alley geographic cluster.

The conditions that allow such platforms to develop include the existence of a generic technology that has potential applications in multiple uses or markets, with readily licensed rights to the use of the technology, and a structured way for buyers and sellers to connect and exchange value. In terms of the combination strategies explored in this book, these conditions are minimal requirements, implying a loose constellation, if any. Apple and Google manage their a constellation of app developers mostly by shaping the platforms used by those developers.

Orchestrating cooperation among businesses directly. Each of Apple's and Google's mobile platforms is also itself the product of explicitly managed collaborations among firms in its stack. This careful management of cooperative relationships is often referred to as *orchestrating* collaboration. It's hard to do. An Israeli start-up called Better Place tried this with electric vehicles. It owned a network of battery-swapping stations in certain locations. Its business plan was to provide batteries on lease to drivers, who would swap out depleted batteries for fully charged ones at these stations. But to get this model to work, the company had to design batteries, cars, and stations that were compatible with each other. To this end, Better Place contracted with Nissan to design and make one of the automaker's all-electric vehicles compatible with Better Place's technology.

This plan required complex orchestration, and in its first rendition, it didn't work. Despite impressive funding by venture capitalists, the high capital costs of rolling out these networks exceeded the capacity of the start-up. At the same time, the Nissan cars didn't sell well in Israel, perhaps because a decline in oil prices lowered the attractiveness of all electric vehicles. Better Place filed for bankruptcy, and the new owners of the assets planned to revise the model to a smaller scale.

Apple, too, stubbed its toe orchestrating collaboration in a constellation, but for different reasons. The company was taken to court for its role in structuring and leading a constellation toward allegedly illegal goals. The court concluded that five large publishers "conspired with each other to eliminate retail price competition in order to raise e-book prices, and that Apple played a central role in facilitating and executing that conspiracy. Without Apple's orchestration of this conspiracy, it would not have succeeded." (The case is still in appeal at the time of publication.)

The public records of this court case suggest how one central firm might orchestrate cooperation in a constellation. We cite it here not to recommend the goals of this orchestration, but as an illustration of a type of organizational mechanism. Orchestrating a constellation of players to achieve procompetitive aims or other beneficial ends involves a mix of advocacy, negotiation, creative contract design, and careful use of bargaining power, tactics Apple used. An orchestra can be led to play peaceful music or jarring music, but the tools and skills of the conductor are likely to be similar.

Assembling components from others into finished systems. Platform and orchestration strategies are indirect ways to shape collaboration among players in a constellation. A more direct strategy is for one company to assemble the products and services of other partners in the stack and to sell this whole system to customers. This strategy looks like vertical integration or a vertical constellation, except that the component-making firms do not sell inputs to the assembler of the system. In effect, the firms in the group sell jointly to a final customer, but one firm takes the lead in coordinating the fit among components.

This model is the traditional approach to complex construction projects, in which a general contractor organizes the work of subcontractors who are responsible for their own individual subsystems. With the emergence of new technologies and rising energy costs, there is increasing competition in building "smart" buildings, grids, and cities. IBM, Cisco, and Johnson Controls have all rolled out various campaigns to deliver these services, which invariably require the companies to combine their own products with those of other companies or each other. These firms cannot just compete on their own; they need to assemble a constellation of firms that play complementary roles in the finished system.

Governance of Constellations

Group strategy, as we just saw, aims at creating network value—an extension of the first law of business combinations. To succeed in that, you need to know where network value comes from and what assets need to be combined. Clearly, however, these steps do not magically create joint value—according to the second law, the group's resources need to be governed effectively. And of course, governance is not a simple matter when there are multiple partners. We'll build on earlier concepts to address the challenge of governing constellations.

The Constellation Spectrum

Like the relationship spectrum of individual business combinations, the many shapes and forms of constellations can also be arranged on a spectrum, from loose to tight. The two dimensions discussed in chapter 2 can now be applied to the constellation as a whole, not just to one interfirm relationship (figure 6-3).

The vertical axis in figure 6-3 again shows a measure of the duration of the constellation. But unlike single combinations, constellations don't just end when a partner leaves, so the concept of duration needs to be modified. In the multipartner situation, we can interpret that axis as the *stability* of the constellation structure—the lower structures change frequently and the higher ones are more stable over time. The horizontal axis shows the extent to which decisions are made jointly by the members, as discussed before for two-party alliances. Along these two axes, we can place various forms of constellations. As before, these placements are not set in stone, but serve to illustrate the range of options available. The terms used to describe similar types of constellations vary widely, though all the terms shown in the figure are in common use.

FIGURE 6-3

| Management Tool |

The constellation spectrum

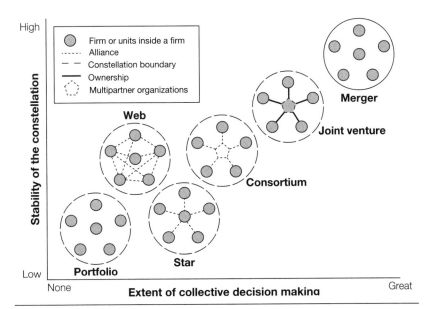

Legend:
- Firm or units inside a firm
- Alliance
- Constellation boundary
- Ownership
- Multipartner organizations

Vertical axis: Stability of the constellation (Low to High)
Horizontal axis: Extent of collective decision making (None to Great)

Labels: Web, Merger, Joint venture, Consortium, Portfolio, Star

As you can see, the constellation forms differ mostly by their internal structure—by which firms are allied to which, and by the nature of those internal linkages. The groupings in the lower left of figure 6-3 are the loosest in terms of the structure of joint decision making, akin to the trade relationships we saw in the relationship spectrum in chapter 2. The groupings on the top right are tight structures with unified decision making, like the merger relationships we saw before.

We have much less experience with constellations than with individual combinations, so it is natural to be confused by the terms people use. We'll explain each of the terms in the figure by way of examples. By understanding the logic of each term better, you can modify the terms to apply the thinking to any industry or company.

Good examples of classic *portfolios* of alliances are those of pharmaceutical firms. These constellations typically involve one or more large firms working with many small biotech start-ups. Management decisions in one alliance usually do not depend much on decisions in other alliances. In fact, a firm with two alliances in the same or in related therapeutic fields may well keep the research progress of one alliance secret from that of the other. In that sense, the members of the portfolio constitute a loose constellation, even when they are allies of one central firm. The members of the constellation help each other compete, but their strategic decisions are only minimally integrated. At the most, these decisions may be subject to common resource constraints, such as if a central firm has to allocate limited funding to several allies.

An important exception to this loose view of a pharmaceutical company portfolio occurs when one central firm maintains several alliances to develop a drug that requires complementary components, such as a compound with a unique delivery mechanism or with a special diagnostic agent. In such situations, the product development decisions in one alliance may well be dependent on decisions in another alliance. The central firm tied to both external firms then may lead the coordination among the separate deals.

Such coordination among alliances is the hallmark of the *star* and *web* constellations in the figure and the other constellations to the right of these two. These two forms are pure cases, so to speak, of a range of ways in which firms inside a constellation can be connected through bilateral partnerships. The alliances may all connect with one central party (the star structure), or there can be separate alliances among more—or all—players in the constellation (the web structure). Of course, hybrid forms exist, too, in which there is a central firm, but also some direct links among the firms on the periphery. (The figure does not show such a hybrid.)

Supply chains often take the form of a star or web constellation. At a minimum, the first-tier suppliers in a chain are connected through alliances with a central firm. For example, Boeing is the central firm in a star network that includes the makers of various airplane subsystems and major components. Some of these suppliers are also connected to each other, and many are at the center of their own star networks consisting of second-tier suppliers, which may not be connected directly to Boeing.

Airbus competes directly with Boeing, but has had to shape the design of its constellation differently. In fact, it illustrates two forms that are further along the spectrum from Boeing's star network. The European aircraft maker evolved from a *consortium* structure at its birth to the multipartner *joint venture* that it is today. The original consortium, known as Airbus Industrie, consisted of the national aerospace companies of Germany, France, the United Kingdom, Spain, and the Netherlands. Each consortium member made certain aircraft components or subsystems, and a central entity coordinated the design, final assembly, and sales of Airbus aircraft. Because this central organization was not a firm, the consortium differed from the classic web structure, as shown in the figure. And in Airbus's case, all the alliance arrangements were contractual, so in financial terms the central unit itself was more of a pass-through entity. It did not earn profits or accumulate equity, and each supplier received its share of profits through transfer pricing. As a result, the power of the central unit was limited, as was its role in unifying decisions and interests among the constellation partners.

Other consortium-like structures are also possible. In the computer industry, standards-setting consortia help members coordinate design decisions, but the consortia do not actually make or sell products. Research consortia among companies and universities help members share information and coordinate R&D. In both situations, the intellectual property that results from consortium activities may be shared by members, or there may be other rules for how the results of the coordination are used. As these examples suggest, consortia can be loose organizations; there is often more joint decision making in a star network with a strong central firm than there is in a multiparty consortium.

For Airbus, the coordination mechanism indeed proved too loose in the face of competition from the star networks of Boeing and of McDonnell Douglas. A few years after the two American firms merged, the Europeans consolidated their Airbus operations into a multipartner joint venture, the European Aeronautic Defence and Space Company. The joint venture at the core of the constellation then became responsible for developing, making, and selling Airbus aircraft. Through a complex shareholding structure, the French state and French and Spanish conglomerates owned a share of the joint venture's equity, as did Daimler; the rest was publicly traded. (Since then, Daimler divested its shares.)

Airbus has not quite evolved to the full merger model shown at the top right of figure 6-3, but it may yet get there. Conceptually, a full *merger* is the natural extension of the progression of structural forms in the figure. But a merger is not necessarily an ideal form in all situations or the best way to manage a constellation. Some constellations do well by staying looser, or there are barriers to their ultimate integration into a single firm.

A complete merger of multiple businesses can also result from sequential acquisitions. This growth strategy is well known— examples range from General Electric to IBM and Cisco. Depending on the roles of these acquisitions, the acquired units may be integrated differently inside their new corporate home. Sometimes, the approach taken mimics the constellation idea discussed here, except that the collection is managed under one ownership roof. IBM has done this over the years in several businesses. It built its global services business on a core of acquisitions from PricewaterhouseCoopers and MindSpring, its packaged software business on the acquisition of Lotus Development Corporation, and its data analytics and mobile businesses on a string of acquisitions of smaller technology companies.

Moving Along the Spectrum

This taxonomy of constellations distills how collections of firms really work. Recall the complexity of the three dominant airline constellations discussed earlier—Star Alliance, oneworld, and SkyTeam—all are consortia in the terminology used here, with a central organization coordinating member activities through contractual ties. In addition, the airlines in each constellation also have bilateral alliances with each other, for code sharing and such. Within the airline networks, some pairs of national airlines have merged, such as United and Continental (in Star Alliance), Delta and Northwest (in SkyTeam), and American Airlines and US Air (in oneworld). Even across national borders, KLM and Air France formed a virtual merger that retains some elements of local control. And some cross-Atlantic alliances have received antitrust immunity from the United States and European authorities, enabling them to create joint ventures on specific routes.

As a result, the airline constellations, like all complex business groupings, cannot be defined neatly as one structural type of constellation or another. They are all constellations in our definition, because the member firms are tied to each other by alliances and compete to some extent as a group. Consequently, they have created governance systems that enable them to make some decisions jointly or at least in coordinated fashion. For example, the central organizations help members schedule connecting flights, share mileage programs, and manage common assets such as the constellation's global brands. But the bulk of the strategic decisions of each member firm are still under the individual firm's sole control or are coordinated with certain other members through bilateral mergers or joint ventures. And the mergers inside the constellations act to consolidate decision making in large swaths of the network. The governance system of the constellation is the sum total of all these decision mechanisms.

The airline groupings have evolved toward the merger end of the spectrum, but other groupings have grown looser, not tighter, over time. In pharmaceuticals, for example, research, clinical trials, and even sales are increasingly outsourced or done with partners instead of in-house by vertically integrated companies. Every move to outsource an operation is, in principle, a move toward a looser constellation structure. This trend overtook the computer industry before it did the pharmaceutical industry, as large companies like IBM and HP started to do fewer and fewer activities in-house and outsourced manufacturing, management operations, and services. Both companies also built consulting arms that sold solutions incorporating hardware from multiple companies, in effect adopting a looser constellation structure for this business than in their traditional hardware businesses. More broadly, the recent trend toward open innovation foresees research conducted in loose constellations, rather than inside large firms under tighter control.

Movements along the constellation spectrum are thus common, as existing groups reorganize to gain competitive advantage. In this sense, a move to tighten or loosen constellation governance differs little from a firm's move to centralize or decentralize its internal operations. Both types of moves are usually efforts to recombine capabilities and resources better—internal capabilities in the case of firms and external capabilities in the case of constellations.

Competing with New Group Structures

Aside from organizational changes in existing constellations, you can also expect new groups to adopt governance structures that differ from those of existing groups if the new structure promises competitive advantages. In fact, challengers in a market very often adopt looser constellation structures and often form larger constellations than dominant players do. This tendency expresses itself in many ways. Leading firms generally have smaller appetites for alliances than do second-tier firms, which more often will seek strength in numbers in challenging the leaders. Similarly, second movers tend to use more open technology strategies than first movers, perhaps licensing their technology more freely to catch up in market share. Even in the absence of established leaders, entrepreneurial firms often seek multiple partners to create wholly new products or services or to stretch their limited internal capabilities.

A constellation with multiple members and relatively loose structure, therefore, often lies at the heart of new competitors' organizational strategies. The battle between Google and Apple over smartphones and tablet computers is a prime example. To make and distribute iPhones and iPads, Apple relies on a set of partners for components, telecommunication services, and complementary software, as noted earlier. But Apple itself makes and sells all the hardware units, and no other company is licensed to produce hardware based on the iOS operating system. With the launch of the first iPhone, Apple was the first mover in this market. This gave Apple a head start on the number of apps that run on its systems and on innovative features.

Google was the second mover. From the start, it adopted an open-systems strategy, licensing its operating system widely and free of charge to any hardware vendor willing to make products to run on the system. The Android constellation clearly has Google at the center of a star-like network, but also includes a consortium-like organization in Android's Open Handset Alliance. Within five years from its launch, this multipartner alliance organization included fourteen telecommunication providers, twenty-three handset manufacturers, twenty-one semiconductor makers, seventeen software companies, and twelve system integrators and consulting companies that helped with commercial applications. Granted, some of these partners had more influence than others: Samsung dominated handset sales, ARM and Qualcomm dominated the microprocessors used in Android handsets. Motorola was an interesting partner in the Android system—Google acquired the company only to sell Motorola's handset business to Lenovo less than two years later. Overall, Google's constellation was much larger than Apple's and in many ways looser in its organization and governance.

As a result of this matchup of Apple's tight constellation with Google's larger and looser groupings, Android rapidly gained market share and overtook Apple's iOS products in terms of units sold. But Android makers, and Google itself, have had a harder time making profits in this business than Apple, partly because the large constellation entails substantial competition between vendors providing similar products or services. This outcome is not uncommon and has often served to restrain first movers from expanding their constellation in response to challengers, for fear of eroding their profitability. On the other hand, the larger market share of the second mover may well eventually translate to higher profits while the first mover's business stagnates. A second-mover constellation challenged Apple's personal-computer business successfully two decades earlier—the IBM PC constellation of IBM, Microsoft, and Intel. Similarly, Sony's Betamax video system was challenged successfully by JVC's VHS constellation, which included Panasonic as a key player. Clearly, the shape of a constellation affects strategic outcomes: it can drive market entry and growth, it helps determine profitability, and it may shape the ultimate future of a business.

Designing and Managing a Constellation

As noted, constellation strategy is a relatively new field. The experience of some pioneers suggests what works and what doesn't, and research suggests some guidelines to success. The most robust recommendations are listed in table 6-1. The common theme here, as in two-party alliances, is that the setup of the constellation must enable later collaboration—the right members need to be included and the collective needs a way to make joint decisions. In addition,

TABLE 6-1

Designing and managing constellations

Constellation strategy

- **Global vision, local gains.** A constellation must create joint value and share this value with each member. In practice, each member must see gains in the global vision that brings the members of the constellation together.
- **The right mix of ingredients.** A constellation is intended to tie together the value blocks needed for a complete system.

Constellation membership

- **Selective membership.** The more members in a constellation, the harder it is to keep them working together. What's more, stricter admission criteria tend to evoke stronger commitment from members. Several constellations have struggled with this size question, often growing wildly and then trimming back.
- **Membership norms.** If the constellation does indeed need to be large, then it pays to find ways to organize with common rules for similar members.
- **Limited internal rivalry.** The challenge of managing a constellation also increases with internal rivalry. Avoiding duplication among members is not always possible or desirable, but internal rivalry can be managed.

Constellation leadership

- **Leadership at the core.** Effective constellations usually cannot be run on a one-member, one-vote model. In practice, one or a few members will lead the constellation because of the members' size or position in the value stack.
- **Strategic sequence and timing of growth.** Constellations do not form in one fell swoop—they grow over time. Consequently, you should pay attention to the sequence of adding members. Some members will attract others. And sometimes, the rise of rival constellations will force the addition of certain members.

however, constellation leaders also face decisions on how to build the group step by step—one deal may need to come before another, or one member will attract another.

Value Sharing in Constellations

Much heat has been expended in debating who gains and who loses when firms join together to compete in groups. Do the larger firms win out? The ones closest to the customer? Those at the center of the movement? The firm that is most—or least—connected to others? The questions continue to fly. But as it turns out, these structural variables matter little. More important than where you sit and whom you know in the group is what you bring to the table.

So here, too, we need to extend our framework beyond two-party business combinations. Like value sharing in these simpler combinations, the sharing of value in constellations is also driven by a bargaining process and intimately tied with group governance and the strategies for creating joint value.

Group Advantage and Member Advantage

To see how value is shared in constellations, let's go back to the basic formula in the preceding chapter (figure 5-3). The profits of a given firm are a share of total profits of the combination. The same formula applies in larger networks with multiple parties, although the calculations get more complex.

The joint value created by a constellation stems from its *group-based advantages*. These advantages depend on the constellation's effectiveness in competing with rival constellations and firms. If we envision a pool of profits available in an industry segment, then rivalry among constellations determines the share that each group appropriates from that pool. This is no different from rivalry among firms in classic industry analysis, except that the competitors here can be firms or constellations of firms.

Just as a firm's competitive advantages are shaped by the strategy and resources of the firm, so it goes with group-based advantages. These are shaped by the resources assembled in the constellation, by how well the constellation is governed, and by the strategy of the group. Further, when the combination yields synergy, each member can be thought of as adding something to the group-based advantages.

Part of the value created by a constellation thus comes from the resources it assembles—the combined scale, market reach, and technical capabilities of the players. This creation of value is the first law of business combinations, on steroids. But assembling resources is not enough, as the second law says—effective governance is critical to generating joint value. Here the constellation needs a unifying vision and must manage internal competition. And group size itself becomes a factor—the larger the group, the harder it is to manage, all else equal. A constellation only gains advantage from member resources if it is able to combine, govern, and direct them effectively.

Group-based advantages are only one part of the equation; *member-based advantages* are the other part. According to the third law of combinations, each member must also earn its share of the joint value produced. We can expect that bargaining among the firms in each constellation will determine the share of total value that each member will earn. Competition among the other firms that complement your business within a constellation adds to your bargaining power. But your direct competition with another member generally erodes that power. As with every combination, therefore, the earnings of each member will depend on the value of the resources added by that firm.

Partner Positioning in Groups

Our framework can help clarify some terms that others have used to describe the role of different players in networks. In *The Keystone Advantage,* Marco Iansiti and Roy Levien distinguished between members who acted as keystones, landlords, and niche players. The keystones had what ecosystems author James Moore called a "choke hold" on their environment. The landlords extracted value through sheer dominance, and the niche players played a specialty role. We no doubt often see these behaviors in the market. In fact, the behaviors are a natural outcome of the fundamental forces we have been discussing. Furthermore, with our broader perspective, we can now see a fuller range of roles that members in a group might play.

The value earned by any given member of a constellation depends on two dimensions—value added and internal rivalry (figure 6-4).

FIGURE 6-4

Management Tool

Value sharing in constellations

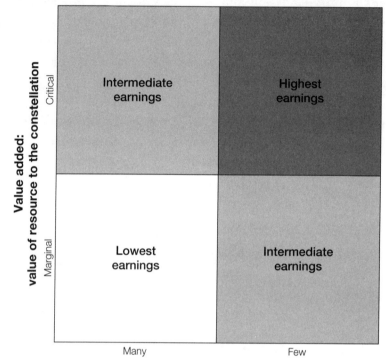

Internal rivalry: number of providers of the resource in the constellation

In terms of value added, some components of a stack are essential to operation; others are optional. In the case of the PC, the operating system and microprocessor were essential. This means that Intel and Microsoft played in the top half of the figure. There, they would have a chance at being a choke point, but that depends on the degree of internal rivalry among the providers of that piece of the stack.

In fact, as discussed, Intel was forced early on by IBM to license its microprocessor design to several manufacturers. So there was indeed internal rivalry among microprocessors, and the Intel processor design was shared widely at relatively low cost with little chance that one provider could exclude others. Today that is the case in the extreme with many technologies accepted by industry standards bodies. Apple and Samsung went to court precisely over this matter—whether a specific Samsung patent ought to be licensed to Apple at low cost, as an industry standard.

Over time, Intel was able to move its position and reduce rivalry for its microprocessor in the PC constellation, moving it from the top left to the top right quadrant. Following this move, its earnings from the PC business grew dramatically and were reflected in a rising market capitalization. Conversely, as IBM's earnings fell as its platform was copied by others, the company moved in the opposite direction from Intel, from the top right to the top left in the figure.

What of the players in the bottom half of the figure? The three founders of the PC constellations were all critical to that stack, as we know. But many applications are not so essential. Constellation members can hardly expect to earn value at the rate enjoyed by the members who add more external value to the group. In the PC world, there are important niche applications in many high-value fields, such as computer-aided design. The providers of these components can expect a decent return from participating in the constellation, as long as there are not many of them. If there are too many providers, then the applications erode to become mere commodities—nice to have, but hardly noteworthy.

Today, in the smartphone field, mapping programs and GPS tracking might be considered niche applications, though they are rapidly becoming more and more important externally and hence are moving upward in figure 6-4. Apple learned the hard way how quickly niche apps can rise in importance when its exclusion of Google Maps from the launch of the iPhone 5 led to consumer protests. The smartphone world also has many players offering near-commodity products—from special ringtones to hardware accessories. The external value of these offerings is often minimal, but what kills the business is the multiplicity of vendors. These low-value, easily replicated apps hence occupy the lower left quadrant of figure 6-4.

* * *

Constellations are emerging in all industries and becoming the norm in some. Competing in constellations is a tricky game. The logic of the game depends on the dynamics of the simpler business combinations discussed earlier in this book. But as the number of partners in a combination grows, the game does become more challenging. Joint value, again, is created from synergy, managed by joint governance, and distributed through internal bargaining. But each of these three steps is more complex than in the simple case.

In the last chapter, we will pull together the ideas in this book. And we'll offer some general guidance that will help you master your own remix strategy.

Chapter 7

Rethinking Strategy

THIS BOOK STARTED BY ARTICULATING A STRATEGIC challenge facing many businesses today—how to create value by combining resources inside and outside the firm. You now have a new perspective, a comprehensive framework, and tools and techniques that you can use to tackle this problem and solve it. But you also have a bigger challenge now—how to make remix strategy part of your everyday business thinking. The remixing of assets to create value cannot be an isolated concern, as it affects every aspect of a business.

Remix strategy affects decisions in five key areas: (1) strategy, (2) competitive advantage, (3) governance, (4) change and innovation, and (5) return on investment. This chapter will show you how the core principles of remix strategy can help you make better decisions in each of these five areas. Each core principle leads to some good management practices that you can adapt to your own situation.

Before we get to these guidelines, though, let's review the central idea of this book. If the central idea is rooted firmly in your mind, you can immediately see the implications and develop your own practices for a business remix. So, bear with me in first examining the intellectual foundation of my recommendations in this chapter.

The Big Idea

No business is ever built completely from scratch. Even so-called brand-new ideas are usually derived from old ideas. New companies often spin out from old companies. Incumbents, too, transform their businesses by mixing and matching internal and external resources.

This business remix is the essence of innovation and entrepreneurship, and it can also revitalize mature companies. By combining internal and external resources smartly, you can start new businesses or change the very core of an existing business. Many of your peers have come to realize that alliances and acquisitions are no longer just tactics to fill gaps in their product lines, or to grow their business on the margin. With a properly executed remix strategy, you can create new value, generate new competitive advantages, and change the way you face competitors.

Take Apple's history as an illustration. Steve Jobs famously created the revolutionary Macintosh computer in the 1980s in part from elements copied from researchers at Xerox (Bill Gates did that to Apple in creating Windows). Later, when Jobs returned to re-create Apple, he combined existing technologies and products into the even more revolutionary iPod, iPhone, and iPad. Virtually all the elements of these new products existed before, outside Apple. For example, touch-screen technology was invented in the 1960s, digital music players were everywhere, telecommunication services were well established, and digital content was already being shared on the web. Jobs mixed and matched these elements brilliantly, of course, infused the remix with Apple's unique design sensibility, and created a new business model that totally transformed Apple. Concretely, Apple used various business combinations to achieve this remix—acquiring software start-ups, allying with component providers such as Samsung, and selling jointly with telecom providers like AT&T and Verizon. Its widely successful iTunes service relies on alliances with content producers such as studios, record labels, and publishers. Most recently, Apple acquired Beats to get into music streaming and is working with IBM to bring apps into the corporate workplace.

If such new combinations of resources can create so much value, it pays to think hard about them. That is why we have developed in this book a roadmap to remix strategy and many practical tools. The three laws of business combinations are your roadmap. The first law is that there must be a prospect for creating joint value from bundling assets—the proverbial $1 + 1 = 3$. The second law is just as critical; without it, the prospect of joint value will not be realized. It requires that the combined assets be governed effectively: $1 + 1 = 1$, to continue with the memory aid. The third law is perhaps the trickiest; it says that the joint value has to be shared in a way that makes it worthwhile for each party to contribute. We visualized this law as $1 + 1 = 1.4 + 1.6$, or any other set of fractions that add up to the 3 in the first formula.

I put these laws in simple terms—and repeat them here—because they need to be clear in your mind as you go forward. Now, let's look at how this approach will help you make better decisions in five core business issues. Five principles follow from the big idea I just sketched. After each principle, you will find broad guidelines for putting these ideas to work in practice.

Strategy

The Principle: Combinations of
Resources Compete, Not Firms

To make good strategic decisions, start by defining carefully which unit competes. That unit sets goals, decides on policies, assembles resources, and ultimately enjoys success or suffers failure in the marketplace. In the traditional approach to strategy, you have two ways to define this unit—at the level of your business or at the level of your corporation as a whole. The scope and content of strategy will be different for business units and entire corporations.

In remix strategy, neither of these units is the primary focus. Instead, the fundamental unit of analysis is the *combination of resources that yield value*. That combination competes with other combinations. Some combinations will gain advantage over others because they encompass just the right resources; others will gain advantage because they manage their collective resources better than others do.

The organization that governs the asset combination may well be a firm. But there are many alternatives to this governance form—constellations of various shapes and sizes that are composed of firms and structured in many ways. The Android constellation, as we saw, competes against Apple's iPhone combination, even though the two groupings are organized in very different ways. ARM uses a constellation of licensees to compete against Intel, which competes much more on its own strength. In airlines, the Star Alliance constellation competes against other constellations, but each group has a slightly different organizational approach and all of them compete at times with single firms such as nonallied airlines. For a long time, Coke and Pepsi pursued different strategies in this regard too, with Coke relying more on independent bottlers and Pepsi owning more of its bottlers.

In every industry, we can find such variety in the organizational form of the competing combinations. This shift in perspective—from firms to asset combinations—is not trivial. It means that the firm and all of its attendant organizational choices are variables in the equation of competition, not fixed parameters. In the views of Edith Penrose and the school of thought she inspired, the firm is a combination of resources managed in a coordinated fashion. Such managed bundles of resources are the keys to success, but they may not always be constituted as a firm. They can come in other forms, too—the firm is a bundle of resources, but a bundle of resources is not always a firm.

The result of flipping these concepts means that the way the bundle is managed itself becomes a tool in competitive strategy. Should Apple be more or less open to partnerships in its quest to compete against Android? Should the airline constellations promote closer integration and joint services and brands, or looser arrangements? How many partners should ARM have? Should Coke invest more in its bottlers to compete against Pepsi? (It has done so.) Such questions are now strategic choices.

The Practice: Think Alliance Strategy, Not Strategic Alliance

If your success will ultimately depend on your combination, then you must start with a comprehensive strategy for bundling external and internal resources. The logic behind every deal needs to be developed rigorously and in detail—which resources are being combined, with what intended effect, at what risk, and so forth. The deal needs to be a function of the strategy for each party, not the other way around. Although this step is self-evident, it is often glossed over in the rush-and-tumble process of doing a deal. Typically, even high-level participants in a combination will have thought more about the structure of the deal than the rationale that's driving it.

Take one large agribusiness company, whose executives were delighted with the research results of its alliance with a small biotech start-up. Their original aim was to acquire new technologies from this start-up. The relationships between the scientific teams were great, the teams were discovering and sharing new information, and the experimental results were positive. This was more than the executives had hoped for when they launched the alliance. There was only one small problem: no one in the company was prepared to use the new technology discovered by the alliance, and some people even saw the technology as a threat to their existing business. Why? The executives had structured a good deal, but had lost sight of the broader strategy around the deal.

The alliance between Amazon.com and Toys "R" Us offers another example. As noted earlier, Amazon.com was keen to enter the toy-selling business. Its deal with Toys "R" Us was an ideal entry route. And for Toys "R" Us, this was a way to join the web-selling craze in a big way. But one court case later, the alliance lay in tatters. Amazon.com did emerge with a thriving toy-selling business, but Toys "R" Us had earlier given up its own e-retailing site and so had no fallback strategy. Again, getting to the deal appeared to have obscured strategies beyond the deal, at least for Toys "R" Us.

These examples show that a deal is never an end in itself. Sometimes, it doesn't seem so, because making a combination work requires focus, dedication, and advocacy. From the "deal fever" of negotiators to the special trust that may develop among relationship managers, so much rides on the workings of the deal itself. Increasingly, careers ride on that too, as managers are assigned special roles in nurturing the health of ongoing combinations. Yet, all this effort ought to be expendable if a business strategy is better served by dissolving a combination. One good partnership

Reengineering Your DNA

Combinations ought to be an essential part of your business strategy, not an afterthought or a special project. In essence, business strategy can be defined as the set of goals and functional policies that collectively shape the way a business uses internal and external resources to position itself in its environment and achieve superior performance.

The phrase "internal and external" in this definition recognizes that strategy increasingly is not just about using what you own. Unfortunately, much of the common thinking in the field downplays the idea of leveraging external resources. Traditionally, strategic thinking has focused much more on internal resources, to the point of exhorting companies to stay true to their "DNA" or their "core" or, more prosaically, their "knitting." This exhortation is bolstered by defining a company's DNA as hard-to-change cultural norms—this makes it seem foolhardy to try to change that core.

This internal focus is often a mistake. Sometimes, a firm does spread itself too thin and reaches far beyond its capabilities. But sticking to your knitting is a bad idea when everyone else is building automatic looms; then it is time to change your core. The dodo bird, after all, stayed true to its DNA until its extinction.

DNA does offer another useful analogy that is not so resistant to change—genetic reengineering. In a natural environment, of course, DNA is constantly being modified through sexual reproduction and chance mutations. But today, biotech firms are also creating new drugs by using recombinant techniques in which researchers take pieces of DNA from one organism and insert dissolved its relationship with hugs and tears and bottles of champagne, but not all combinations are so lucky.

How do you avoid letting the deal take over the strategy? Start by articulating the ultimate goal. Then define all the policies and actions that may be needed to reach it. Combinations might be among these actions, but they are likely to go hand in hand with changes in the broader organization. For example, other units that

them into another. Similarly, genetically modified seeds are controversial in the food chain, but taking specific segments of DNA from one seed and inserting them in another seed's DNA can create new plants that withstand disease and drought better, or that give higher yields. The idea of recombinant DNA is a metaphor for how the core of a business can be reengineered.

Such reengineering is now critical. In response to shifting competitive conditions, most firms now have to reach outside their boundaries to tap into external resources. Classic recent examples include pharmaceutical giants reaching outside for biotech expertise, or computer hardware companies bringing in software capabilities. No wonder that the rate of alliance formation has been so high in these two specific industries.

Reaching outside for new resources is also critical in companies seeking to raise their competitive position in a business they know well and that is not changing particularly fast. Better management of supply chains, horizontal constellations, and ecosystems of complementary players may allow new or second-tier firms to challenge industry leaders or help the leaders become even more successful. In this sense, they are changing their competitive DNA. Cultural norms may well be hard to shift on their own, but you can remix the resources you use to compete, and in the process, change even those cultural norms. This innovation process starts with understanding the value that is available from combinations, and then creating the conditions for success.

are not directly involved in the combination may need to wind down competing projects, gear up to offer help, or open up to external ideas. And managers up and down the line, in and out of the combination, may need to be kept informed about the rationale for, and the progress of, the deal.

Ultimately, your success with a remix strategy requires that you design deal elements with your goal in mind before signing. You need to prepare your organization to support and leverage any combinations you're creating. You must understand your partners' goals, and vice versa. Moreover, you need to manage performance with those goals in mind, rather than just tracking the completion of operational tasks. Finally, you'll want to manage the evolution of the combination (and the relationships) with the ultimate value to the company in mind (see the sidebar "Reengineering Your DNA").

Competitive Advantage

The Principle: The Right Combination Yields Advantage

You have a strategy so that you can gain a competitive advantage that can yield superior performance. There can be many sources of competitive advantage, such as low-cost operations or a powerful brand image. How do you create such an advantage? Traditional strategic thinking prescribes that you own resources and engage in activities that may yield the advantage you seek.

Remix strategy adds a twist to this prescription. It says that you can derive advantage from the way you combine resources, including resources that you don't own. We have seen how to do this in earlier chapters. But you may still feel that a reliance on external resources presents a new problem. If external resources are so important in your strategy, might your dependence on them not neutralize your potential advantage over another firm? After all, both you and your competitors may have access to the same external resources. The answer is no, you can still create a unique advantage—but you must create it through the smart use of your combinations. (As an analogy, that's how a painter using generic materials can create a unique picture.)

We have argued here that the way two resources are matched shapes the joint value that they can generate. In addition, the way the combination is governed determines whether the potential joint value is reached or falls short of the promised synergy. These two factors leave much room for firms to differ in terms of the advantages that they might derive from a combination, even if they have the same external resources available to them.

The match as the source of advantage. Because every firm has a different set of internal resources, the match that each can make with a given external resource will differ too. This idea is well known in acquisitions; one acquirer might be able to make more out of a given target than another because of how that target will fit into its business. Such a purely *combinatorial* advantage depends less on how the combination is governed than on what is combined with what. Chapter 3 explained how to identify these kinds of match-made advantages.

Relationship management as the source of advantage. Firms accessing external resources may also differentiate themselves from rivals with their *relationship* advantage—the ability to govern and integrate an external resource to yield maximum value. In acquisitions, some firms have special skills in post-integration management; in alliances, some firms are partners of choice because of their relationship-management capabilities. Chapter 4 explained how effective governance can give you an advantage.

This distinction focuses a spotlight on a current puzzle in the field of strategy. When does a given resource—an asset or a capability—yield competitive advantage to a firm? In short, the traditional argument is that certain scarce and valuable resources can set the firm apart from others. Examples are specific brand names or unique assets or capabilities in certain fields. But sometimes even these core resources can be copied or developed by others over time. Or, the providers of these key resources might extract all the value they generate for the firm, leaving little for the bottom line.

A more recent school of thought argues that the particular combination of resources within a firm sets it apart from the others, not the characteristics of the resources themselves. For example, imagine two firms that can hire the same kinds of engineers and salespeople, have access to the same capital and technology markets, and sell to similar sets of buyers. Even then, the firms may well differ in how they mix and match these inputs and in the depth of the specific capabilities they choose to build from their common set of assets. As a result, the same resource may yield a certain competitive advantage to one firm and not to another.

The Practice: Look Beyond Chemistry, Trust, and Other Marriage Analogies

If the first important element of remix strategy is setting the goal, the second one is selecting the right external resources. These resources will come from an acquisition target, a potential partner, a possible supplier or buyer, or a collection of complementary firms, depending on the form of the combination. One broad criterion should shape your choice of partners—the likelihood that a combination with this firm or group of firms will in fact offer the resources that are needed to generate joint value. Not only does the external party need to have the resources, but the combination needs to provide access to these resources. A partner may have exactly what you need, but not be willing to deal. Conversely, eager partners may have weak resources.

It requires sensitive, personal effort on your part to select a business partner and maintain the relationship. But you also face difficult analytical, legal, and management work. You need to turn every stone and ask tough questions. This critical approach may seem like bad relationship manners in a strictly personal sphere. It's not in business. It's good practice.

Chapter 4 gave a framework for selecting partners and structuring the relationship. Here are additional ways to make sure that you make the right match and sign a productive contract:

- **Evaluate carefully the partner's true resources and capabilities.** Your evaluation may include external analysis by independent parties. Legal clauses seldom protect against a partner simply not having what you thought they did.

- **Explore options with alternative partners.** Engaging in multiple negotiations may be touchy or ruled out by an agreement. But even then, you can evaluate those options in your internal analysis. The lack of a serious evaluation of alternatives is a sure sign of a poor partner search.

- **Protect yourself through the legal terms of the deal by building in concrete mechanisms for joint governance.** A personal touch, good intentions, and enthusiastic teams are never enough. These need to be supported by a clear division of rights and duties, effective communication channels, and good escalation procedures, just in case.

- **Trust your partners, but only after you structure the relationship and set up good management practices.** By itself, trust is not reliable. Your trusted personal counterpart may leave, or circumstances may change to make commitments costly. But you can manage the relationship to ensure good communication and encourage mutual forbearance and reciprocity.

- **After the deal is signed, expect your partners to pursue their interests and use their leverage.** Their self-interest may drive them to do something surprising, no matter what is said in the courtship. You may be pleasantly surprised later by your partners' forbearance in your favor, but you shouldn't be surprised if they pursue their own strategic interests.

Ultimately, serious business partners will respect your serious due diligence work. And you should expect it of them.

This kind of analysis is an antidote to blind-love syndrome (see the sidebar "Good Chemistry Can Lead to Bad Decisions"). But due diligence is hard even in the absence of blinders. You never have an open window into a counterpart's strategy, for the same reason that you don't share all of your strategy with them. Still, that just means that every morsel of information about your counterpart's strategy becomes more important.

As an astute practitioner of remix strategy, you can milk these morsels of information and build scenarios to understand a counterpart's strategy. Ask yourself questions that might seem disloyal

Good Chemistry Can Lead to Bad Decisions

Chemistry can be dangerous. Not the kind that I did as a teen with my chemistry set, but the kind that makes grown-up CEOs fall in love. Whenever I hear that two CEOs are striking a deal in part because they get along well personally, I cringe.

One large research organization experienced the danger of CEO chemistry firsthand. I heard the story after the fact, when a key alliance had failed. The opening of the story was already ominous: the companies began talking and found common ground because a scientist from a medical device firm had joined the research organization. True, that is how the idea for a deal may first arise. But in this case, it was the main reason for the in-depth conversations that followed, with little if any analysis of alternative partners.

In these discussions, the CEOs indeed hit it off swimmingly. There were full-court-press visits to each other's headquarters, and deal details were worked out rapidly. The research organization promised to invest in special research over several years to develop the technology needed to combine with that of the medical device firm, which was to employ this technology in its own product line. And that product line was a top priority of the CEO of the device firm.

Work started, investments were made . . . and then the medical device firm's CEO was replaced. Why the executive left is if raised at the actual negotiating table. How have the partners behaved previously with partners similar to you? What other options do they have or can they develop? What factions inside their organization may militate for or against your relationship? Why, really, do they want a deal with your firm? Why not deal with your competitors instead? And so on.

Questions such as these are not disloyal at all. They ensure that you will have a good understanding of your partner, which in turn enables you to negotiate and manage a more productive combination.

immaterial and unrelated to the project. But the new CEO had different ideas, and the former top-priority product line was scrapped. What's worse, because the organizations had relied so much on the personal commitments of their leaders, the contract did not call for reimbursement or other arrangements should the product be dropped. The possibility of a divorce like this had just not occurred to anyone—the couple had been so much in love.

I've seen many variations on this story. Sometimes it is not the early love that is the problem, but the very reliance on love itself. One US industrial company worked well with its Japanese partner because of a key alliance leader who spanned the bridge. As an American living in Japan, he opened doors back home for the Japanese firm, smoothed conflicts, and put out brush fires on both sides. His success led him to a promotion up the ladder in the US firm, leaving the partnership without a full-time godfather. Again, the partners did not have a broad contractual or organizational process to manage their relationship, as it had depended mostly on the excellent personal touch of one man. After a few years, as new competitive stresses arose on both sides of the Pacific, the partners found themselves in conflict in China's new market, and the alliance eventually disbanded.

Governance

The Principle: Govern What Matters,
Even If You Don't Own It

You know you have to pay attention to governance—regulatory agencies and your shareholders will remind you of that if you mess it up. Governance, in the usual business parlance, refers broadly to the way decisions are made about the use of the corporation's assets. But I don't restrict the term to how a board of directors makes decisions or, more importantly, I don't confine it to the scope of the corporation. In this book, the term refers to how you best manage a combination of assets to create value. This key question in remix strategy differs from the usual concern with governance, because the combination of assets often includes resources that don't fall in the usual scope of the board of directors.

Remix strategy does sometimes call for full ownership of resources. Traditional acquisitions remain common and effective ways to generate value from new combinations. But sometimes an acquisition is not the best way to recombine resources, as we have seen. Often, it's not even a practical, feasible, or legal option. What then? Well, then the combination has to take the form of something short of acquisition, even if that form may be challenging to manage. (Of course, managing acquisitions effectively is challenging too.) Alliances, constellations, and other types of external relationships are additional options for how firms can recombine resources.

You can expand the strategic options available to your firm by keeping an open mind about precisely how resources should be recombined. As noted earlier, too many firms restrict themselves to certain types of external relationships or shun them altogether out of a fear of losing control. Apple did that with the Macintosh computer, ruling out clones or licensees, while the IBM PC took over the world with a constellation of vendors. The lessons from this experience may have driven Steve Jobs to seek partners in the rollout of iTunes and Apple's mobile devices. Google has been taking this broad-collaboration strategy further still, as we have seen.

Because the assets critical to your success often lie outside your firm's boundaries, corporate governance cannot stop at those boundaries. A narrow legal definition of governance might be restricted to assets owned and controlled by the corporation. But, as we have seen, the bundle of assets that is relevant for success in the market often includes assets in partnerships outside your firm. Your *economic* definition of governance, therefore, must pay attention to these external assets too. Eli Lilly's board knew this when it encouraged the firm's executives to invest in alliance man-agement. Effective governance today includes the governance of a company's partnerships, supply chains, and joint ventures.

Governance of combinations is an organizational strategy—akin to the way firms need to organize internally to implement strategic goals. A slew of organizational choices inside firms affects the success of various strategies. For example, depending on your firm's strategy and situation, you may prefer to manage internal resources in a centralized or decentralized way. You may encourage close cooperation between certain units, each of which represents a different combination of resources. Or you may allow some units to compete or at least to offer parallel services to different segments of the market.

We may be tempted to say that the governance of constellations is simply an extension of organizational strategy, but there's nothing simple about it. Constellation design and management are particularly complex because of the multiple and separate interests usually involved. Furthermore, there are usually better or more familiar mechanisms for managing resources inside firms than across firms. Internal management relies on bureaucratic power, incentives and controls, routines and processes, among other factors. Cross-firm management uses all these tools, but in an environment that is a mixture of contracts and ownership rights.

Here again, a narrow legal approach to governance is not suffi-cient (see the sidebar "The Contract is Too Important to Be Left to the Lawyers").

The Practice: Don't Compartmentalize the Three Laws

Effective governance also requires broadening the perspectives of deal makers and managers. They focus all too often on the acquisi-tion or the merger or the alliance, rather than the act of combining

The Contract Is Too Important to Be Left to the Lawyers

When you are traveling in an unfamiliar area, a printed or elec-tronic map is invaluable. But its value is limited in two ways. First, roads or landmarks may be shown in the wrong place or shown even when they no longer exist. Second, the map may have gaps—pathways, obstacles, and features that are not mapped.

The same is true of the contracts that govern combinations. Without a doubt, you need competent lawyers writing your con-tracts. Nevertheless, most successful, complex business relation-ships are governed by contracts that are incomplete, as discussed in chapter 4.

Lawyers generally hate to hear the term *incomplete contract,* especially in mixed company—in front of their business colleagues. That their contracts can never cover all contingencies is a dirty little secret the lawyers tend to keep among themselves. More-over, the term *incomplete* sounds as if the lawyers didn't cross their t's and dot their i's. They prefer other terms, like *open-ended* and *evolving* contracts, though those too may suggest a weakness in the legal foundation—a weakness that may not exist. In reality, a contract is strong precisely when it has a way to bend in the face of change.

resources that lies behind each of these combinations. This narrower view often leads managers to jump to well-worn deal types, rather than thinking first about the actions and behavior they want to promote. And doing that makes these leaders even more vulnerable to losing sight of the ultimate goal.

You are better off following Dwight Eisenhower's dictum that "plans are useless, but planning is invaluable." In military strategy, plans are always upended in battle. But the dictum also means that the act of planning matters more than a particular

In business relationships, the contract obviously represents a sliver of the rules and patterns of behavior expected of the partners. There are gaps from the start. But the situation is worse than that—the territory keeps changing, with new features arising unexpectedly. How can a contract foresee a particular new technology emerging or one of the partners changing its strategy?

The only way for you to travel in such varying territory is to be alert at the wheel. In business terms, you need to manage the relationship as a whole—in particular, the parts that are the gaps in the formal contractual map. In the well-mapped territory, you can drive on autopilot; in the other parts, you need to sense the environment in real time, react on the spot, and be ready to create new plans to reach your goals. Managing a complex business relationship is therefore never just a matter of executing or monitoring a legal contract.

So as a business leader, you must first shape the kind of relationship you want—your vision of the territory you wish to travel through—and then lawyers can create a contract that helps in managing the legal aspects of this relationship. Even then, much will need to be left to agreements and planning that never make it into the written contract.

solution—evaluating goals, alternatives, sequences, processes, and the like, prepares you to be a good problem solver in the moment.

For business combinations, hard thinking about the logic of combining resources will matter more than the ultimate form of a particular deal. This scrutiny is all the more important because complex deals are rarely completed as planned. They are often renegotiated and change in response to circumstances—just like Eisenhower's "plans."

Unfortunately, many corporations have turned this logic upside down. They are organized to manage specific types of deals, not to manage the process of finding, evaluating, and implementing different combinations. Acquisitions may be done by a mergers-and-acquisitions (M&A) unit and advised by specialized investment banking firms. Some alliances are formed by a business-development unit; others are considered channel deals handled by sales units. Supply alliances are probably handled by the procurement office. Legal staff is often similarly specialized by deal type.

In such an organization, deals are tracked early on as belonging to one type (and unit) or another. A new opportunity to combine resources with an external party may then be branded prematurely as an acquisition project; the plan then becomes to acquire, not to carry out a combination through the best means possible. Of course, the M&A team then takes over, with investment bankers making sure the team stays on target. (Investment bankers are usually paid less for deals short of acquisitions.)

With such an approach, deal types are organized in silos, making it hard to determine the best structure for a combination. Specialized units for each kind of deal tend to split the company's efforts and wisdom rather than integrate them. Acquisitions, alliances, and simpler transactions each have their place. But you can best find that place by exploring the trade-offs between them without prejudice. Even during your negotiations with a partner, the shape of the deal may change from one kind to another. Like Eisenhower, you are best served by focusing on the reasoning of what you want to achieve in a combination rather than on one particular way to do so.

Deliberate coordination is essential to addressing all the aspects of the three laws, and there are any number of effective ways to implement this coordination. Some companies have all their deals go through a common screening; others assign all deal-making to one unit, regardless of the type of deal. In other companies, multiple units are coordinated through councils and processes. In any case, be wary of keeping deal design in too-narrow a circle of decision makers.

To organize your own agenda, consider table 7-1. Each of the three laws of business combinations draws on a different discipline and involves decisions that may be the responsibility of different management units. To manage remix strategy successfully, your organization must find ways to integrate these different ways of thinking. You can adapt the table to help your organization's process for doing so.

TABLE 7-1

Management Tool

Thinking—together—about remix strategy

Law of business combinations	Which unit is typically responsible?	Which strategies or activities are related?	Which decision criteria can be used?	Which disciplines and functions help?
Identify potential joint value	Business unit, business development, and corporate strategy	Marketing and operations strategies	Fit with goals, position, and resources	Economics of the business, forecasting
Govern the collaboration	Legal staff and the units that will own the combination	Incentives and governance policies	Decision making practices, risk management	Organizational behavior, legal framework, project management
Share the value created	Finance staff and business units	Valuation goals and methods	Hurdle rates, margin goals, option values	Negotiation and valuation techniques

Change and Innovation

The Principle: Remix Strategy Helps You Move Fast

You deal daily with change in your business environment—rapid, uncertain, and disruptive change. How you manage this change has become critical to success. Some strategists conclude that competitive advantage has become inherently unstable and that only a strategy that keeps moving fast can give you an edge over your rivals. As a result, you need to pursue opportunities and react to competitors with flexibility and agility. Remix strategy is a perfect tool to help you manage change.

Remix strategy is also ideally suited to generate innovation, as envisioned by Joseph Schumpeter a century ago. Product innovation often relies on external resources, as discussed above for the case of Apple. In addition, firms use remix strategy to transform their business models; IBM entered software and services through alliances and acquisitions. Remix also creates its own new form of competition, as we have seen with the groupings in airlines. Finally, whole new industries can come into being through combinations, as is happening today with the new wave of smart, connected devices creating the internet of things.

At the root, making business combinations is a speedy way to reposition your company. Some types of business combinations will give you more flexibility than others will, though. Acquisitions and mergers usually represent firmer commitments to a direction than do alliances and constellations, which can be tweaked more readily over time. Exiting an alliance is usually less costly than reversing a merger.

Switching partners, adding partners, and just growing a constellation can be important strategic moves in a world in which combinations of resources compete against each other. In fact, the easy-in, easy-out nature of alliance constellations often leads to competition for partners, much as rivals sometimes compete in acquisition bidding wars.

Consider the periodic switches of allegiance in the airline constellations. Continental switched from its alliance with Delta's SkyTeam group to join United's Star Alliance group before actually merging with United a year later, and US Airways exited Star Alliance before merging with American Airlines. Sometimes, such switches are contentious and fail to happen. Delta fought hard, but without success, to lure Japan Airlines (JAL) away from the oneworld constellation of American Airlines.

Switches like these can take place more readily in the airline industry than in industries where partner products and technologies are tied to each other over time. For the airlines, there are exit fees for dropping out of a constellation, but beyond that, the switch is mostly a matter of changing branding, mileage programs, scheduling, and rearranging gates. In a constellation with strong technical ties, such as Wintel (Intel and Microsoft in the PC world), threats from one side or another to strike out with new partners can be as deeply threatening as in the airline industry, but more difficult to carry out.

Rearranging a constellation internally can also have a significant impact. Google, as noted, had grown its Android constellation rapidly to enter the smartphone market in competition with Apple. But as a result, the Android world threatened to become fragmented and somewhat overpopulated. Google's move to acquire Motorola Mobility was in part an effort to bolster one of its handset makers and enable closer integration between software and hardware. At the same time, however, this move alienated some of Google's handset allies, who wondered if Google would begin to play favorites among them. In response to this reaction (and because of Google's relative inexperience in making hardware products), Google soon sold Motorola's handset assets to Lenovo. This further reorganization of the constellation may also have been prompted by Samsung's growing power as a handset producer. Internally, therefore, a constellation such as Android can evolve rapidly, partly because individual companies follow their own strategies to gain power within the group.

As a corollary to these switches, new combinations can also block rivals. In principle, every new alliance creates a new, friendly relationship and may generate several new enemies—the firms that weren't selected or those that were closed out of future partnerships. For this reason, every new alliance can create *barriers to collaboration* for future suitors. Managers are not likely to admit to such motives; you won't see this tactic as a rationale in press releases. But these tactics often appear to be behind some deals. For example, Google invested $1 billion in AOL–Time Warner, probably to keep AOL out of Microsoft's orbit. A few years later, Mic-

Flexibility Makes Risk Your Friend

With change comes uncertainty and risk. One way to deal with the risk of new combinations is to think of them as real options. Like a *financial* option, a *real* option buys you a chance now, at low cost, to make a decision later on a larger investment. As the names imply, financial options give you a chance to buy or sell financial assets, and real options let you buy or sell real assets, such as operating a business or a manufacturing plant. Buying a real option, therefore, means investing a small amount in a deal that can pave the way for an expanded investment in more resources.

Many—though not all—business combinations can be seen as small steps on the way to a larger investment. Of course, big acquisitions don't come in bite-size chunks, so the real-option approach won't work there. But small acquisitions do, as do shared investments in large assets, alliances with limited equity outlays, minority investments in a business, and other partnerships. Some joint ventures, for example, are transitional steps toward a full acquisition or divestment. So alliances may be the first steps toward greater and deeper collaboration between firms. Or under different conditions, each of these options may be disbanded—many alliances and joint ventures end that way too.

The advantage of looking at your business combinations as real options is that it gives you a way to manage the risk ahead.

rosoft tied up with Yahoo! partly to share costs in search-engine technology, but no doubt also to keep Yahoo! out of Google's orbit. None of these tie-ups could be called watertight defenses against a determined foe, but the maneuvers are relatively low-cost ways to block a rival.

Participating in a constellation can quickly expand your range of competitive moves, not just the choices you have for organizing resources. This added flexibility of your strategy helps you manage uncertainty and risk in the environment (see the sidebar "Flexibility Makes Risk Your Friend").

The option gives you a way to respond to risk, but doesn't tie your hands. If things turn up, you expand the deal; if things turn down, you disband it. This ability to act in the future in response to new information is itself valuable.

With this type of approach, risk is managed and the flexibility of your combination becomes a benefit, not a burden. In this way, a combination may have an *option value* that goes beyond the expected returns. Instead of just judging combination proposals against a static hurdle rate, then, ask these questions:

- Which opportunities does one alliance or small acquisition create, even if we might decide later not to use them?

- Which market or technical information can we gather by making a small investment now, and how will this information will help us later in larger combinations?

- How can a combination serve as a pilot test for a larger strategy?

- Which combinations are to some extent reversible?

- How might an alliance or small combination prevent a rival from entering a new field, even when we are not yet certain of our strategy in this field?

The Practice: In a Combination Wave,
Follow the Logic, Not the Fashion

Because they are such flexible tools, alliances and mergers often spread like wildfire. Whenever key players in an industry begin to use business combinations for one reason or another, their rivals often are not far behind. This pattern happened in airlines, computers, pharmaceuticals, banking, media, communications, and other industries. Why? And should you follow such a fad when it hits your business?

You should follow the logic of the wave, not the management fashion. Consider the following good reasons before you decide to join a combination trend:

- **Responding to change in the business environment.** The simplest explanation of a combination wave is that firms are reacting to common changes in their business environment. For example, when the emergence of a new technology favors the formation of alliances, most firms in the industry will seek partners. Maybe your rivals know something— check it out.

- **Matching the capabilities of rivals.** Firms often follow each other's strategic moves. Doing so might lower a firm's chances of moving ahead or—more importantly—falling behind its rivals. Think about how the combinations of your rivals are changing your business, and consider if you need to follow suit.

- **Pursuing first-mover advantages.** Sometimes, being first is the key to success. When an industry has high economies of scale, high customer switching costs, or steep experience curves, competitors can be expected to try to establish a dominant market share early. You can use combinations to shorten the time needed to establish a lead position. Or, if you are a latecomer, you can more rapidly erode the position of the lead firm.

- **Striking preemptively.** There may be advantages to preemptive strikes in tying up, because of the limited opportunities for collaboration at any point in time. Tying up early gives you the best choice of partners and preempts your rivals from tying up with an attractive partner. The preemptive partnerships in effect become a barrier to collaboration for rivals.

Are there limits to how far you should go with these strategic reactions? Yes. Every combination wave has its limit. The simplest constraint on the wave is overcrowding of the field. The pool of eligible partners will diminish because of the boom in alliance formation itself. Saturation in the industry generates a kind of strategic gridlock that limits your combination options.

Other limits to growth of constellations stem not from the external environment, but from internal constraints. Managers often cite their own lack of "bandwidth" as a constraint on alliance formation or to merger integration. Negotiating each agreement requires effort, and major alliances require the continual, direct, and personal involvement of top management. These demands on management increase with the size of the group and the complexity of the deals.

In addition, cooperation becomes increasingly difficult as the number of members in a constellation rises. And conflicts of interest will add to the coordination costs of the group and limit the degree to which the group can be integrated to implement a common strategy. When such friction arises, constellation leaders often respond by restructuring the group. In fact, just like single alliances, constellations with multiple members are often reshaped in response to new challenges.

Return on Investment

The Principle: Value Is Earned at Two Levels— the Combination and Its Members

The ultimate goal of your strategy, of course, is to achieve superior performance. So, you naturally want to evaluate strategic options by their promised contribution to that performance. Here again, in the new world of group versus group—or combination versus combination—sticking to traditional metrics can lead to misguided decisions. In this world, performance needs to be measured at different levels in a combination.

Should you evaluate the performance of the resource combination as a whole or of its constituent parts? An analogy: What matters more in baseball—the success of a team or a player's individual statistics, or perhaps the contribution that a player makes to the performance of others? It all depends on your point of view. Team owners will think differently than players will.

In some forms of resource combination, a "team owner" will be interested mostly in the success of the combination as a whole. When firms or a common set of shareholders own a combination of resources, this is often the case. But what if the elements of the combination are owned by different interests? That will usually be the case in a constellation of related, but independent firms. Each firm is then likely to measure success on its own terms—that is, the firm will aim for a return on its own resources. But paradoxically, this return will depend on the performance of the group as a whole.

The return ultimately earned by a resource owner stems from the interaction of two factors, as shown in chapter 5. The first factor is the extent to which the combination creates joint value in competition external to the grouping. How does the resource combination as a whole perform? (Have potential scale and scope advantages paid off? What about the potential value of integrating closely complementary components in a business system? Was that value realized?) The second factor is the extent to which each member adds value, and the bargaining position that each member commands inside the combination. (Did each partner add the value it was expected to? Was one partner's contribution greater than another's? And if so, should this partner take more value out of what has been earned?)

These two factors offer a way to understand what economists like to call the *double-margins* puzzle. When two firms occupy successive positions in an industry value chain, and each has some market power in its market, both will try to earn a profit margin over their costs. As a result, the final price in the market will usually be higher than if the two firms were merged, so much so that the chain may price itself out of the market. In other words, the firms really need to manage the value chain with an eye, first, to the total pie and only after that think of how to divide the pie.

Xerox and its partner Fuji Photo Film faced this classic problem in their low-end laser-printer business. Xerox's wholly owned operations in the United States had resources in marketing and sales in this business, and the Fuji Xerox joint venture had R&D and manufacturing resources in Japan. As a constellation, the two companies competed against a single firm—Canon, which had comparable resources in the two markets, but managed its business as an integrated chain. Xerox and Fuji Xerox at first faced the classic double-margins problem; each arm of the constellation sought a markup on its own costs, making the product uncompetitive with Canon's products.

The solution was to combine the business in a partnership that consolidated all costs in the chain and final revenues, with a formula to disburse the ultimate profits. In this way, the partners were able to focus first on the total value chain and, only after that, on the division of profits. This innovation, in addition to closer integration of R&D and marketing, led to substantial improvement in the Xerox group's position in this specific market.

In remix strategy, situations such as that of Xerox and Fuji aren't just curious puzzles in economics textbooks; they're the norm. Whenever firms get together to compete as a group, they need to focus on two elements of remix strategy: (1) the competitive advantage of the group over other external rivals and (2) their own competitive advantage over other members inside the group.

The principle of multilevel competition recognizes that in the end, firms will demand a return on their own resources, whether as rivals or as members of rival groups. The game of strategy may have changed—with complex constellations now battling against firms—but we still keep score the old way.

The Practice: Recalibrate Your Return-on-Investment Benchmarks When Evaluating Combinations

Many companies set the benchmark for a new project in deceivingly simple terms: the hurdle rate of return on investment. Technically, this hurdle rate is based on the company's cost of capital. If a new project earns returns above this rate, it's a go.

Business combinations complicate matters, because in many ways they are not strictly comparable to other investment options. To make sure you evaluate combination projects correctly, step back and be clear on which benchmark is relevant to them.

Few investments are worth making if their expected return falls short of the firm's cost of capital. But an actual investment project can earn much higher returns, especially when it exploits a strong competitive advantage. That is why the traditional core businesses of a successful multibusiness firm typically have higher returns than its peripheral or newer businesses.

Because business combinations share some features with peripheral businesses, you need to evaluate the combinations with the same caution. This is not to say that combinations with external resources are less important to strategy than the core—in fact, you may need to expand the periphery to maintain a competitive advantage in the core. Often, however, the firm does not own and control the full set of capabilities needed within these projects to excel in the market. The firm's own capabilities are incomplete in this sense and are more productively used in tandem with those of another firm.

As a result, the returns on business combinations are often lower than the returns on the firm's core businesses, which are usually wholly owned. Again, a firm should not use its historical experience in the wholly owned business as a guide. The hurdle rate for business combinations ought to reflect the best internal use of the capabilities being devoted to the combination. In a recent IBM survey on innovation practices, the best performing firms reported using lower hurdle rates for innovation projects than for traditional projects; their less-innovative peers used the same or higher hurdle rates for both types. This may seem counterintuitive, because innovation projects are inherently risky. But requiring innovation projects to meet the hurdle rate of the core business is sure to starve them of investment.

Google's strategy on combinations illustrates these points. Early on, Google's business was famous for its laser-like focus on its core of internet search and associated advertising. Today, however, Google's interests stretch far beyond this core. The company still makes the bulk of its profits in search and makes little to nothing on its peripheral businesses, including the popular Android smartphone operating system. Google has invested in large and small business combinations in the periphery, from the acquisition of YouTube to the (free) licenses to Android users. The returns on these combinations surely fell short of Google's profits in the wholly owned business.

But each of these combinations was a step in Google's strategy to expand beyond its core business. Both YouTube and Android extended Google's role in markets beyond its traditional core of text search on desktop computers. Some combinations were probably intended to protect wholly owned assets or to block the advance of rivals. At the same time, each of these moves was a real option that allowed Google to pursue various roads in the future (see the sidebar "Flexibility Makes Risk Your Friend" earlier in this chapter).

Google financials do not allow a breakdown of the profitability of these new businesses, much less of each combination. But the new businesses clearly could not be justified solely on the basis of a traditional return-on-investment calculation measured against the yardstick of the company's wholly owned business.

The problem is compounded when firms use simpler metrics to judge success, such as return on sales or operating margins. Often, for example, the margins on an in-licensed product are lower than on an internally developed one. But these lower margins may be balanced by the lower development cost of the licensed product.

Collect Enough, but Not Too Much

Some analysts of group competition suggest that the best stance for leading firms in a group or constellation is to extract "enough, but not too much," to maintain the health of the group as a whole. Such a prescription seems sensible, even if it is a bit ambiguous. What are the upper ("too much") and lower ("enough") limits on what a firm ought to earn from its resources devoted to group-based competition? You now have the concepts to think about this.

The lower limit on a firm's earnings in a combination is the easiest to define. As noted at the beginning of this chapter, virtually all business combinations are actually recombinations of resources with a prior use or at least an alternative use. The resource earnings in that external option establish a floor on what they should earn in any new combination. If these firms cannot extract "enough" value from the group, they will leave the collective. Continental Airlines, for example, got a better deal in Star Alliance than it had in SkyTeam, so the airline left.

Whatever you do, be careful of taking "too much" value from the combination, even if you can. If one party extracts too much,

Still, many companies make the mistake of taking too narrow a look at the returns of potential combinations. For example, a firm might dismiss entrepreneurial strategies prematurely when the expected returns cannot be justified according to strict standards developed for the core business. Or they see the relationship risk of combinations as an additional reason to be conservative. A conservative approach may work, as long as the wholly owned business remains strong and keeps producing high returns. Sometimes, however, when the core business declines, it is already too late to change course. And, when involving many partners, some firms neglect to consider the overall health of their constellation (see the sidebar "Collect Enough, but Not Too Much"). Better to take a wide and long view when evaluating remix strategies.

the competitive advantage of the group as a whole may deterio-
rate. For example, Coke for many years earned the bulk of its profits from the production of the beverage concentrate, which it sold
to its independent bottlers. Using its market power in the supply
chain, it managed to raise the price of this concentrate even while
the final price of the bottled cola drinks declined in real terms.
The strong bargaining position of Coke versus its bottlers enabled
this disparity. But it also helped starve the bottlers of profits to
the point where many of them had to cut back on investments and
services. In the end, this also hurt Coke's own strategy, as healthy
bottlers were a key channel to the market for the system as a
whole.

The Coke constellation survived, partly because Coke bought
up many of its bottlers and increased its investment in those distribution channels. If it had not done so, Coke's own business would
have been at risk. The upper limit on a firm's earnings in a group,
therefore, may well be set by the survival of the group itself.

Remix Strategy Is in Your Hands

I hope that you have arrived at this point in the book feeling confi-
dent that you have command of a new way of thinking about business combinations and strategy, and that you have an arsenal of
tools to help you apply your thinking in practice. (The main tools
are presented as a collection after this chapter.)

Combining assets in new ways is a powerful route to creating
value and is more common and more effective than many people
think. Following Joseph Schumpeter's vision, I equate this method
of creating value with entrepreneurship writ large—not just the
launch of new firms, but also the turnaround and restructuring
of mature businesses. You can mix and match assets to make a

strong, new business and to remodel an old business into something better.

What matters most, though, is what you ultimately make of the ideas in this book. Recombine these ideas with your own and with those of others. The theme of this book applies not just to business strategy. Mixing and matching is a way of life in the arts, in invention and innovation, and in personal life. The real value of this book for you will emerge from your own remix.

Complete Collection of Remix Strategy Tools

THE FOLLOWING PAGES PRESENT THE MANAGEMENT tools that were introduced in the chapters, together with notes about how to use them. Each tool was introduced and explained in the main text, so you may find it useful to revisit them there for broader context and to find examples of applications. In a few instances, the tools or notes that follow are slightly modified from the corresponding figures in the text.

When using these tools, you need to adapt them to the situation at hand. They are generic starting points for you to develop your own practices. In reality, every business combination involves complexities that are not covered by these tools—regulations, legal frameworks, cultural considerations, personalities, and the like. As you navigate these complexities, these tools will help you stay focused on the strategic goal of creating value for your business.

The management tools presented here are organized as follows:

Roadmap to Remix Strategy

First Law: Identify Potential Joint Value

Second Law: Govern the Collaboration

Third Law: Share the Value Created

All Three Laws: Competing in Multipartner Groups

All Three Laws: Coordinating Key Decisions

Roadmap to Remix Strategy

Tool 1: The three laws of business combinations

**Identify potential
joint value**

First Law
The combination
must have the potential to
create more value than
the parties can alone

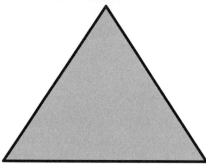

**Govern the
collaboration**

Second Law
The combination
must be designed
and managed to realize
the joint value

**Share the
value created**

Third Law
The value earned by
the parties must motivate
them to contribute to the
collaboration

Use this tool to guide your decisions of when, how, and why to form business combinations. The laws shown are necessary and sufficient conditions for success in any business combination, regardless of its form or purpose.

(See page 16 in the main text for further discussion.)

Roadmap to Remix Strategy

Tool 2: Key decisions in remix strategy

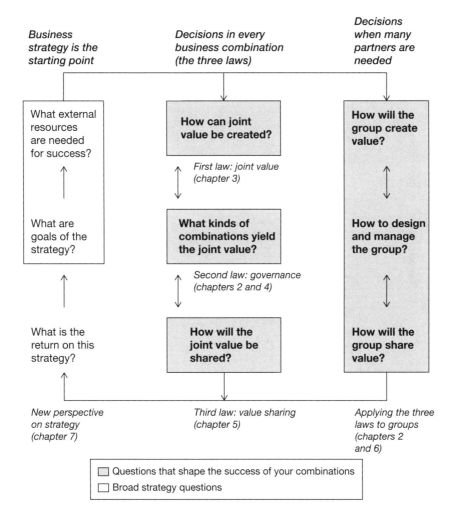

Business
strategy is the
starting point

Decisions in every
business combination
(the three laws)

Decisions
when many
partners are
needed

What external
resources
are needed
for success?

How can joint
value be created?

How will the
group create
value?

First law: joint value
(chapter 3)

What are
goals of the
strategy?

What kinds of
combinations yield
the joint value?

How to design
and manage
the group?

Second law: governance
(chapters 2 and 4)

What is the
return on this
strategy?

How will the
joint value be
shared?

How will the
group share
value?

New perspective
on strategy
(chapter 7)

Third law: value sharing
(chapter 5)

Applying the three
laws to groups
(chapters 2
and 6)

☐ Questions that shape the success of your combinations
☐ Broad strategy questions

Use this tool to identify the sequence of decisions you need to make
in remix strategy and to see which parts of the book can help you in
these decisions. The principles that should guide your answers to
these questions can be applied to single deals as well as to groups
of deals. This book focuses on the questions that shape the success
of your combinations (gray boxes), and it provides a new perspective on the broad strategy questions (white box).

(See page 24 in the main text for further discussion.)

Roadmap to Remix Strategy

Tool 3: The relationship spectrum

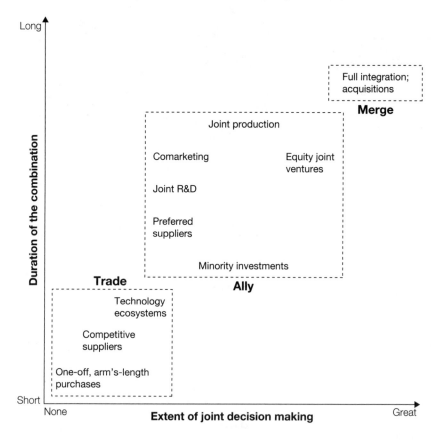

Use this tool to assess what kind of combinations you have and may need in the future. The exact terms used to describe different types of combinations vary by industry. What matters more are the terms *trade, ally,* and *merge.* Firms *trade* when they simply buy and sell goods, or services. They *ally* when they work together more closely, but remain separately owned units. And they *merge* when they combine all resources under one roof. Tool 8 explains these terms further.

The relationship spectrum does not say which form is best; moving higher in the chart does not imply greater value creation. The context and intent of a combination dictate which form will be more effective; tools 9 and 10 will help with that decision.

(See page 35 in the main text for further discussion.)

Roadmap to Remix Strategy

Tool 4: Mapping your relational footprint

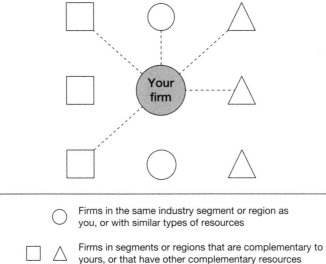

○	Firms in the same industry segment or region as you, or with similar types of resources
□ △	Firms in segments or regions that are complementary to yours, or that have other complementary resources
- - - - -	Possible linkages that may create value—acquisitions, alliances, or other types of combinations

Use this tool to map your current or prospective relational footprint. Each chart and footprint will be unique, reflecting the capabilities, goals, and competitive position of the companies involved. To explore the landscape of deals that may lie ahead for you, start with a (large) blank page, and take the following steps:

1. Define the goals and the resources needed for success. This may include access to markets and technologies.

2. Map your current combinations in this domain. Include alliances and recent acquisitions.

3. Map potential alliances and acquisitions that you may need to gain access to new resources or markets.

4. Evaluate critical links in the current and prospective footprint. Which deal might need to be done before others?

5. Map your rivals' footprints and compare them with yours.

(See page 49 in the main text for further discussion.)

First Law: Identify Potential Joint Value

Tool 5: Sources of joint value

Generic sources of joint value	Why value may be created when firms combine
Increased scale	• Savings in production cost from larger volume of operations • Increased market power from larger volume of sales or purchases • Specialization and focus that enables efficient scale of operations • Network effects from larger community of users
Increased scope	• Savings from sharing common resources in back office • Increased demand from cross- and joint-selling
Improved coordination	• Reduced uncertainty about supply and demand • Greater incentive for investment in specific assets • Reduced risk of dependence and holdup • Increased tailoring of output and activities
Expanded options	• Ability to hedge against uncertain outcomes in the future • Ability to respond to new information as it becomes available • Flexibility to change course as strategies and environment evolve

Use this tool to identify the source of joint value in a combination. For example, if increased scale seems to be the main purpose of the combination, drill down into the details to see why this is—production savings, market power, focus, or network effects. Knowing the concrete mechanism by which value will be created will help you determine which resources need to be combined and how the combination should be managed.

(See page 64 in the main text for further discussion.)

First Law: Identify Potential Joint Value
Tool 6: Dissecting the value stack of a business

Concept: the value stack of a business		
Outputs		• Product • Service
Activities		• Operation that transforms inputs into outputs
Resources	**Capabilities**	• Skills • Know-how • Organization
	Assets • Intangible • Tangible	• Brand • Rights • Technology • Capital equipment • Land

Use this tool to assess the roots of competitive advantage in your own organization and those of your partners. The value stack is comparable to the well-known value-chain template, which is another way to think about the key parts of a business. This tool shows that competitive advantage may stem from specific resources, activities, and outputs (the details in the right-hand columns are illustrative). Inside a business, these elements are often complementary: certain resources work best with other resources and with certain activities. The tool does not show who owns what in the value stack, but just shows that all the parts of the stack have the potential to create value for someone. This same scheme is also used in tool 7.

(See pages 72–74 in the main text for further discussion, which includes an example from the oil industry.)

First Law: Identify Potential Joint Value

Tool 7: Finding promising combinations

Value stack elements		Value stacks of two complementary businesses	
		Business A	Business B
Outputs			
Activities			
Resources	Capabilities		
Resources	Assets • Intangible • Tangible		

Shaded value blocks are sources of competitive advantage for each firm (illustrative)

Use this tool to identify and evaluate which resources need to be linked in potential combinations. Compare the value stacks of your business with those of one or more complementary businesses. Examine what value blocks in each business you might need to combine to create joint value. The gray boxes illustrate how the competitive advantage of Business A and Business B may differ; joint value often comes from linking these different value blocks. This tool will help you see the relevant blocks that need to be combined; tools 8, 9, and 10 will help you decide on the form of the combination.

(See page 81 in the main text for further discussion.)

Second Law: Govern the Collaboration

Tool 8: Three relationship models: trade, ally, and merge

	How joint value is created	How the relationship is governed	How value is shared
Trade	Coordination of activities through exchange of outputs from independent parties	Each party is responsible for its own decisions, which are based on price signals	Arm's-length sharing: terms of trade (mostly prices) set at the start, and parties' own costs determine profitability of transactions
Ally	Coordination of activities through exchange of outputs and resources among parties that share some interests	Parties influence each other's behavior through contractual agreements and management communication	Pay as you go: terms of trade and returns to resource sharing are adjusted over time through profit-sharing mechanisms
Merge	Coordination of activities through unified management and interests	The behaviors of the parties are shaped by control from a common owner and by intracompany policies	Pay now, profit later: acquisition price provides return to seller of an asset; buyer retains the rights to residual profits—and losses

Use this tool to assess and select from various combination options. This tool is an overview of the principal features of the three main relationship models referred to in tools 3 and 9. The table is generalized; in reality, your deals may have slightly different features or may be hybrids that lean one way or another. But it shows how the three laws may play out in each of the three relationship models. For example, if you select an alliance, that shapes in part how joint value is created, how collaboration is governed, and how value is shared. Conversely, if you prefer certain governance characteristics, that preference drives you to select one of the relationship models.

(See page 90 in the main text for further discussion.)

Second Law: Govern the Collaboration

Tool 9: How joint value shapes governance

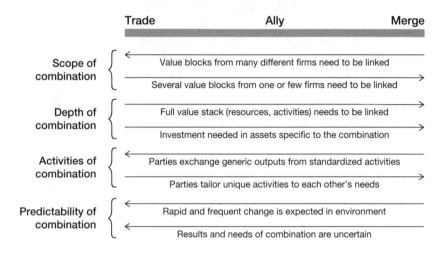

Use this tool to evaluate which combination form is best suited to the value-creation strategy of the combination. The conditions necessary to generate joint value dictate the best governance model for the combination. But different conditions in one deal may well dictate different choices. The best way to think about this choice is as a series of controls that can be dialed up or down in response to certain conditions.

This tool shows the most important of these control dials that shape governance. For example, when multiple value blocks are needed from many different firms, governance should tend toward the left of the scale (first arrow from top). However, if the parties need to invest in specific assets, governance should tend toward the right of the scale (fourth arrow down). The final choice depends on such trade-offs along the variables shown in the figure. Use this tool with tool 10, which focuses on the choice between trade (vendor) and ally (partner).

(See page 95 in the main text for further discussion.)

Second Law: Govern the Collaboration

Tool 10: Choosing between a vendor and a partner relationship

Condition	Vendor: complete contract may be possible and effective	Partner: well-managed, open-ended contract is likely needed
Technology	Mature, stable	New, rapidly changing
Prices, costs	Known, good forecasts	Uncertain, volatile
Customer requirements	Detailed specifications can be formulated	Detailed specifications still unknown or likely to change
Competitive environment	Stable markets, commodity-like	Dynamic markets, differentiated
Task requirements	Well understood, predictable	Uncertain, to be determined
Investment needed	Generic assets, equally valuable without the deal	Specific assets, most valuable in the deal
Dependence on this relationship	Low; many possible counterparts	High; few other potential partners

Use this tool to assess the best form of a combination that falls in the trade-to-ally range of the relationship spectrum in tool 3. The choice between a partnership (ally) and a vendor relationship (trade) is shown to depend on the conditions that apply in each category. For example, if the technology is new and changing rapidly, a partnership is a better choice than a vendor relationship, because the agreement will surely have gaps that need to be governed. On the other hand, if the technology is mature and stable, then clear contract specifications will more likely be possible, and a partnership may well be overkill—a simpler vendor relationship is less costly to manage. This table complements the broader analysis in tool 9.

(See page 109 in the main text for further discussion.)

Second Law: Govern the Collaboration

Tool 11: Assessing partner fit

Consideration (based on the three laws of business combinations)	How partner compares to your firm	Fit with potential partners		
		A	B	C
What is the potential for joint value? (first law)	**Complementary capabilities:** each party has what the other needs			
Can we work together to realize this potential? (second law)	**Compatible attitudes and broad strategy:** these don't need to be identical, but they must not conflict			
	Common vision for project: there is agreement on goals for the collaboration itself			
	Limited competing interests: direct and indirect conflicts are minimal or contained			
What will be the returns to each party? (third law)	**An acceptable balance of returns:** needed to provide incentives for commitment from both sides			

Use this tool to assess your fit with a partner in an alliance. This assessment may be useful in deciding whether or not to form the alliance, or in designing and managing the alliance. A good fit between alliance partners needs to fulfill all three laws of business combinations. The table shows criteria that apply to each law. For each criterion shown, one partner may seem a better fit than another, and these rankings may well vary by criterion. For example, two firms with great complementary capabilities (the first criterion), may not have compatible strategies (the second criterion) or may have competing interests (the fourth). To select a partner or to structure the deal with a given partner, you need to weigh the trade-offs among these criteria.

(See page 110 in the main text for further discussion.)

Second Law: Govern the Collaboration
Tool 12: Designing and managing alliances

Alliance Design

- **Provide incentives for collaboration at all key levels and functions.** Collaboration with an outside party is not natural for many employees. Salespeople, engineers, and managers of business units need to receive tangible benefits from working with the external party.
- **Define what is in and what is out of the alliance.** Rivalry between partners may sometimes exist, but it will hurt collaboration if competition is not kept out of the scope of the collaboration. This strategy demands excellent contract design, as well as careful thinking about strategic direction.

Alliance Operations

- **Define partner roles.** A division of labor, and sometimes a division of decision-making authority, can focus each partner on what it does best. For example, one partner might run local factories in a joint venture, but both partners will share planning and investment decisions.
- **Create processes for making joint decisions.** The open-ended contracts that are typical of alliances rely on excellent decision processes in the alliance itself and between the parent companies. For joint ventures, these processes are defined in corporate bylaws. In other alliances, you may have agreements on how decisions will be made and what issues will get escalated.

Relationship Management

- **Manage the joint business as well as the relationship itself.** The two tracks, or roles, may demand different skills and personnel. Distinguish between the technical success of an alliance and the health of the relationship itself.
- **Build and maintain trust on purpose.** Negotiate good contracts, deepen personal contacts, and act reliably and with reciprocity. Yes, these practices are easier said than done, but trust does not appear magically; it must be built and nurtured with concrete management tools.
- **Allocate sufficient resources to alliance management.** None of the above practices can be done on the cheap. Yet, under-resourcing alliance management is the single most common mistake that even large and rich companies make.

This tool helps you design and manage an alliance. The key to success here is to design and manage the alliance to support the collaboration that is needed to create joint value. Further details depend on the circumstances of each alliance—the specific best practices for an alliance will vary between companies and industries. The successful principles listed here are a guide to developing your own practices.

(See page 114 in the main text for further discussion.)

Third Law: Share the Value Created

Tool 13: Determinants of how value is earned in combinations

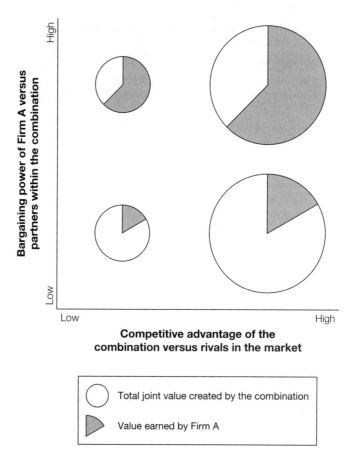

Use this tool to diagnose what value will ultimately accrue to each party in a combination. These earnings depend on competitive processes at two levels. The competition between your combination and its external rivals (horizontal axis) determines the total joint value created by the combination—the size of the pie, so to speak. Bargaining between your firm and your partners (vertical axis) then affects what share of that total pie you earn. To understand and manage your value-sharing relationships, keep an eye on both of these processes.

(See page 145 in the main text for further discussion.)

Third Law: Share the Value Created

Tool 14: Partner positioning in combinations

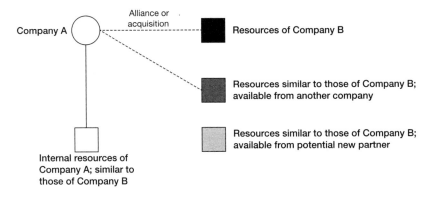

Use this tool to assess the relative bargaining power between you and your partners in a combination, whether it is an alliance or an acquisition. This simple diagram is intended to show you key elements in partner positioning. Imagine that Company A (circle) needs resources (squares). It decides to form an alliance with, or to acquire, Company B (black square). In addition, however, those resources may also be available internally or from other companies. The more of these options that Company A has, the stronger will be its bargaining position in sharing value with Company B. In an acquisition, the price of the deal will be affected by this bargaining power; for an alliance, the value-sharing arrangement will be affected.

(See page 141 in the main text for further discussion.)

Third Law: Sharing the Value Created
Tool 15: Taming co-opetition

- **Be realistic: see co-opetition for what it is.** All too often, the possibility of conflict between partners is not faced honestly when businesses are planning a partnership. Conflict is understandably a sensitive topic. But it needs to be addressed first in your own planning and then in conversations with your prospective partner.
- **Be cautious: avoid co-opetition, if you can.** With few exceptions, being in competition with your partner is not helpful for a combination. When the cost of competition appears high, you may do well to avoid the partner or even the alliance itself.
- **Be preemptive: squash co-opetition up front, if you can.** If you cannot avoid it—perhaps because competitive conditions leave you no choice— then you can try to squash the competition up front through a full merger or an asset swap that in effect puts all the competing assets under one roof.
- **Be smart: manage co-opetition, if you can't avoid it.** If a merger doesn't work—and, again, you could not avoid forming a combination with a competitor—then try to structure the alliance so as to minimize competition. For example, territorial boundaries (where legal) can keep the partners out of each other's way.
- **Be bold: in exceptional situations, ignore the above advice and jump in.** In some situations, competitors may indeed work together toward a common goal, such as strengthening the infrastructure or ecosystem of their industry. This kind of co-opetition does little to give one party the edge over the other, but may lift all boats.

Use this tool to evaluate whether and how to collaborate with a competitor. Such collaboration is seldom a preferred option and is fraught with risk, but sometimes the benefits outweigh the risks— especially if you manage them with proper safeguards.

(See page 136 in the main text for further discussion.)

All Three Laws: Competing in Multipartner Groups

Tool 16: The constellation spectrum

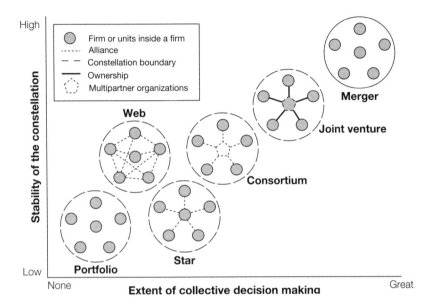

Use this tool to assess what kind of constellation structure you might need. In the figure, gray circles are firms and the larger dashed circles denote the constellation as a whole. (The merger picture is different, as the group is bound together by common ownership, so the gray circles are business units inside the larger firm.) Inside each constellation, the linkages between firms are alliances of various sorts—from looser contractual alliances (dotted lines) to tighter equity investments (solid lines).

As with the relationship spectrum (tool 3), you can adapt this tool to your industry and company. As suggested by the diagram, the constellation forms differ mostly due to their internal structure—by which firms are allied to which, and by the nature of those internal linkages.

(See page 173 in the main text for further discussion.)

All Three Laws: Competing in Multipartner Groups

Tool 17: How joint value shapes constellations

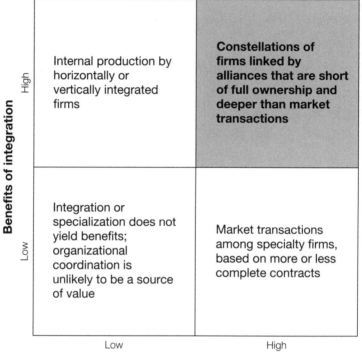

Use this tool to decide how best to bundle a set of complementary resources, or firms, to create competitive advantage in the market. Your decision depends on the balance of two economic forces. Under certain conditions, a constellation of partners is likely to be the best way to create joint value—specifically, when both integration and specialization offer advantages (gray quadrant). At other times, integrated firms (top left quadrant) or independent specialty firms trading with each other (lower right quadrant) are better choices. When neither factor is important (lower left quadrant), then these organization choices are unlikely to affect value creation.

(See page 166 in the main text for further discussion.)

All Three Laws: Competing in Multipartner Groups

Tool 18: Designing and managing constellations

Constellation strategy

- **Global vision, local gains.** A constellation must create joint value and share this value with each member. In practice, each member must see gains in the global vision that brings the members of the constellation together.
- **The right mix of ingredients.** A constellation is intended to tie together the value blocks needed for a complete system.

Constellation membership

- **Selective membership.** The more members in a constellation, the harder it is to keep them working together. What's more, stricter admission criteria tend to evoke stronger commitment from members. Several constellations have struggled with this size question, often growing wildly and then trimming back.
- **Membership norms.** If the constellation does indeed need to be large, then it pays to find ways to organize with common rules for similar members.
- **Limited internal rivalry.** The challenge of managing a constellation also increases with internal rivalry. Avoiding duplication among members is not always possible or desirable, but internal rivalry can be managed.

Constellation leadership

- **Leadership at the core.** Effective constellations usually cannot be run on a one-member, one-vote model. In practice, one or a few members will lead the constellation because of the members' size or position in the value stack.
- **Strategic sequence and timing of growth.** Constellations do not form in one fell swoop—they grow over time. Consequently, you should pay attention to the sequence of adding members. Some members will attract others. And sometimes, the rise of rival constellations will force the addition of certain members.

Use this tool to shape the design and management of a constellation. Further details depend on the circumstances of each grouping—the specific best practices for a constellation will vary by industry and over time, as the constellation develops. The successful principles listed here are a guide to developing your own practices

(See page 181 in the main text for further discussion.)

All Three Laws: Competing in Multipartner Groups

Tool 19: Value sharing in constellations

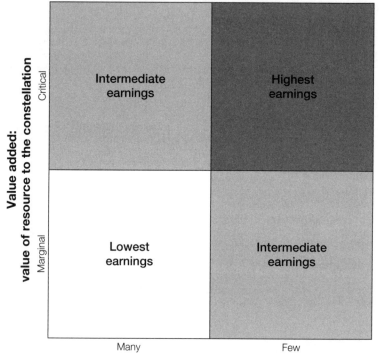

Use this tool to assess the profits that each player might earn from a constellation. The basic formula for earnings is the same as for any single combination (see tool 13). In a group, your share of value depends on the interaction between the competitive importance of the resource you add to the constellation and how many other providers bring in the same or similar resources.

(See page 184 in the main text for further discussion.)

All Three Laws: Coordinating Key Decisions

Tool 20: Thinking—together— about remix strategy

Law of business combinations	Which unit is typically responsible?	Which strategies or activities are related?	Which decision criteria can be used?	Which disciplines and functions help?
Identify potential joint value	Business unit, business development, and corporate strategy	Marketing and operations strategies	Fit with goals, position, and resources	Economics of the business, forecasting
Govern the collaboration	Legal staff and the units that will own the combination	Incentives and governance policies	Decision making practices, risk management	Organizational behavior, legal framework, project management
Share the value created	Finance staff and business units	Valuation goals and methods	Hurdle rates, margin goals, option values	Negotiation and valuation techniques

Use this tool to sort out how your organization will address the key questions in remix strategy. Each of the three laws of business combinations draws on a different discipline and involves decisions that may be the responsibility of different management units. To manage remix strategy successfully, your organization must find ways to integrate these different ways of thinking.

(See page 205 in the main text for further discussion.)

Further Reading

CHAPTER 1

Ideas

My inspiration for the idea of business remix comes from Joseph A. Schumpeter, *The Theory of Economic Development* (originally published in German 1911; English trans. London: Oxford University Press, 1934). Though I first read this book as an undergraduate, I have since learned how its core insight about business combinations can be put to use in management. Schumpeter is better known for his work on creative destruction, which appeared in a later book. Scholars of entrepreneurship, however, have regularly referred to Schumpeter's concept of business combinations.

Following the Great Recession, interest in reshuffling assets rose among firms, for reasons sketched briefly in the text. See also the contemporary advice on the matter in Richard Dobbs, "Are You Still the Best Owner of Your Assets?" *McKinsey Quarterly* (November 2009).

As noted, the concept of remix is akin to what has been called "recombination" in the literature. This idea has been referred to by various business writers on entrepreneurship and innovation, although none addressed recombinant strategy in depth. For an early application in economics, see Martin Weitzman, "Recombinant Growth," *Quarterly Journal of Economics* (May 1998). Rebecca Henderson and Kim Clark define architectural innovation as a recombination of components in "Architectural Innovation: The Reconfiguration of Existing Product Technologies and the Failure of Established Firms," *Administrative Science Quarterly* 35 (1990). An application of this concept to organizational design is in D. Charles Galunic and Kathleen M. Eisenhardt, "Architectural Innovation and Modular Corporate Forms," *Academy of Management Journal* (December 2001).

Following Schumpeter, students of entrepreneurship have used the concept of recombination too; for example, see Ola Olsson and Bruno S. Frey,

"Entrepreneurship as Recombinant Growth," *Small Business Economics* 19 (2002). Closely related is the "make do with what is at hand" approach to innovation in Ted Baker and Reed E. Nelson, "Creating Something from Nothing: Resource Construction Through Entrepreneurial Bricolage," *Administrative Science Quarterly* 50 (2005). See also the "brokerage" approach in Andrew Hargadon and Robert I. Sutton, "Technology Brokering and Innovation in a Product Development Firm," *Administrative Science Quarterly* 42 (1997); and the same authors' case study of IDEO in "Building an Innovation Factory," *Harvard Business Review,* May–June 2000.

Aggregating and extending these views, some authors' theories of the firm or of value creation revolve in part on the recombination of assets. See Bruce Kogut and Udo Zander, "Knowledge of the Firm, Combinative Capabilities, and the Replication of Technology," *Organization Science* (August 1992); D. Charles Galunic and Simon Rodan, "Resource Recombinations in the Firm: Knowledge Structures and the Potential for Schumpeterian Innovation," *Strategic Management Journal* 19 (1998); and Peter Moran and Sumantra Ghoshal, "Markets, Firms, and the Process of Economic Development," *Academy of Management Review* 24 (1999). A recent discussion of the impact of recombination on leadership is in Joseph L. Badaracco, *The Good Struggle: Responsible Leadership in an Unforgiving World* (Boston: Harvard Business Review Press, 2013).

The recombination (or reconfiguration) of capabilities or assets also is featured in some literature on the "dynamic capabilities" of firms; see especially David Teece, Gary Pisano, and Amy Shuen, "Dynamic Capabilities and Strategic Management," *Strategic Management Journal* 18 (1997); and David J. Teece, "Explicating Dynamic Capabilities: The Nature and Microfoundations of (Sustainable) Enterprise Performance," *Strategic Management Journal* 28 (2007). A brief, good review of this literature is Constance E. Helfat and Margaret A. Peteraf, "Understanding Dynamic Capabilities: Progress Along a Developmental Path," *Strategic Organization* 7 (2009). A statistical study of recombination within semiconductor firms is Gianluca Carnabuci and Elisa Operti, "Where Do Firms' Recombinant Capabilities Come From? Intraorganizational Networks, Knowledge, and Firms' Ability to Innovate Through Technological Recombination," *Strategic Management Journal* 34 (2013). For the role of alliances in restructuring a company, see Koen Dittrich, Geert Duysters, and Ard-Pieter de Man, "Strategic Repositioning by Means of Alliance Networks: The Case of IBM," *Research Policy* (2007).

Each of the three laws introduced in this chapter rests on a rich body of prior work, which will be discussed in the following chapters and in the references below. The overall framework is new. Previous frameworks that introduce a related set of factors are in Jeffrey H. Dyer and Harbir Singh, "The Relational View: Cooperative Strategy and Sources of Interorganizational Competitive Advantage," *Academy of Management Review* 23 (1998); Dovev Lavie, "The Competitive Advantage of Interconnected Firms: An Extension of the Resource-Based View," *Academy of Management Review* 31 (2006); and J. Adetunji Adegbesan, "On the Origins of Competitive Advantage: Strategic Factor Markets and Heterogeneous Resource Complementarity," *Academy of Management Review* 34 (2009). On acquisitions specifically, Mark L. Sirower offers a related approach in *The Synergy Trap: How Companies Lose the Acquisition Game* (New York: Free Press, 1997).

Evidence

The data on business combinations is not comprehensive, with acquisitions being covered much better than alliances. For a review of the available data on alliances, see Melissa A. Schilling, "Understanding the Alliance Data," *Strategic Management Journal* 30 (2009).

A detailed and critical account of the DaimlerChrysler merger is Bill Vlasic and Bradley A. Sterz, *Taken for a Ride: How Daimler-Benz Drove Off with Chrysler* (New York: HarperBusiness, 2001). A good case study of the Renault-Nissan alliance is Sara Gaviser Leslie and Robert A. Burgelman, "The Renault-Nissan Alliance in 2008," Case SM-166 (Stanford, CA: Stanford Graduate School of Business, 2008). These two mergers are compared briefly with other auto mergers in "Marriages Made in Hell," *The Economist,* May 19, 2009.

The Disney-Pixar history is told well in David J. Collis, Juan Alcacer, and Mary Furey, "The Walt Disney Company and Pixar Inc.: To Acquire or Not to Acquire?" Case 709-462 (Boston: Harvard Business School, 2009), and its accompanying "The Walt Disney Company and Pixar Inc.: To Acquire or Not to Acquire? An Update," Case 709-489 (Boston: Harvard Business School, 2009). The larger transformation of Disney is described in Michal Lev-Ram, "Empire of Tech," *Fortune,* January 1, 2015, pp. 4858.

CHAPTER 2

Ideas

Make-or-buy analysis is well known, and the alliance option is now often added in many companies. A managerial approach focusing on the alliance option, derived from Cisco's experience, is in Steve Steinhilber, *Strategic*

Alliances: Three Ways to Make Them Work (Boston: Harvard Business Review Press, 2008). A framework to the full range of options is Laurence Capron and Will Mitchell, *Build, Borrow, or Buy: Solving the Growth Dilemma* (Boston: Harvard Business Review Press, 2012); and Laurence Capron and Will Mitchell, "Finding the Right Path," *Harvard Business Review,* July–August 2010. A recent study about how companies typically mix these modes is Phanish Puranam, Ranjay Gulati, and Sourav Bhattacharya, "How Much to Make and How Much to Buy? An Analysis of Optimal Plural Sourcing Strategies," *Strategic Management Journal* 34 (2013).

David Ricardo's principle of comparative advantage is a foundation of modern economics, as are other concepts he introduced. See his *On the Principles of Political Economy and Taxation* (London: John Murray, 1817), ch. 7, available at www.econlib.org/library/Ricardo/ricP.html.

In an earlier book, I explored the theoretical basis for the distinction made here between firms and constellations as ways to bundle resources; see Benjamin Gomes-Casseres, *The Alliance Revolution: The New Shape of Business Rivalry* (Cambridge, MA: Harvard University Press, 1996). My definition of a constellation or an "alliance group" or "alliance network" (Benjamin Gomes-Casseres, "Group Versus Group: How Alliance Networks Compete," *Harvard Business Review,* July–August 1994) is related to the concepts of several other authors.

Closely related concepts to my idea of constellations are the "strategic blocks" in Nitin Nohria and Carlos Garcia-Pont, "Global Strategic Linkages and Industry Structure," *Strategic Management Journal* (summer 1991); the "webs" in John Hagel, "Spider Versus Spider," *McKinsey Quarterly* 1 (1996); and the "business groups" in the literature on emerging markets (see, e.g., Tarun Khanna and Jan W. Rivkin, "Estimating the Performance Effects of Business Groups in Emerging Markets," *Strategic Management Journal* 22 [2001]; and Tarun Khanna and Yishay Yafeh, "Business Groups in Emerging Markets: Paragons or Parasites?" *Journal of Economic Literature* [June 2007]). My definition of a constellation is more restrictive than these concepts and closer to the "constellations" of G. Lorenzoni and Oscar A. Ornati, "Constellations of Firms and New Ventures," *Journal of Business Venturing* 3 (1988), who appear to have been the first to use that term, and to those of Richard Normann and Rafel Ramírez, "From Value Chain to Value Constellation: Designing Interactive Strategy," *Harvard Business Review,* July–August 1993.). For a review of this literature, see Ranjay Gulati, "Alliances and Networks," *Strategic Management Journal* 19 (1998).

Social network analysis has become a popular tool in business. Many images showing networks in one context or another are available by a simple web search. The depth of analysis behind these images varies. The more technical analyses demand a familiarity with tools and concepts in the field. As usual, *Wikipedia,* q.v. "social network analysis," last modified February 10, 2015, https://en.wikipedia.org/wiki/Social_network_analysis, offers a good introduction. A classic primer for researchers is John Scott, *Social Network Analysis: A Handbook* (London: Sage, 1991). A nice application to understand company organization is in Henry Mintzberg and Ludo Van der Heyden, "Organigraphs: Drawing How Companies Really Work," *Harvard Business Review,* September–October 1999. A recent analysis that distinguishes nicely between the ego and network perspectives is Maxim Sytch and Adam Tatarynowicz, "Exploring the Locus of Invention: The Dynamics of Network Communities and Firms' Invention Productivity," *Academy of Management Journal* 57 (2014).

The relational footprint tool at the end of the chapter is one that I have used regularly with companies, but it has not been published before. A related tool is in James Bamford and David Ernst, "Managing an Alliance Portfolio," *McKinsey Quarterly* 3 (2002).

Evidence

Scott McNealy's tweet was on Twitter, April 22, 2011, https://twitter.com/scottmcnealy, (accessed January 22, 2014).

Airline alliances are in the news daily; a recent review is "Friends With Benefits: Global Alliances Have Shortcomings, Now as Always. But Losing Their Relevance? No." *Airline Weekly,* April 22, 2013. Not surprisingly, antitrust authorities are good sources of comprehensive and publicly accessible studies. See the final order of the US Department of Transportation regarding the accession of Continental to Star Alliance's antitrust immunity, signed by Christa Fornarotto, Acting Assistant Secretary for Aviation and International Affairs, Order 2009-7-10, Docket OST-2008-0234,: www.regulations.gov. An economic study commissioned by the US Department of Justice is William Gillespie and Oliver M. Richard, "Antitrust Immunity and International Airline Alliances," Economic Analysis Group Discussion Paper EAG 11-1, February 2011.

News about Google's partnerships and network is also widely reported. A review of Android's context and evolution is Amanda Silverman et al., "Google's Android: Will It Shake Up the Wireless Industry in 2009 and Beyond?" Case SM-176 (Stanford, CA: Stanford Graduate School of Business, 2009). Analysis and evidence of how Google's acquisition strategy contributes to its innovation in hardware and software is Rex Chen, Kenneth L. Kraemer, and Prakul Sharma, "Google: The World's First Information Utility?" *Business & Information Systems Engineering* (January 2009).

CHAPTER 3

Ideas

Chester Barnard's *The Functions of the Executive* (Cambridge, MA: Harvard University Press, 1938) is still worth reading for its treatment of the fundamentals of organizational design and management. A modern treatment, including an application of the idea of complementarity to manufacturing, is in Paul Milgrom and John Roberts, "Complementarities and Fit: Strategy, Structure, and Organizational Change in Manufacturing," *Journal of Accounting and Economics* 19 (1995).

The relationship between complementarity and organizational ties was sketched in one of the earliest pieces about alliances, G. B. Richardson, "The Organisation of Industry," *The Economic Journal* (September 1972). An explicit examination of the role of complementarities in making resources valuable is Jens Schmidt and Thomas Kiel, "What Makes a Resource Valuable? Identifying the Drivers of Firm-Idiosyncratic Resource Value," *Academy of Management Review* 38 (2013).

The concept of synergy is critiqued in Mark L. Sirower, *The Synergy Trap: How Companies Lose the Acquisition Game* (New York: Free Press, 1997).

James D. Thompson's classic is *Organizations in Action* (New York: McGraw-Hill, 1967). His ideas are applied to value chains in Charles B. Stabell and Øystein D. Fjeldstad, "Configuring Value for Competitive Advantage: On Chains, Shops, and Networks," *Strategic Management Journal* (1998).

Originally, the term *stack* was used in software coding to designate a data structure; today it also refers to a solution stack composed of hardware and software components. See, for example, Jim Rapoza, "How the Stacks Stack Up: Open-Source and .Net Stacks Perform Well, but a Mix of the Two Won Big in Labs' Tests, *eWeek,* July 10, 2006. A discussion similar to mine connects the idea to economic complementarities and to business combinations: Lucia Silva Gao and Bala Iyer, "Analyzing Complementarities Using Software Stacks for Software Industry Acquisitions," *Journal of Management Information Systems* (fall 2006). Intel's former CEO Andrew S. Grove discusses the strategic implications of the solution stack in computers in his *Only the Paranoid Survive* (New York: Doubleday, 1996), ch. 3. A nice example of the stack in the "internet of things" business is in Michael E. Porter and James E. Heppelman, "How Smart, Connected Products Are Transforming Competition," *Harvard Business Review,* November 2014.

There is extensive literature on the economics of each of the sources of joint value discussed—scale, scope, coordination, and future options.

A good textbook on strategy or microeconomics will discuss at least the first three; for example, see Garth Saloner, Andrea Shepard, and Joel Podolny, *Strategic Management* (New York: John Wiley & Sons, 2001). The fourth—the value of future options—is a more specialized topic; see Timothy A. Luehrman, "Strategy as a Portfolio of Real Options," *Harvard Business Review,* September 1998.

Edith Penrose's *The Theory of the Growth of the Firm* (White Plains, NY: Oxford University Press, 1959) is still worth reading as the foundation of the resource-based view of the firm, though this view was not developed further until the 1980s. These ideas entered the current strategy literature in force following Birger Wernerfelt, "A Resource-Based View of the Firm," *Strategic Management Journal* 5 (1984). Interestingly, Wernerfelt later lamented in a retrospective that most of the research citing resource-based advantages of firms neglected to account for the strategic value of resources that were not wholly owned by the firm, such as in licensing and joint ventures; see Andy Lockett et al., "The Development of the Resource-Based View: Reflections from Birger Wernerfelt," *Organization Studies* 29 (2008). An overview of theory in this field is in Jay B. Barney and Delwyn N. Clark, *Resource-Based Theory: Creating and Sustaining Competitive Advantage* (New York: Oxford University Press, 2007).

Michael E. Porter's work on the activities view of the firm is in his *Competitive Advantage: Creating and Sustaining Superior Performance* (New York: Free Press, 1998), which also introduces the model of the value chain discussed in this chapter. A concise exposition of the activities view is Michael E. Porter, "What Is Strategy?" *Harvard Business Review,* November 1996. An interesting picture of Disney's activity map, drawn by the company's internal analysts in 1957, appears in Todd Zenger, "What Is the Theory of Your Firm?" *Harvard Business Review,* June 2013.

The two schools of thought in strategy—activities versus resources—are reflected in the management literature, although few articles try to combine the two concepts. Saloner, Shepard, and Podolny, *Strategic Management,* the textbook cited above, explains both schools of thought and combines them in a different way than in this book. A good discussion of the resources view, with another attempt to integrate the two schools, is David J. Collis and Cynthia A. Montgomery, "Competing on Resources," *Harvard Business Review,* July 2008.

I am unaware of prior attempts to use the idea of a solution stack to model the building blocks of advantage in a firm. But IBM has developed a related approach it calls component business modeling (CBM); the company has applied for a patent for this methodology and uses it in its management consulting practice. IBM's first publication on CBM is George Pohle, Peter

Korsten, and Shanker Ramamurthy, *Component Business Models: Making Specialization Real* (Somers, NY: IBM Institute for Business Value, 2005). The patent application is by Guy Jonathan James Rackham, "System and Method for Alignment of an Enterprise to a Component Business Model," USPTO application 20050246215 (2005); at least six other patent applications have followed on various ways to use the CBM methodology. This book does not draw directly on this parallel work.

Related to the building-blocks model I propose is work that analyzes the modularity of firms and industries. A major work in this field is Carliss Y. Baldwin and Kim B. Clark, *Design Rules: The Power of Modularity,* vol. 1 (MIT Press, 2000). See also Carliss Y. Baldwin, "Where Do Transactions Come From? Modularity, Transactions, and the Boundaries of Firms," *Industrial and Corporate Change* 17 (2007). The idea of modularity in business draws in part on architectural design concepts rooted in the classic Christopher Alexander, *Notes on the Synthesis of Form* (Cambridge, MA: Harvard University Press, 1964). More recent and applied analysis of modularity across industries is in Melissa Schilling, "The Use of Modular Organizational Forms: An Industry-Level Analysis," *Academy of Management Journal* 44 (2001).

Evidence

Alfred D. Chandler Jr.'s masterwork on the role of scale and scope in corporate advantage in the twentieth century is *Scale and Scope: The Dynamics of Industrial Capitalism* (Cambridge, MA: Harvard University Press, 1990).

Evidence on alliances between for-profit and not-for-profit entities is in Global Environmental Management Initiative and Environmental Defense Fund, "Guide to Successful Corporate-NGO Partnerships," GEMI and EDF, 2008, www.gemi.org/resources/gemi-edf%20guide.pdf.

The organization of the oil and gas value chain in the tables is stylized and illustrative. An example of the value chain data, with application to joint ventures, is Ernst & Young, *Navigating Joint Ventures in the Oil and Gas Industry* (Ernst & Young, 2011). Some of the reasons behind the de-integration of the oil and gas firms are discussed in Ernst & Young, *The Oil Downstream: Vertically Challenged?* (Ernst & Young, 2012, http://www.ey.com/GL/en/Industries/Oil—Gas/The-oil-downstream—vertically-challenged—overview).

Some research has tried to tease out when divestments create value; for example, see Tomi Laamanen et al., "Performance of Acquirers of Divested Assets: Evidence from the U.S. Software Industry," *Strategic Management Journal* 35 (2014). A review of both sides of the acquisition-divestment process is Melissa E. Graebner, Kathleen M. Eisenhardt, and Philip T. Roundy, "Success and Failure in Technology Acquisitions: Lessons for Buyers and Sellers," *Academy of Management Perspectives* (August 2010).

Philip Evans and Thomas S. Wurster, in *Blown to Bits: How the New Economics of Information Transforms Strategy* (Boston: Harvard Business School Press, 1999), discuss how digital technologies led to the de-integration of firms in information industries. Firms in other industries, too, have become less integrated over time. For the example of pharmaceuticals, see Oliver Scheel, Jim O'Keefe, and Tim Wintermantel, *Unleashing Pharma from the R&D Value Chain,* A.T. Kearney, July 2013.

CHAPTER 4

Ideas

The fundamental idea behind the second law, discussed in this chapter, is that the organizational form of the asset bundle will affect the joint value created by shaping the incentives for cooperation. For a formal model of this argument—but a model applied to internal firm organization—see Wouter Dessein, Luis Garicano, and Robert H. Gertner, "Organizing for Synergies," *American Economic Journal: Microeconomics* (November 2010).

The Nobel Prizes awarded for transaction cost economics were to Ronald H. Coase (1991), for his seminar work, and to Oliver E. Williamson (2009), for his extensions and elaborations of the theory. The literature on this topic is extensive, but most of it is in technical economics journals. Ronald H. Coase's original statement is accessible to the general reader; see his "The Nature of the Firm," *Economica* (November 1937). Similarly, Oliver E. Williamson's classic *Markets and Hierarchies: Analysis and Antitrust Implications* (New York: Free Press, 1975) is also readable and not overly technical. Williamson's Nobel Prize lecture summarizes the development of the field; see his "Transaction Cost Economics: The Natural Progression," *American Economic Review* (June 2010). For an excellent treatment of core ideas in modern organizational economics, see John Roberts, *The Modern Firm: Organizational Design for Performance and Growth* (Oxford, UK: Oxford University Press, 2004). A useful clarification about the advantages and disadvantages of firms and markets is Robert Gibbons, "Taking Coase Seriously," *Administrative Science Quarterly* 44 (1999). An alternative view, related to my emphasis on joint decision making in the text, is Birger Wernerfelt, "Governance of Adjustments," *Journal of Business* 77 (2004).

Legal scholars have also addressed transaction costs, often with data on actual contracts and useful clarifications of how courts handle these problems. See Gillian K. Hadfield, "Problematic Relations: Franchising and the Law of Incomplete Contracts," *Stanford Law Review* (April 1990); Alan Schwartz, "Relational Contracts in the Courts: An Analysis of Incomplete Agreements and Judicial Strategies," *Journal of Legal Studies* (June 1992); Robert E. Scott, "A Theory of Self-Enforcing Indefinite Agreements," *Columbia Law Review* (November 2003); and Stefanos Mouzas and Michael Philip Furmston, "From Contract to Umbrella Agreement," *Cambridge Law Journal* (March 2008).

Good examinations of the transaction-cost and relational-contracting approaches, with applications to alliances, are Jean-François Hennart, "Explaining the Swollen Middle: Why Most Transactions Are a Mix of 'Market' and 'Hierarchy,'" *Organization Science* (November 1993); and George Baker, Robert Gibbons, and Kevin Murphy, "Strategic Alliances: Bridges Between 'Islands of Conscious Power,'" *Journal of the Japanese and International Economics* 22 (2008).

The academic literature at times mistakenly pitted the resource-based view of the firm against transaction-cost economics as alternative theories of the firm. Most scholars now realize that the two approaches are complementary and that they address different aspects of one phenomenon. That is the approach I take in this book. Other articles that compare or synthesize these two fields are Kathleen R. Conner, "A Historical Comparison of Resource-Based Theory and Five Schools of Thought Within Industrial Organization Economics: Do We Have a New Theory of the Firm?" *Journal of Management* 17 (1991); Jay Barney, "How a Firm's Capabilities Affect Boundary Decisions," *Sloan Management Review* (spring 1999); Robert Gibbons and Rebecca Henderson, "Relational Contracts and Organizational Capabilities," *Organization Science* (September–October 2012); and Nicholas S. Argyres and Todd R. Zenger, "Capabilities, Transaction Costs, and Firm Boundaries: An Integrative Theory," *Organization Science* (September–October 2012). Another synthesis, applied to the theory of the multinational enterprise (a branch of the theory of the firm) is Jean-François Hennart, "Down with MNE-Centric Theories! Market Entry and Expansion as the Bundling of MNE and Local Assets," *Journal of International Business Studies* 40 (2009); and Jean-François Hennart, "Emerging Market Multinationals and the Theory of the Multinational Enterprise," *Global Strategy Journal* 2 (2012).

Evidence

The blinders I have observed about how to structure combinations is not just anecdotal; there is broad evidence that governance preferences are shaped by the personal experiences of managers. See Jeffrey J. Reuer et al., "Executive Preferences for Governance Modes and Exchange Partners: An Information Economics Perspective," *Strategic Management Journal* 34 (2013).

Boeing's experience with the Dreamliner is widely reported. A comprehensive description is in Douglas E. Olesen, Richard L. Nolan, and Philip M. Condit, "Boeing 787: The Dreamliner," Case 305-101 (Boston: Harvard Business School, 2005). The coordination problems with suppliers are reported in J. Lynn Lunsford, "Boeing Scrambles to Repair Problems with New Plane," *Wall Street Journal,* December 7, 2007, and in "Nightmareliner," *The Economist,* September 3, 2011.

The description of various degrees of cooperation in airline alliances is based on my discussions with industry executives. See also Dawna L. Rhoades and Heather Lush, "A Typology of Strategic Alliances in the Airline Industry: Propositions for Stability and Duration," *Journal of Air Transport Management* 3 (1997); and Zhi H. Wang and Michael Evans, "Strategic Classification and Examination of the Development of Current Airline Alliance Activities," *Journal of Air Transportation* (2002).

Researchers have explored how goals and tasks of a combination shape its form: Ranjay Gulati, Paul R. Lawrence, and Phanish Puranam, "Adaptation in Vertical Relationships: Beyond Incentive Conflict," *Strategic Management Journal* 26 (2005); and Lihua Wang and Edward J. Zajac, "Alliance or Acquisition? A Dyadic Perspective on Interfirm Resource Combinations," *Strategic Management Journal* 28 (2007).

Recent empirical analyses of how goals and tasks shape alliance design (and, sometimes, performance) are Joanne E. Oxley and Rachelle C. Sampson, "The Scope and Governance of International R&D Alliances," *Strategic Management Journal* 25 (2004); Rachelle C. Sampson, "R&D Alliances and Firm Performance: The Impact of Technological Diversity and Alliance Organization on Innovation," *Academy of Management Journal* 50 (2007); Prashant Kale and Phanish Puranam, "Choosing Equity Stakes in Technology-Sourcing Relationships: An Integrative Framework," *California Management Review* (spring 2004); Glenn Hoetker and Thomas Mellewigt, "Choice and Performance of Governance Mechanisms: Matching Alliance Governance to Asset Type," *Strategic Management Journal* 30 (2009); Farok J. Contractor, James A. Woodley, and Anke Piepenbrink, "How Tight an Embrace? Choosing the Optimal Degree of Partner Interaction in Alliances Based on Risk, Technology Characteristics, and Agreement Provisions," *Global Strategy Journal* 1 (2011); and Dovev Lavie, Pamela Haunschild, and Poonam Khanna, "Organizational Differences, Relational Mechanisms, and Alliance Performance," *Strategic Management Journal* 33 (2012).

The classic study of business combinations in the aluminum industry is John A. Stuckey, *Vertical Integration and Joint Ventures in the Aluminum*

Industry (Boston: Harvard University Press, 1983). The biofuels context of the Chevron-Weyerhaeuser joint venture is described in Joseph B. Lassiter et al., "Khosla Ventures: Biofuels Gain Liquidity," Case 812-035 (Boston: Harvard Business School, 2012). The joint venture's relationship with KiOR is described in KiOR's 2013 10-K Securities and Exchange Commission filing. KiOR's failure is described in Steven Mufson, "Billionaire Vinod Khosla's big dreams for biofuels fail to catch fire," *The Washington Post,* November 28, 2014. A critical review of the Chevron venture is in Ben Elgin and Peter Waldman, "Chevron Defies California on Carbon Emissions," *Bloomberg Sustainability* (April 18, 2013).

The long-term partnership of Oracle and HP, ironically, is documented in their court filings, which, of course, also provide details of their conflicts. By early 2015, the case was pending trial, but much has already come out during pretrial hearings. See court proceedings following this original complaint: California Superior Court for the County of Santa Clara, "Hewlett-Packard Company vs. Oracle Corporation," Case No. 1-11-CV-203163 (June 15, 2011); and Oracle's cross-complaint (December 2, 2011). Evaluation of the facts on both sides and of the relevant law is in Judge James P. Kleinberg's August 28, 2012, decision, which ruled on certain pretrial issues.

The case of the American telecom company cited is Mark Keil, Steve Simonson, and John J. Sviokla, "BellSouth Enterprises: The Cellular Billing Project," Case 193-150 (Boston: Harvard Business School, 1996).

CHAPTER 5

Ideas

Roger Fisher and William L. Ury, *Getting to YES: Negotiating Agreement Without Giving In* (New York: Penguin Books, 1981), is a classic that has spawned an industry of followers. A good application of its approach to management and strategy is David A. Lax and James K. Sebenius, *The Manager as Negotiator: Bargaining for Co-operation and Competitive Gain* (New York: Free Press, 1987). A modern handbook to complex negotiations, including multipartner deals such as those discussed later in this book, is Andrew Trask and Andrew DeGuire, *Betting the Company: Complex Negotiation Strategies for Law and Business* (Oxford, UK: Oxford University Press, 2013).

Frederic M. Scherer's analysis of bilateral monopoly is in his classic text *Industrial Market Structure and Economic Performance* (2nd ed. 1980; Houghton Mifflin).

Adam M. Brandenburger and Barry J. Nalebuff, *Co-opetition* (New York: Currency Doubleday, 1997), elaborate on the ideas of value added and co-opetition. The term *co-opetition* was coined earlier by Ray Noorda, CEO of Novell in the 1980s; he died in 2006. His obituary highlights the term; see "Ray Noorda," obituary, *Independent* (London), November 1, 2006, www .independent.co.uk/news/obituaries/ray-noorda-422415.html.

Analysis of value in strategy was advanced substantially by theory developed in Adam M. Brandenburger and Harborne W. Stuart Jr., "Value-Based Strategy," *Journal of Economics & Management Strategy* (spring 1996); and, more technically, in the same two authors' "Biform Games," *Management Science* (April 2007).

Various sources of power in a relationship are also explored in Anne Lytle, Jeanne M. Brett, and Debra L. Shapiro, "The Strategic Use of Interests, Rights, and Power to Resolve Disputes," *Negotiation Journal* (January 1999). Their treatment is related to the distinction I made between different influences on value sharing in this chapter.

The bargaining perspective is applied to the resource-based view of the firm in Steven A. Lippman and Richard P. Rumelt, "A Bargaining Perspective on Resource Advantage," *Strategic Management Journal* 24 (2003); and in Glenn MacDonald and Michael D. Ryall, "How Do Value Creation and Competition Determine Whether a Firm Appropriates Value?" *Management Science* (October 2004).

The race-to-learn idea is introduced in Gary Hamel, Yves L. Doz, and C. K. Prahalad, "Collaborate with Your Competitors—and Win," *Harvard Business Review,* January 1989. Further elaboration is in Yves L. Doz and Gary Hamel, *Alliance Advantage: The Art of Creating Value Through Partnering* (Boston: Harvard Business School Press, 1998).

Several strategies for bargaining with complementing parties over value sharing are discussed in David B. Yoffie and Mary Kwak, "With Friends Like These: The Art of Managing Complementors," *Harvard Business Review,* September 2006; this piece also provides evidence on the interaction between Intel and Microsoft and advocates the use of various forms of bargaining power.

Evidence

An interesting analysis of the balance of cooperation and competition in music production is Greg Clydesdale, "Creativity and Competition: The Beatles," *Creativity Research Journal* 18 (2006). A similar, interesting analysis of contracting modes and problems in music production is Cédric Ceulemans, Victor Ginsburgh and Patrick Legros, "Rock and Roll Bands, (In)complete Contracts, and Creativity," *American Economic Review: Papers and Proceedings* (May 2011).

Calouste Gulbenkian's story is told well in Daniel Yergin, *The Prize: The Epic Quest for Oil, Money, and Power* (New York: Simon and Schuster, 1991).

Michael Lewis, *Moneyball: The Art of Winning an Unfair Game* (New York: W. W. Norton, 2004), exemplifies and explains the modern thinking around the value added of baseball players. The illustrative calculations cited in my discussion are from Dan Brooks, "Daniel's Data," accessed February 3, 2014, https://sites.google.com/a/brown.edu/daniel-s-data/project-2-baseball.

The Boston Scientific and Medinol alliance is described in court documents and news reports, which are summarized and excerpted in Todd D. Rakoff, "The Case of the Medical Stent," case PSW004-SM (Cambridge, MA: Harvard Law School, 2010), http://casestudies.law.harvard.edu/the-case-of-the-medical-stent. Quotations in my discussion are from the court findings in United States District Court, Southern District of New York, "Medinol Ltd. v. Boston Scientific et al.," October 28, 2002, and December 2, 2004. Additional information, focusing on Medinol's side of the story, is from Moran Bar-Kochva, "Kobi Richter: Boston Scientific's CEO Admitted to Me That the Company Tried to Steal Medinol's Intellectual Property," *Globes* (Rishon Le-Zion, Israel), October 21, 2001.

The Fuji Xerox and the Honeywell-Yamatake cases are discussed in detail in my book *The Alliance Revolution: The New Shape of Business Rivalry* (Cambridge, MA: Harvard University Press, 1996).

Court papers are again the best source for data on the alliance between Amazon.com and Toys "R" Us. The quote from Judge Margaret McVeigh is from her opinion in Superior Court of New Jersey, "Toys R.Us.Com LLC vs. Amazon.com," March 1, 2006, in Superior Court of New Jersey, C-96-04.

The Intel story is described well in several Harvard Business School cases on the company; the most recent case is Ramon Casadesus-Masanell, David B. Yoffie, and Sasha Mattu, "Intel Corp.: 1968–2003," Case 703-427 (Boston: Harvard Business School, 2002; revised 2010). The early phases of ARM's licensing strategy are described in Willy Shih, Chintay Shih, and Chen-Fu Chien, "Horizontal Specialization and Modularity in the Semiconductor Industry," Case 609-001 (Boston: Harvard Business School, 2008; revised 2009).

Several studies have succeeded in dissecting electronics value chains to identify who captures value in them. See Greg Linden, Kenneth L. Kraemer, and Jason Dedrick, "Who Captures Value in a Global Innovation Network? The Case of Apple's iPod," *Communications of the ACM* (March 2009); and the same authors' "The Distribution of Value in the Mobile Phone Supply Chain," Personal Computing Industry Center, University of California, Irvine, October 2010, http://pcic.merage.uci.edu/ papers/2010/CellPhoneProfitability_Oct2010.pdf.

Several recent statistical studies use the bargaining and value-added perspectives to explore how value is created and shared in alliances. See especially J. Adentunji Adegbesan and Matthew J. Higgins, "The Intra-Alliance Division of Value Created through Collaboration," *Strategic Management Journal* 32 (2010); and Dovev Lavie, "Alliance Portfolios and Firm Performance: A Study of Value Creation and Appropriation in the U.S. Software Industry," *Strategic Management Journal* 28 (2007). Related studies are Jonghoon Bae and Martin Gargiulo, "Partner Substitutability, Alliance Network Structure, and Firm Profitability in the Tele-communications Industry," *Academy of Management Journal* 47 (2004); and Olivier Chatain, "Value Creation, Competition, and Performance in Buyer-Supplier Relationships," *Strategic Management Journal* 32 (2010).

CHAPTER 6

Ideas

Ronald H. Coase cites the buttermilk analogy in "The Nature of the Firm," *Economica* (November 1937). The actual quote Coase used came from D. H. Robertson and S. Dennison, *The Control of Industry* (Cambridge, UK: Cambridge University Press, 1923; reprint 1960).

A growing body of literature recognizes the commonalities between firms and other ways to combine resources. A recent survey of these fundamentals is Phanish Puranam, Oliver Alexy, and Markus Reitzig, "What's 'New' About New Forms of Organizing?" *Academy of Management Review* 39 (2014). Theoretical models of the firm that can be used to understand other forms of organization are Patrick Bolton and Mathias Dewatripont, "The Firm As a Communication Network," *The Quarterly Journal of Economics* (November 1994); and Raghuram Rajan and Luigi Zingales, "The Firm As a Dedicated Hierarchy: A Theory of the Origins and Growth of Firms," *The Quarterly Journal of Economics* (August 2001), 843, which recognizes explicitly that the economic and legal definitions of the firm may be different. See also the case study analysis in Nicolai J. Foss, "Selective Intervention and Internal Hybrids: Interpreting and Learning from the Rise and Decline of the Oticon Spaghetti Organization," *Organization Science* (May–June 2003).

The discussion of constellation structure draws on the large literature on social networks. A theoretical exposition of various network structures is in Allen Wilhite, "Economic Activity on Fixed Networks," in *Hand-

book of Computational Economics, vol. 2, ed. Leigh Tesfatsion and Kenneth Judd (New York: Elsevier, 2006). Recent studies of how network structure affects behavior are Allan Afuah, "Are Network Effects Really About Size? The Role of Structure and Conduct," *Strategic Management Journal* 34 (2013); and Maxim Sytch and Adam Tatarynowicz, "Friends and Foes: The Dynamics of Dual Social Structures," *Academy of Management Journal* 57 (2014). A good application of social network analysis to alliance strategy is Henrich Greve, Tim Rowley, and Andrew Shipilov, *Network Advantage: How to Unlock Value From Your Alliances and Partnerships* (San Francisco: Jossey-Bass, 2014).

A few studies of network structure address the effects of network positioning on performance; see especially Henrich Greve, Tim Rowley, and Andrew Shipilov, *Network Advantage: How to Unlock Value from Your Alliances and Partnerships* (San Francisco: Jossey-Bass 2014). An application to the theory of the firm is in Bruce Kogut, "The Network as Knowledge: Generative Rules and the Emergence of Structure," *Strategic Management Journal* 21 (2000); an analysis of advantages and disadvantages of constellations, drawing on cases, is Remo Hacki and Julian Lighton, "The Future of the Networked Company," *McKinsey Quarterly* 3 (2001). Recent statistical studies are Melissa A. Schilling and Corey C. Phelps, "Interfirm Collaboration Networks: The Impact of Large-Scale Network Structure on Firm Innovation," *Management Science* (July 2007); Dovev Lavie, Christoph Lechner, and Harbir Singh, "The Performance Implications of Timing of Entry and Involvement in Multipartner Alliances," *Academy of Management Journal* 50 (2007); and Andrew Shipilov, "Firm Scope Experience, Historic Multimarket Contact with Partners, Centrality, and the Relationship Between Structural Holes and Performance," *Organization Science* (January–February 2009).

A separate body of research addresses how firms manage their alliance portfolios. Managerial approaches are in James Bamford and David Ernst, "Managing an Alliance Portfolio," *McKinsey Quarterly* 3 (2002); Salvatore Parise and Amy Casher, "Alliance Portfolios: Designing and Managing Your Network of Business-Partner Relationships," *Academy of Management Executive* 17 (2003); and Dovev Lavie, "Capturing Value from Alliance Portfolios," *Organizational Dynamics* 38 (2009). A theoretical approach is in Pinar Ozcan and Kathleen M. Eisenhardt, "Origin of Alliance Portfolios: Entrepreneurs, Network Strategies, and Firm Performance," *Academy of Management Journal* 52 (2009).

Another body of research addresses the competition between groups of firms. My own work on this topic is in the following publications: "Group Versus Group: How Alliance Networks Compete," *Harvard Business*

Review, July–August 2004; *The Alliance Revolution: The New Shape of Business Rivalry* (Cambridge, MA: Harvard University Press, 1996); "Competitive Advantage in Alliance Constellations," *Strategic Organization* (August 2003); and "How Alliances Reshape Competition," in *Handbook of Strategic Alliances,* ed. Oded Shenkar and Jeffrey J. Reuer (Thousand Oaks, CA: Sage, 2006). Others have written theoretical and empirical papers on this theme; see T. K. Das and Bing-Sheng Teng, "Alliance Constellations: A Social Exchange Perspective," *Academy of Management Review* 27 (2002); Tim J. Rowley et al., "Competing in Groups," *Managerial and Decision Economics* 25 (2004); Javier Gimeno, "Competition Within and Between Networks: The Contingent Effect of Competitive Embeddedness on Alliance Formation," *Academy of Management Journal* 47 (2004); and Sergio Lazzarini, "The Impact of Membership in Competing Alliance Constellations: Evidence on the Operational Performance of Global Airlines," *Strategic Management Journal* 28 (2007).

James F. Moore's book on ecosystems is *The Death of Competition: Leadership and Strategy in the Age of Business Ecosystems* (New York: HarperCollins, 1996). His most recent book, available on the web, speaks eloquently about ecosystems' health and provides good data on the ARM Holdings example; see his *Shared Purpose: A Thousand Business Ecosystems, a Worldwide Connected Community, and the Future,* May 2013, www .arm.com/files/pdf/Shared_Purpose.pdf. A separate body of work studies geographic clusters; for a recent review, which also draws organizational implications, see Andaç T. Arikan and Melissa A. Schilling, "Structure and Governance in Industrial Districts: Implications for Competitive Advantage," *Journal of Management Studies* (June 2011).

Adam Smith's original analysis of the division of labor and the value of specialization is in his *An Inquiry into the Nature and Causes of the Wealth of Nations,* book 1, chapter 1, available at www2.hn.psu.edu/faculty/jmanis/ adam-smith/wealth-nations.pdf, accessed August 8, 2014.

Marco Iansiti and Roger Levien's book is *The Keystone Advantage: What the New Dynamics of Business Ecosystems Mean for Strategy, Innovation, and Sustainability* (Boston: Harvard Business School Press, 2004); a companion piece by the same authors is "Strategy as Ecology," *Harvard Business Review,* March 2004.

Other approaches to how companies create and earn value from group-based strategies are David Evans and Richard Schmalensee, *Catalyst Code: The Strategies Behind the World's Most Dynamic Companies* (Boston: Harvard Business School Press, 2007); Satish Nambisan and Mohanbir Sawhney, "Orchestration Processes in Network-Centric Innovation," *Academy of Management Perspectives* (August 2011); Thomas Eisenmann et al.,

"Platform Envelopment," *Strategic Management Journal* 32 (2011); and Llewellyn Thomas et al., "Architectural Leverage: Putting Platforms in Context," *Academy of Management Perspectives* 28 (2014).

Evidence

The evolution of Airbus is covered in many sources. One report focusing on the challenges of managing the consortium is Carol Matlack, "'Major Screwup' at Airbus," *BusinessWeek,* June 29, 2006.

Corning International's use of alliances is described in Christopher A. Bartlett and Ashish Nanda, "Corning, Inc.: A Network of Alliances," Case 391-102 (Boston: Harvard Business School, 1990; revised 1992). But I learned the most about this strategy from conversations with Thomas McAvoy, former president of the company.

MasterCard and Visa's alliance strategies are described in James D. Bamford, Benjamin Gomes-Casseres, and Michael S. Robinson, *Mastering Alliance Strategy: A Comprehensive Guide to Design, Management, and Organization* (San Francisco: Jossey-Bass, 2003), ch. 22.

An interesting discussion of the Tin Pan Alley cluster, with a comparison to today's app industry, is in Dennis K. Berman, "Tin Pan Valley: The Coming Shakeout for App Makers," *Wall Street Journal,* June 13, 2012.

The July 10, 2013, court ruling in "USA vs Apple" (12-cv-02826-DLC) is informative about how Apple went about creating its iTunes constellation. It is available at www.justice.gov/atr/cases/f286700/286727.pdf.

A characterization of Chrysler's network is in Jeffrey H. Dyer, "How Chrysler Created an American Keiretsu," *Harvard Business Review,* July 1996.

CHAPTER 7

Ideas and Evidence

The story of Apple's iPod, iPhone, and iPad line is widely reported. A careful exposition of how the development of the digital music industry led to the iPod is in Willy C. Shih, "MP3 Portable Audio Players and the Recorded Music Industry," Case 608-119 (Boston: Harvard Business School, 2009). An early report on Apple's alliances in this business is Peter Burrows, "Apple's Partner Paradox," *Bloomberg Business Week,* July 3, 2007.

There is a large body of literature on how companies might best organize their alliance strategies. Much of it is written for managers. My own book on this topic is James D. Bamford, Benjamin Gomes-Casseres, and

Michael S. Robinson, *Mastering Alliance Strategy: A Comprehensive Guide to Design, Management, and Organization* (San Francisco: John Wiley/Jossey-Bass, 2003). See also Prashant Kale, Jeffrey H. Dyer, and Harbir Sing, "Alliance Capability, Stock Market Response, and Long-Term Alliance Success: The Role of the Alliance Function," *Strategic Management Journal* 23 (2002); and the same authors' "How to Make Strategic Alliances Work," *MIT Sloan Management Review* (summer 2001). For a focus on contract design, see Nicholas Argyres and Kyle J. Mayer, "Contract Design as a Firm Capability: An Integration of Learning and Transaction Cost Perspectives," *Academy of Management Review* 32 (2007). For a focus on the alliance portfolio, see Koen H. Heimericks, Elko Klijn, and Jeffrey J. Reuer, "Building Capabilities for Alliance Portfolios," *Long Range Planning* 42 (2009).

Various strategies for addressing change in the environment, including business combinations, are discussed in Dovev Lavie, "Capability Reconfiguration: An Analysis of Incumbent Responses to Technological Change," *Academy of Management Review* 31 (2006). On the need for agile strategies and the instability of competitive advantage, see Rita Gunther McGrath, *The End of Competitive Advantage: How to Keep Your Strategy Moving as Fast as Your Business* (Boston: Harvard Business Review Press, 2013). McGrath has also been an early proponent of applying real-options analysis to strategic decisions, discussed in the sidebar "Flexibility Makes Risk Your Friend."

An analysis of the spread of alliances in various businesses is in Benjamin Gomes-Casseres, "The Logic of Alliance Fads: Why Collective Competition Spreads," in *Law, Economics and Organization of Alliances and Joint Ventures,* ed. Joseph McCahery and Erik P.M. Vermeulen (Cambridge, UK: Cambridge University Press, forthcoming). Evidence of how new technologies can cause a wave in alliance formation (and the effects on innovation) is in Melissa A. Schilling, "Technology Shocks, Technological Collaboration, and Innovation Outcomes," *Organizational Science* (forthcoming).

Commonly used measures of firm performance, costs, and profits are poor at capturing the value of alliances, because they focus on wholly owned and majority-owned activities. For a view that incorporates more of the firm's relational footprint, see John K. Shank, "Strategic Cost Management: New Wine, or Just New Bottles?" *Journal of Management Accounting Research* (fall 1989); John K. Shank and Vijay Govindarajan, "Strategic Cost Management: The Value Chain Perspective," *Journal of Management Accounting Research* (fall 1992); and Gianni Lorenzoni, John Shank, and Riccardo Silvi, "Networked Organizations: A Strategic Cost Management Perspective," working paper 99-109 NB, Babson College, Babson Park, MA: July 21, 1999.

On the divergence between how firms evaluate projects in the core business and in peripheral businesses, see Joseph Lampel and Jamal Shamsie, "Probing the Unobtrusive Link: Dominant Logic and the Design of Joint Ventures at General Electric," *Strategic Management Journal* 21 (2000).

Evidence on how innovative companies use a lower hurdle rate on innovation than do less-innovative companies is in IBM Institute for Business Value, *"More than magic: How the most successful organizations innovate,"* December 2014, p. 10, available at http://public.dhe.ibm.com/common/ssi/ ecm/gb/en/gbe03625usen/gbe03625usen.pdf, accessed March 8, 2015.

Index

Note: Page numbers followed by *f* refer to figures. Page numbers followed by *t* refer to tables.

Acknowledgments

My mother and father left behind a library of more than 2,200 books. Ruth, my mother, loved fiction and cookbooks, and Charlie, my father, devoured nonfiction books (and wrote two of his own). The appreciation my parents instilled in me for good reading and effective writing was the wellspring of this book.

My wife and daughter fueled my progress in the writing of this book more than they know. Their nonbusiness perspective was always refreshing—and a challenge to be met in the exposition of complex ideas and concepts. They cheerfully celebrated each draft that was half-done, then done, then redone, then done again, and so on, again and again. Susan and Rachel, now this book is really done—and I dedicate it to you.

I was lucky to have the support of Melinda Merino, my editor at Harvard Business Review Press. Melinda's patience, evident soon after she first bought into my ideas, was exceeded only by her superb guidance when a draft finally appeared on her desk. Her editorial and production team of Dave Lievens, Courtney Cashman, Patty Boyd, and Stephani Finks helped make this book shine, and Julie Devoll, Nina Nocciolino, Lindsey Dietrich, and their marketing colleagues helped give it readership.

In keeping with its theme, this book is a remix of ideas—the best ideas about business competition and collaboration that I learned from scholars, teachers, mentors, and friends. This remix process has been going on in my mind for about thirty years, so it is hard to pin down where I learned what. My previous two books give sources that contributed to my thinking along the way. The chapters of this book and the section entitled Further Reading attempt to signal my debt to the classics in social science and to current management scholars.

I have also learned a great deal from managers, colleagues, and students in my work at Harvard and Brandeis and in my research interviews and consulting with executives across a wide range of industries. As models of alliance leadership, Thomas MacAvoy of Corning, Yotaro Kobayashi of Fuji Xerox, and my friend Tomás Kohn of Ideal Alambrec have made lasting impressions on my thinking. Louis Wells, David Yoffie, Peter Petri, Jean-François Hennart, Jeremy Ahouse, and James Bamford have been reliable sources of wisdom over the years. They also reviewed parts of my book drafts, as did Larry Kanarek, Mel Blake, Joel Schwartz, and four anonymous referees. Rosabeth Moss Kanter, Mike Bellissimo, Cees Bijl, Russ Buchanan, Martin Fleming, Ashok Krishna, Nigel Sheail, and Steve Steinhilber were kind enough to read an advance copy and endorse the book. My MBA students at Brandeis debated my ideas in the classroom; several served as research assistants along the way. Brandeis University and the Asper Center for Global Entrepreneurship supported my research for this book, as well as the work of my research assistants and my writing coach, Regina Maruca.

Masha masha danki is how I now say a heartfelt thank-you to all these allies—in Papiamentu, the language of my native Curaçao. On this Dutch island in the Caribbean, populated by people from around the world, I first learned that "remix" of cultures is a beautiful way of life.

Benjamin Gomes-Casseres
Lexington, Massachusetts
May 2015

About the Author

BENJAMIN GOMES-CASSERES has been studying, teaching, and consulting on the strategy of business combinations for thirty years. His work has focused on alliances and multipartner constellations, with special attention to innovation strategy. He has studied business combinations in a range of industries, from information technology and pharmaceuticals to automobiles, airlines, and energy.

Gomes-Casseres is a professor at the International Business School, Brandeis University and previously was a professor at Harvard Business School. Before that, he was an economist at the World Bank. He has published his research in two books, *The Alliance Revolution* and *Mastering Alliance Strategy,* and in articles, handbook chapters, blogs, and videos. He speaks for and consults widely with companies seeking to create value from external resources and to improve the way they manage business partnerships.

Gomes-Casseres earned a DBA in international business from Harvard University, an MPA in economic development from Princeton University, and a BA in history and in economics from Brandeis University. A native of Curaçao, he speaks four languages. On many clear nights, he can be found stargazing, his hobby since childhood.